Harriet R. Feldman, PhD, RN, FAAN, is dean and professor at the Lienhard School of Nursing at Pace University. She is also Chairperson of the University's Institutional Review Board. She was one of the founding editors of *Scholarly Inquiry for Nursing Practice* and is currently editor of *Nursing Leadership Forum,* both published by Springer Publishing. Dr. Feldman received her nursing diploma from Long Island College Hospital School of Nursing, bachelor's and master's degrees from Adelphi University, and her PhD from New York University. She also received a certificate for her attendance at the Management Development Program at Harvard University. She has served in leadership positions in a number of local, state, and national professional groups, presented and consulted widely both nationally and internationally, and published extensively in books and refereed journals. Her most recent book, coauthored with Dr. Sandra B. Lewenson is entitled *Nurses in the Political Arena: The Public Face of Nursing* (Springer Publishing) and was named an *American Journal of Nursing* Book-of-the-Year.

STRATEGIES FOR
*N*URSING
*L*EADERSHIP

STRATEGIES FOR NURSING LEADERSHIP

Harriet R. Feldman, PhD, RN, FAAN

Editor

 SPRINGER PUBLISHING COMPANY

Springer Publishing Company, Inc.
536 Broadway
New York, NY 10012-3955

Acquisitions Editor: *Ruth Chasek*
Production Editor: *Elizabeth Keech*
Cover design by *Susan Hauley*

01   02   03   04   05/5   4   3   2   1

Library of Congress Cataloging-in-Publication Data

Strategies for nursing leadership / Harriet R. Feldman, editor.
  p.   ; cm.
  Includes bibliographical references and index.
  ISBN 0-8261-1414-8
    1. Nursing services—Administration.   2. Leadership.
  [DNLM: 1. Leadership—Collected Works.   2. Nursing—organization & administration—Collected Works.   3. Nurse Adminstrators—Collected Works.   WY 105 S898 2001]
  I. Feldman, Harriet R.   II. Title: Nursing leadership forum.
  RT89 .S775 2001
  362.1'73'068—dc21

                                                                    00-069815

Printed in the United States of America by Maple-Vail Book Manufacturing Group

This book is a compilation of articles previously published in the journal *Nursing Leadership Forum* (Springer Publishing Company).

Contents

Contributors

Barbara A. Backer, DSW, RN
Professor
Department of Nursing
Lehman College
Bronx, New York

Fay L. Bower, DNSc, FAAN
Nurse Consultant
Clayton, California

Susan Brusilow, CFRE
Assistant Administrator of
    Development
Fairfax Hospital
Falls Church, Virginia

Barbara Callaghan, MSN, RN
Patient Care Administrator
Fairfax Hospital
Falls Church, Virginia

**Kathleen Leask Capitulo, MS,
    RN, FACCE**
Clinical Director
Maternal Child Health Care
    Center
Mount Sinai Hospital
New York, New York

Cynthia Caroselli, RN, PhD
Clinical Director
Mount Sinai Hospital
New York, New York

Virginia R. Cassidy, EdD, RN
Professor
School of Nursing
Northern Illinois University
DeKalb, Illinois

**Ruth Davidhizar, RN, DNS, CS,
    FAAN**
Dean of Nursing
Bethel College
Mishawaka, Indiana

Sandra S. Deller, BA
Special Assistant to the Vice
    President
Director of Major Gifts
Case Western Reserve University
Cleveland, Ohio

Kathleen M. Dirschel, PhD, RN
Vice President for Education
    and Director, Cochran
    School of Nursing
St. John's Riverside Hospital
Yonkers, New York

Karen DuBois, MSN, RNC
Director of Content
    Development for
    NursingCenter.com
Lippincott Williams & Wilkins
New York, New York

Margaret K. Edwards, RN, MSN
Coordinator of the Oncology
    Rehabilitation Program
Greenville Hospital Systems
Greenville, South Carolina

Claire M. Fagin, PhD, RN, FAAN
Dean Emeritus and Professor
    Emeritus
School of Nursing
University of Pennsylvania
Philadelphia, Pennsylvania

**Joyce J. Fitzpatrick, PhD, MBA,
    RN, FAAN**
Elizabeth Brooks Ford Professor
    of Nursing
Frances Payne Bolton School of
    Nursing
Case Western Reserve University
Cleveland, Ohio

Harriet Forman, EdD, RN
Nursing Spectrum Retention
    Consultant
Nursing Spectrum
Pompano Beach, Florida

**C. Alicia Georges, MA, RNC,
    FAAN**
Lecturer
Department of Nursing
Lehman College
Bronx, New York

Martha Greenberg, RN, PhD
Assistant Professor and
    Chairperson
Lienhard School of Nursing
Pace University
Pleasantville, New York

Louise S. Jenkins, RN, PhD
Director of Graduate Studies
School of Nursing
University of Maryland
Baltimore, Maryland

Barry Jay Kaplan, MFA
Medical Writer, Novelist,
    Playwright
New York, New York

Jessica K. Kirkpatrick
Office Manager
Comprehensive Physical
    Therapy Associates
Chapel Hill, North Carolina

Mary Kirkpatrick, RN, EdD
Professor of Adult Health
    Nursing
East Carolina University
Greenville, North Carolina

Rosemarie Kovac, BSN, RN
Nursing Unit Director for
  Obstetrics
St. John's Queens Hospital
Elmhurst, New York

Nora E. Ladewig, RN, MSN
St. Luke's Medical Center
Milwaukee, Wisconsin

**Elizabeth R. Lenz, PhD, RN,
  FAAN**
Anna C. Maxwell Professor of
  Nursing Research
Associate Dean for Research
  and Doctoral Studies
Columbia University
School of Nursing
New York, New York

Claire Manfredi, EdD, RN
Associate Professor
Villanova University
College of Nursing
Villanova, Pennsylvania

**Diana J. Mason, PhD, RNC,
  FAAN**
Editor-in-Chief
American Journal of Nursing
New York, New York

**Cynthia Peden-McAlpine, PhD,
  RN, CS**
Assistant Professor
School of Nursing
University of Minnesota
Minneapolis, Minnesota

Gertrude Rodgers, MSN, RN
Chief Executive for External
  Affairs
Fairfax Hospital
Falls Church, Virginia

**Kathleen D. Sanford, DBA, RN,
  FACHE**
Vice President for Nursing
Silverdale Campus
  Administrator
Harris Memorial Hospital
Bremerton, Virginia

**Carolyn Hope Smeltzer, RN,
  EdD, FAAN, FACHE**
Principal
Integrated Health Care Practice
PricewaterhouseCoopers LLP
Chicago, Illinois

Sylvene Spickerman, RN, MSN
Professor Emeritus
East Carolina University
Greenville, North Carolina

**Theresa Stephany, RN, MS, CS,
  CRNH**
Nurse
Kaiser-Permanente
Hayward, California

**Mary Crabtree Tonges, MBA,
  MSN, RN**
Consultant
Center for Case Management,
  Inc.
South Natick, Massachusetts

Norma Ness Turini, MPA, RN
President
Smart Management Strategies
Atlantic Highlands, New Jersey

Linda D. Urden, DNSc, RN, CNA
Associate Professor
School of Nursing
Indiana University
Indianapolis, Indiana

Penny M. Vigneau, MSW, RN
Health Care Consultant
PricewaterhouseCoopers LLP
Detroit, Michigan

Constance E. Young, EdD, RN
Associate Professor of Nursing
  Programs
Sacred Heart University
Fairfield, Connecticut

Foreword

As the first editor of *Nursing Leadership Forum*, my initial reaction to this book (and its sister compilation, *Nursing Leaders Speak Out*), was delight—and a little pride that so many valuable articles had been spawned by the journal. Seeing a book's table of contents produces a cumulative impression that one doesn't get in the ongoing effort of turning out one issue after another. And, yes, there was a touch of personal vanity. I'll confess I was tempted to count how many articles were published on my watch and how many on Harriet's—but I refrained from that adolescent enterprise, remembering how grateful I was to have such a competent and motivated colleague as Harriet to take over "my baby" when it was time for me to move on to other endeavors.

The selection of articles for this book testifies that, in some small way, the journal succeeded in achieving our envisioned niche. It was titled *Nursing **Leadership***, not *Nursing **Administration***, for good reason. As the selected articles reveal, we wanted to catch that elusive and individual spark that effective leaders evince—more a snapshot of leadership than dictates for how to be a good administrator. Even the articles that might sound like strict "rules and regulations"—take Fitzpatrick's contributions on fundraising—end up revealing the person, and his/her drive, determination, and vision.

This book will not only be enlightening for the reader, but, equally important, fun to read. What is more intriguing than to ferret out those bits and pieces that comprise a nurse leader's personality? Of course, we won't decide to be just like Fitzpatrick, or Cassidy, or Davidhizar, or any of the other authors. Instead, we'll each ask, how will that work for me?

Chapter 1 of this book starts out most appropriately with Harriet Forman's discussion of leadership by the pen, and that makes all these authors leaders. They were each willing to "lay it on the line" in their very personal act of writing. I think of the brave article by DuBois, who tells us how it is for a novice to grow in the computer technology world, and I think of the vast ranges of leadership demonstrated here, right up to the final article by Fagin, whose professional mastery probably enables her to write as easily as she breathes. I remember working with many of these authors, some struggling to say just what they meant, others for whom this sort of sharing was already a familiar task. Whatever each author's process, I think the reader will find a wonderful and sage book of practical advice offered through the unique eyes and efforts of every author.

BARBARA STEVENS BARNUM
RN, PhD, FAAN

Introduction

The last half of the 1990s and beginning of the 21st century have ushered in a new look at leadership. Leadership has become a topic of increasing interest among nurses and other professionals—even among the general public. Why is this? For nurses, it might be a sign of the growing maturity of the profession. Because of dramatic changes in health care, nurses have been challenged to more actively participate in and lead organizational and policy initiatives. Nurses are on the job every hour of every day of the week and are often called upon to make decisions alone, to supervise the work of an increasing number of paraprofessionals and other ancillary workers, and to accommodate numerous demands by patients, other professionals, and high level administrators. They must have leadership skills to be able to succeed in these arenas. As providers of care, teachers, researchers, and managers, nurses realize that they need to know the "ins and outs" of leadership.

This book offers insights and practical advice on leadership in nursing from nearly 40 experts in education, administration, clinical practice, and research. The book collects in one place some of the best articles published in the journal *Nursing Leadership Forum* since its inception in 1995. The journal was founded as a forum for nursing leaders to share their experience and knowledge of leadership and the many shapes it can take. As Barbara Barnum, founding editor of the journal, noted, "Today nurse leaders can be found at every level, in every sort of practice . . . Nursing leadership takes many forms. Sometimes it comes from the thinker . . . sometimes it comes from the political activist . . . sometimes it comes from the person who can phrase a question in a new way." The experts in this book range from nurse executives and educators to journalists, consultants, and business owners.

The book is organized into four sections. The themes of change, empowerment, leadership, vision, and self-development are found throughout the articles in each section. "Getting Started" sets the stage for the discussion to follow. In this section leaders such as Harriet Forman and Joyce Fitzpatrick discuss what brought them to nursing, the risks that they took, and their perspectives on leadership. In the next section, "Developing Leadership Skills," concrete strategies and skills needed for nurse leaders are described, such as developing a business plan, making a speech, fundraising, succession planning, and finding time for yourself. "Enhancing Patient and Employee Satisfaction" deals with the sensitive task of human relations in leadership, which for nurses includes relationships with patients as well as staff. Some of the critical topics covered in this section are empowerment, organizational climate, patient and employee satisfaction, and shared governance. The final section, "Coping With Changing Institutions," reflects the reality of today's health care work environment—where institutional mergers, reorganization, or even closure have become a challenge to the largest health care profession, nursing. In the final chapter, Claire Fagin addresses change from the health policy standpoint, and suggests an advocacy role for nurses in the political arena.

Strategies for Nursing Leadership offers an opportunity to learn from our colleagues who have used exciting and challenging strategies to advance people and organizations. These individuals have played an important role in laying the groundwork for the leadership era, and their passion, experience, and words provide guidance for each of us to develop our own unique skills as leaders.

HARRIET R. FELDMAN
PHD, RN, FAAN

PART I

Getting Started

CHAPTER 1

Nursing Leadership With the Pen: Two Peas in a Pod

Harriet Forman

When I was a little girl growing up in Brooklyn, I learned early on that I was a leader. When I said, "Let's go to the beach" or "Let's go to the movies," I always had company, because many of the kids within earshot would say, "We'll go, too!"

But I didn't always *want* company. Sometimes I wanted to be alone. One of the places I liked to go to solo was the Museum of Natural History on the Upper West Side of Manhattan. I'd set out on a weekend morning armed with a book to read during my journey and maneuver through the subway system—an adventure unto itself—all the while preparing myself for the wonders of nature preserved from earliest times.

Often, while I traveled to the museum, dreams of my future would interrupt my reading, and two themes would invariably recur. In one, I could see myself in a garret, starving and threadbare, pecking away at a typewriter. Like Jo in *Little Women,* and Katrin in *I Remember Mama,* I was going to be a writer.

Mind you, I had never seen a garret, except in movies, and I was fortunate enough never to have had to wear threadbare clothes. But sure as anything, I could see myself composing the great American novel—I could see myself, that is, until another image superimposed itself upon that of the young woman hunched over a typewriter. That other image was of me as a nurse, and that image turned out to be the stronger of the two.

Note: Originally published in *Nursing Leadership Forum,* Vol. 1, No. 1, 1995. New York: Springer Publishing Company.

So when it came time in high school to focus, I focused with a vengeance. I concentrated on one thing and one thing only. I focused on nursing. And while studying and working my way through a grueling 3-year diploma program, my leadership propensities both got me into trouble *and* limited the fallout.

But in the days of my youth, who thought about leadership? Certainly not my friends, and certainly not me. All we thought about was having a little fun and not getting into trouble—not getting into too *much* trouble, that is, because a little trouble was inevitable. You couldn't really have fun if you didn't take a few chances. And taking a few chances meant then what it means now: Unavoidably, you'll cross a line or two along the way, and despite the fact that you're not looking for it, trouble will eventually find you.

Looking back from the vantage point of having been relied upon to think of "things to do," and then to lead the way; of having done many things in the company of others and many things alone; of having pushed the outer limits until I've encountered some difficulty and of somehow working through those dilemmas; of accomplishing many things and racking up a few failures, I often think that therein lies a definition of leadership:

> . . . the ability to envision a path or direction; to motivate others to follow; to join with others to reach a common goal; to work alone when solo action is called for; to withstand trouble and failure; and to refuse to be crushed by either.

In today's world, effective, visionary leadership in nursing is needed perhaps more than ever before. We are at a crossroads. Take one path and nursing will remain a vital part of health care delivery under a reformed system. Take another avenue and we might well cease to exist, at least as we know ourselves to be today.

For the first time in our history we are enjoying the public's eye. We are being talked about on Capitol Hill, and our opinions are being sought by those in power and by those advising those in power. If our leaders lead us down the path defined by this attention—into case management, fiscal responsibility, primary health care, continuous quality improvement, appropriate preparation, differentiated practice, and the like, then I believe that we can indeed look forward to a long and fruitful future. But the enemy is at the gate, or perhaps more accurately stated, the enemy lurks within.

There are those among us who continue to say that a nurse is a nurse irrespective of education and training, and that nurses have equal worth in all categories and in all specialties. There are those among us who say that because of our special education and experience, certain duties and responsibilities are "beneath" us. There are those among us who say that cross-training of lower paid, lesser prepared individuals can serve to replace higher paid RNs, and there are those among us who say that nursing care can and should be delivered by these cross-trained employees.

Whom shall we follow? The bottom line must be met, and patient safety and satisfaction must be ensured. Therefore, we must pursue the leader down the path we determine to be the one heading for these goals. For the readers of this new publication, perhaps a better way to pose this concept is to say, "We must proactively *lead* our colleagues down the path toward nursing's active participation in meeting, and perhaps even in beating, the bottom line; toward nursing's continued viability; and toward nursing's ongoing presence in the lives of patients who require *nursing care*."

But who are these leaders? How do we identify them? Instead of "they," might they be "us"? Might they be nurse executives, nurse managers, *and* nurse editors? How does leadership equate and translate to both these roles?

As a practicing clinical nurse, I cared for a relatively small number of patients. And care I did. My patients felt cared for, my supervisors were confident in my skills, and I felt fulfilled. I *loved* being a nurse. As the years flew by, my personal needs changed and I needed more money to support my family than was available to bedside nurses. So despite my reluctance to leave that venue, I gained entrée into nursing administration. And lo and behold I discovered that, although I had only a rare opportunity to "lay on hands," I could facilitate the nursing care provided to many more patients. I knew that even on my best days as a staff nurse, I couldn't directly care for more than 8 to 10 acutely ill patients. As a nurse administrator, though, I could *influence* the care provided to 50 times that number, and in my next position as chief nurse executive, I was able to reach 80 times that number.

For the next 12 years, like many of my nurse executive/nurse manager colleagues, I led, nurtured, educated, motivated, convinced, and cajoled, and had an impact on hundreds of nurses and thousands of patients. And then a new door opened, one that took me out of a health delivery institution and into a different vehicle of leadership. This, too, was a pathway to make an impression, to have an impact, to assert leadership abilities, and, not insignificantly, to live out another dream.

My instrument—the written word—considered by many to be "mightier than the sword," is a communication device that does not fade into oblivion but, if pertinent, pointed, and poignant, endures both in its inscribed form and in the hearts and minds of its readers. I don't work from a garret, and the keyboard over which I am frequently hunched is that of a personal computer. As the executive editor of a nursing publication with a wide circulation, my words, and the words contained within each edition, have the potential to influence more nurses than I ever dreamed possible.

I am sometimes asked whether I ever miss the clinical arena—the nurse leader situation, that is—and the truth of the matter is that I don't miss it because I have never really left it. Editorial leadership requires no less vision, strength, commitment, skill, or savvy than does clinical or administrative leadership. In fact, I believe that all three have the potential to be equally potent.

Nurse leaders come in all shapes and sizes, and they come in many forms. Through manuscript selection, their own writings, and what they choose to cover, editors set the tone of their publication. They define its mission and its character. Nurse executives, by selecting staff members, patient care models, skills mix designs, and leadership styles, set the tone, the mission, and the character of their organizations. Is it possible that the leadership qualities needed to ensure success in these seemingly disparate endeavors are as alike as, shall we say, two peas in a pod?

CHAPTER 2

The Art of Legendary Leadership: Lessons for New and Aspiring Leaders

Claire Manfredi

Leadership has been a topic of interest in our society and the subject of numerous studies, particularly over the last half of the 20th century. Bass (1990) observes that there are almost as many different definitions of leadership as there are persons who have attempted to define the concept, and acknowledges over 7,500 research studies, papers, and monographs on this topic (p. xv). Over the years, leadership has been defined in terms of traits, personalities, situations, tasks, roles, power, positions, interactions, perceptions, group process, and followership (Manfredi & Valiga, 1994).

Leadership is a "universal phenomenon in humans and in many species of animals" (Bass, 1990, p. 4). How one gains an understanding of the complexities of leadership is a question often posed by those who have undertaken the task of examining the concept and communicating the process to others.

Legendary tales have been handed down from generation to generation and serve a useful role in our society. They represent accepted beliefs, values, and attitudes that give a people identity (Cavendish, 1982). They often serve as raw material for scholarly discourse in a variety of disciplines (Ashliman, 1987), and provide valuable insights into human nature and our understanding of complex phenomena. It was with this purpose in mind that the writer created the leader-

Note: Originally published in *Nursing Leadership Forum*, Vol. 1, No. 2, 1995. New York: Springer Publishing Company.

ship legend that follows. This legend was constructed to serve as a catalyst for new and aspiring leaders as they examine and consider the complexities of leadership and prepare for leadership roles in the future.

Once upon a time, centuries ago in a tiny village far away, the Mayor who had served as the leader of the village for many years, passed away. Shortly after the burial, the town elders gathered to discuss the selection of a successor. A call went out to all of the residents in the village for volunteers to succeed the village leader. After a period of time, three candidates came forward. Since there was no job description and there were no selection criteria, the Council of Elders decided to test the leadership of the candidates by placing them in charge of the village for a period of 1 month. The candidate who was accepted by the residents and successful in leading the village for 1 month would be appointed the new leader of the village. And so the selection process began.

Candidate #1 believed that the best way to lead a village was to keep the village stable; so the word *change* was deleted from the language. The village motto became: "No need to grow; support the status quo." At the end of the month, the residents were so bored and disenchanted they developed their own motto: "Candidate #1 must go; and so must the status quo."

Candidate #2 believed that one must create structure in order to lead. So rules were written and regulations were drafted. Unfortunately, Candidate #2 believed that rules were made for subjects only, not for leaders. So, day after day the candidate was observed violating all of the policies that had been put into place. At the end of the month the subjects created a bonfire with the 700 volumes of rules and regulations that had been generated during the brief reign of Candidate #2.

Candidate #3 believed that leaders know what is best for the general public, and that villagers cannot be trusted to make decisions or develop ideas. So for 1 month, Candidate #3 made all of the decisions and never consulted the residents of the village. At the end of the month, the villagers were finally able to make one decision: They decided they definitely did not want Candidate #3 to lead them.

Obviously, all three candidates were rejected by the villagers. When the Council of Elders gathered to consider an alternative, they began to discuss the requisite qualities and characteristics of a leader, and the role of the town leader in the future. Soon, discussion turned to argument and argument turned to heated debate. Not only were the elders unable to come to agreement about the role of the town leader, but they succeeded in generating almost as many definitions and descriptions of leadership as there were residents in this tiny village. The elders realized they needed time to examine this complex phenomenon known as leadership, so they decided to retreat to a quiet hideaway in the mountains to engage in discourse and come to resolution. They emerged 1 month later with a document entitled "The Village Leader." This document identified five roles for the leader in providing direction for the tiny village:

Leaders create visions
Leaders create climates
Leaders create conflict
Leaders create change
Leaders create leaders

One cannot help but be impressed with the wisdom of the Council of Elders in their visionary concept of the roles required for successful leaders. Most students of leadership would agree that these roles are as relevant today as they were when they were identified in that tiny village centuries ago. As one examines these roles, it becomes evident that they serve as a challenge for new leaders and those who aspire to leadership roles in the future.

LEADERS CREATE VISIONS

Leaders frequently engage in the process of traveling into the future. When an individual plans a vacation, the months or weeks prior to the trip are often spent in a process the town elders might have humorously referred to as "anticipatory vacationalization." These would-be travelers envision the arrival, the setting, the climate, the activities, the people they will meet, and the places they will explore. Like vacationers, leaders dream of possibilities and envision the future. They spend a great deal of effort "gazing across the horizon of time . . ." (Kouzes & Posner, 1987, p. 9). They, too, anticipate arriving at a new and unfamiliar destination, experiencing a unique setting and climate, and exploring previously unknown territories. And, like the dreams of the vacationer, the dreams of the leader generate enthusiasm and excitement. LaPierre (1965) identifies three groups in society who bring about the diffusion of ideas: innovators (those who create the ideas), advocates (those who sell the ideas), and adopters (those who implement the ideas). In most instances, the leader is the innovator, the creator of the idea who works with followers to bring the idea to fruition. In some instances, however, the leader is the advocate or adopter, recognizing the value in the creative idea of another and working with followers to promote and implement the idea. "The leader's primary contribution is in the recognition of good ideas, the support of those ideas and the willingness to challenge the system . . ." (Kouzes & Posner, 1987, p. 8). New and aspiring leaders are challenged to be comfortable as advocates and adopters in identifying new and innovative ideas and assisting others to shape dreams into realities. Yet, they must also strive to entertain ideas about the unthinkable, the impossible, the inconceivable, the unusual, and the unimaginable. When leaders dare to dream, the visions of today can become the realities of tomorrow. "The first basic ingredient of leadership is a guiding vision" (Bennis, 1994, p. 39).

LEADERS CREATE CLIMATES

Leaders build teams and create an esprit de corps that generates excitement within followers. As Candidate #2 soon learned, leaders cannot operate in isolation, nor can they expect from followers what they themselves are unwilling to give. Dreams and visions are more exciting when they can be shared with others, and they can only be achieved through the commitment and support of knowledgeable, informed followers. Followers will go to great lengths to bring visions to fruition if they truly believe in the leader and the vision. Obviously, leaders must earn that commitment and support, and they can do so by creating a climate wherein followers can challenge ideas and are encouraged to speak the truth. The truth is not always what leaders want to hear, but it may be what they need to hear if they are to bring about the changes that will lead to a better future. Truth is related to authenticity, a concept that has been linked with leadership. Leaders are authentic when they "discern, seek, and live into truth, as persons in diverse communities and in the real world" (Terry,

1993, p. 112). Authenticity is extremely difficult for leaders who live in a society where conformity is celebrated and acquiescence is applauded. "Too many would-be leaders smooth out their rough edges and round out their sharp corners until they resemble all the other pebbles in the stream" (Safir, 1990, p. 16). New and aspiring leaders are challenged to use their rough edges and sharp corners as they strive for authenticity, and they should nurture and foster these skills in the "pebbles" they meet along the way.

LEADERS CREATE CONFLICT

Promoting and facilitating the status quo only serve to stifle creativity and impede the healthy process of change and growth. Leaders must be willing to challenge existing ideas, structures, processes, and visions. They must feel comfortable raising questions, and, unlike Candidate #3, they should encourage followers to question and challenge as well. Unfortunately, in a society where conflict management seminars abound and conflict resolution strategies proliferate, it is difficult to envision generation of conflict as a role requirement for leaders. Yet, the well-known phenomenon of groupthink occurs when too little conflict exists within decision-making groups, when people are unable or unwilling to speak out (Janis, 1982). Conflict-generating strategies can be as simple as providing new information or promoting discussion of an idea or trend. Too much conflict can lead to chaos and too little conflict can lead to stagnation. New and aspiring leaders are challenged to devise innovative strategies for generating conflict, and for managing and channeling the upheavals these strategies may produce. Living with uncertainty is no easy task, yet it is essential if leaders are to eventually bring about a new order. Conflict is an antecedent of change.

LEADERS CREATE CHANGE

Candidate #1 failed to realize that one key role for a leader is that of change agent. Leaders sow the seeds of change; they initiate discussions and engage in dialogue to stimulate thought and stretch the imagination of followers. In many respects, leaders create the window of possibility through which followers see a future crafted by the leader. The role of the leader is to work with followers to open that window to enable a changed future to emerge. Frequently, change represents a monumental threat to the status quo. "Change means movement. Movement means friction. Only in the frictionless vacuum of a nonexistent abstract world can movement or change occur without that abrasive friction of conflict" (Alinsky, 1971, p. 21). Figure 2.1 represents the relationship between conflict, status quo and change, and can be a useful tool for change agents. New and aspiring leaders need to realize that too little conflict can lead to apathy and too much conflict can lead to chaos. They must become skilled at creating a climate wherein the status quo is balanced by healthy conflict. Some degree of conflict along with a "safety net" of status quo, signals the ideal environment for change, and the ideal time for change agents.

LEADERS CREATE LEADERS

There are many people of talent and competence in our society today who would eagerly embrace leadership roles if they had reason to believe they would be supported and nurtured in the process (Clark & Clark, 1994). What, then, are we doing to prepare our leaders for tomorrow, and who is undertaking this monumental task? Leaders come from the ranks of followers (Rosenback & Taylor,

FIGURE 2.1 Conflict/status quo model.

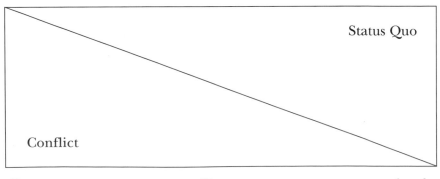

1993). The preparation of leaders for the future falls to those who are currently exercising leadership. They are charged with the responsibility of reaching into the follower ranks and grooming potential leaders who will provide a new direction and create a new order. The terms *coaching* and *mentoring* have often been associated with this process of creating new leaders. Coaches are cheerleaders; they encourage, they generate excitement, they bolster self-confidence and self-esteem, and they urge continued effort and improvement. It is often from the sidelines that coaches bring out the best in individuals. Mentors, on the other hand, play a more intimate role in the personal growth and development of a protégé. They guide, direct, open doors of opportunity, provide insight and honest feedback, and impart wisdom and knowledge. Mentors provide a prototype of one particular leadership path but never attempt to influence others in the selection of that path. Instead, after close scrutiny, the protégé may choose another path or create a path where one did not exist. New and aspiring leaders must first become comfortable with their own leadership role. It is difficult to encourage and groom others when one is in the process of learning, growing, and becoming. As the comfort level increases, the leader can seek out others and use such skills as coaching, mentoring, or both. The end result of the leader's efforts is manifested by the follower's choice of direction: selecting a new path or creating a path where none previously existed. This is the ultimate indicator of success: the preparation of a new leader who will forge in a different direction, carve out a new role, and create a new order.

It seems appropriate now to bring the legend to a close. Campbell (Maher & Briggs, 1989) indicates there are two ways of living a mythologically grounded life. One is to live the "way of the village" and remain with the villagers. The other is to move out and seek adventure elsewhere (Maher & Briggs, 1989). New and aspiring leaders need not abandon the old and familiar; often they can introduce sufficient conflict to precipitate change in even the most comfortable of surroundings. However, they may wish to move on to new and uncharted territory in order to test their ability to deal with uncertainty. The challenge for the leader, then, is to decide whether to remain with the villagers and learn from the legends of the past, or move to new and unfamiliar ground and create the legends of the future.

REFERENCES

Alinsky, S. (1971). *Rules for radicals: A pragmatic primer for realistic radicals.* New York: Random House.

Ashliman, D. L. (1987). *A guide to folktales in the english language* (pp. ix–xv). New York: Greenwood Press.

Bass, B. M. (1990). *Bass & Stogdill's handbook of leadership: Theory, research, & managerial applications* (3rd ed.). New York: The Free Press.

Bennis, W. (1994). *On becoming a leader.* New York: Addison-Wesley.

Cavendish, R. (1982). *Legends of the world* (pp. 9–13). New York: Schocken Books.

Clark, K. E., & Clark, M. B. (1994). *Choosing to lead* (p. 161). Charlotte, NC: Leadership Press.

Janis, I. (1982). *Groupthink: Psychological studies of policy decisions and fiascoes.* Boston: Houghton-Mifflin.

Kouzes, J. M., & Posner, B. (1987). *The leadership challenge.* San Francisco: Jossey-Bass.

LaPierre, R. (1965). *Social change.* New York: McGraw-Hill.

Maher, J. M., & Briggs, D. (1989). *An open life.* New York: Harper & Row.

Manfredi, C., & Valiga, T. (1994). Foreword. *Holistic Nursing Practice, 9*(1), vi.

Rosenback, W. E., & Taylor, R. L. (1993). *Contemporary issues in leadership* (3rd ed.). Boulder, CO: Westview Press.

Safir, W. (1990). Prolegomenon. In W. Safir & L. Safir (Eds.), *Leadership* (p. 16). New York: Simon and Schuster.

Terry, R. (1993). *Authentic leadership: Courage in action.* San Francisco: Jossey-Bass.

CHAPTER 3

Storytelling: An Approach to Teaching Leadership Values

Mary Kirkpatrick, Sylvene Spickerman,
Margaret K. Edwards, and Jessica K. Kirkpatrick

Storytelling is not a traditional way to learn about leadership, but it is an excellent way to learn what is important or significant. Reasons for telling stories are listed in Table 3.1. Storytelling is the individual's account of an event used to create a memorable picture in the mind of the listener. According to the National Association of Storytelling (1994), storytelling is for all ages. Storytelling, yarnspinning, and the telling of fables, myths, and tales are the means by which our history, values, and culture are preserved. Values of individuals and institutions are supported through storytelling. Stories in the form of parables and allegories relate these values and messages.

Storytelling is not new in health care (Neuhauser, 1993). It is one way to orally communicate effectively. Storytelling forces one to become a better, more active listener because one must listen to what

TABLE 3.1 Reasons to Tell a Story

Simple—Understandable	Spread the word
Timeless—ageless	Fun, we all like stories
Demographic	Memorable—You don't forget
Way to empower	A great sales tool
Form of recognition	Recruitment and hiring tool

Note: Originally published in *Nursing Leadership Forum*, Vol. 2, No. 3, 1996. New York: Springer Publishing Company.

is being said aloud, as well as to what is being implied. Storytelling causes the listener to be an active participant in imagining what it is really like to put oneself in the other person's shoes. Storytelling causes listeners to "listen with their bones," reflecting on every detail of what is being said. And listeners can imagine according to their own perspective what they think it would be like if they were in the story.

A major part of leadership education is assisting individuals to learn to communicate, including listening. Storytelling is a strategy that will advance these goals. This chapter relates stories applicable in health care that enhance the teaching of leadership by making materials interesting and meaningful. The intent is to show how nurses can communicate meaningful stories that let others know and recognize the influence of the nurse.

CHARACTERISTICS AND PURPOSE OF STORIES

Stories are told in the classroom, on the stage, at the bar, in the backyard, in the pulpit, at the fireplace, in the halls, and the list continues. Stories are told to entertain, relieve tension, build camaraderie and teamwork, clarify values and relate "how things are done here," or teach the rules and regulations of an organization (Neuhauser, 1993). Yet, storytelling as an approach to leadership conjures up a totally different reaction. Are you sure it will work? Are you sure it will be effective? Scandinavian Airlines, Armstrong International, and General Electric are only a few of the successful companies that, in reinventing their corporations, have told many stories to teach morals and values, pass along traditions, train and recognize employees, and manage their employees. According to Neuhauser (1993), two main purposes of stories in organizations are grounding or clarifying key values, and instructing and demonstrating the way to do things. The essential characteristics of the group storytelling process, according to Sarosi and O'Connor (1987) are:

> the oral retelling of vivid remembered experiences; the attempt at "storytelling listening," listening with bones, using the whole body as the ear; the suspension of judgment, explanations, and interpretation during the immediate storytelling process; and the presence of 6 to 18 participants in a quiet room sitting down, with a facilitator who sets the stage and models a good story. (p. 31)

STORIES TEACH VALUES

With the increasing emphasis in health care on customer service and excellence, stories can be used to teach health care providers to go the extra mile in showing that they care more and desire to satisfy the customer. The airline industry is known for its focus on customer service. Carlzon's *Moments of Truth* (1987) attempts to ground this value in numerous quick cameo stories. In demonstrating that the SAS airline strives to be the "best airline in the world," Carlzon defines the "moment of truth" as the first 15 seconds which impresses the customer with the value of the service (p. 3). He relates the story of a passenger who arrives at the airport without his ticket, inadvertently having left it in the hotel room. The ticket agent issues the passenger a temporary ticket, calls the hotel, and the ticket is delivered before the passenger embarks on his flight. The agent walks up to the passenger, and says calmly, "Have a good flight! Here's your ticket." Such excellent customer service should make this passenger a major advocate for SAS airlines.

Nurses could adapt similar stories to convey their own motto of customer service: "We care more!" For example, a billboard for a hospital carries the above motto. A young woman wrote back to the nurses in that hospital to demonstrate to them what it would take for the motto to become real to their customer. The story follows:

Imagine you are a single, 21-year-old woman, in the holding area of the operative suite of a 50-bed orthopedic hospital 2,000 miles from family. A loneliness hits you, much like the "Outward Bound" experience of being alone in the Smokey Mountains for three days and nights by yourself. Your only friend has left, but what exactly was she to say to someone getting ready to go under the knife, "Good luck!" The nurse is hooking you up to what seems like a "web of wires and eternally beeping machines." Across from you is a mother-daughter pair, and you distinctly feel a need for your mother—not because you are scared, but just to have her experience this event with you. Imagine someone coming to you with a warm, friendly voice with the caring eyes and concern of a mother. She says, "I am Jackie, your recovery room nurse. I will stay with you till the surgery begins, then I will be back for you before you wake up." Suddenly you know you are going to be okay. What a relief! Someone is holding your hand, saying she cares about what you are feeling and thinking.

You can make it! This event is definitely the "Moment of Truth," where grounding occurred in the first 15 seconds by the nurse proving to this patient that people at this hospital care more! (Kirkpatrick & Kirkpatrick, 1995)

In the book, *Managing by Storying Around*, Armstrong (1992) takes the approach that storytelling is one way to communicate and manage. Armstrong's leadership by "storying around" is fun, simple, entertaining, empowering, timeless, and promotes self-management. Armstrong tells the story of changing the work environment by removing all time clocks, and reestablishing trust between employees and employers. What would happen if nursing service removed all the time clocks in the hospital? Nursing would be communicating the message that since nurses can be trusted in life and death situations with patients, they surely can be trusted to report their time correctly. The integrity of nurses parallels that of other professionals. After all, time clocks don't stop cheaters; they just destroy trust and erode responsibility.

A story commonly circulated in health care facilities to promote the value of teamwork is the story of geese flying north for the summer. The story goes like this:

This spring when you see geese heading back north for the summer flying in a "V" formation, you might be interested in knowing what scientists have discovered about why they fly that way. It has been learned that as each bird flaps its wings, it creates an uplift for the bird immediately following. By flying in a "V" formation, the whole flock adds at least 71% greater flying range than if each bird flew on its own. Whenever a goose falls out of formation, it suddenly feels the drag and resistance of trying to go it alone and quickly gets back into formation to take advantage of the lifting power of the bird immediately in front. When the lead goose gets tired, he rotates back in the wing and another goose flies point. The geese honk from behind to encourage those up front to keep up their speed. Finally, when a goose gets sick or wounded by a gunshot and falls out, two geese fall out of formation and follow him down to help protect him. They stay with him until he is either able to fly or until he is dead, and then they launch out on their own or with another formation to catch up with their group. (Armstrong, 1992)

What if nurses, and all members of the interdisciplinary health care team were supported thusly! An increased efficiency of 71% would make it obvious that we work as a team or fall and fail as a team. Each member of the team would care enough to lend a helping hand when needed, irrespective of the task.

Joel Barker's (1990) video, "Discovering the Future: The Business of Paradigms," is often used in nursing leadership classes. His "kick in the pants" story is about a Swiss watch manufacturing company whose leaders rejected the idea of manufacturing the quartz watch because their traditional paradigm of what a watch should be did not fit the new model. Watches were supposed to have a winding stem, and Swiss watches were the best in the world with a costly price tag. Japan and the United States seized the moment, and the Swiss manufacturer lost control of the watch manufacturing market. This story gives the message to viewers to take off their blinders, avoid tunnel vision, expand their horizons, and develop new and different ways of doing things. The message is particularly pertinent in work redesign in hospitals where paradigm shifts are occurring and nurses' resistance may leave them behind the team that is moving ahead to make things happen differently.

A story read by nurses and circulated in some hospitals is Byham's *ZAPP!* (1988). *ZAPP!* tells the experience of a supervisor, Joe Mode, who learns what it's like to be zapped (energized, enthusiastic, responsible) as compared with being sapped (drained, controlled, with lowered self-esteem and pride) in an organization. Emphasis in this book is on the principle of effective communication, listening to people at the grass roots and responding to their needs through coaching and mentoring (ZAPPING) rather than through punishing and harassing (sapping) them. Here leadership becomes divergent and the leadership characteristics of all members of the team are enhanced through coaching, mentoring, and communicating. Similar to the leadership role of facilitator in Robert Greenleaf's *Servant Leadership* (1991), team members become leaders to empower themselves and each other.

Stories are a great way to communicate values the organization cherishes and rewards. Remember, one cannot lead without communicating. In client-focused care, stories told by patients in the community may affect the reputation of the hospital and caregivers. For example, one hospital excluded fathers from participating in the birth of their children. Unwilling to give up their rights as consumers, Lamaze-educated parents took their business elsewhere, going to a medical center 35 miles away to deliver their babies. Stories about the excellent experience clients were having at the distant hospital began to filter back to the local health care providers. The stories were communicated to the physicians and administrators; a quick reversal in the hospital policy encouraged the fathers' presence at birth. Communicated stories create change! Failure to listen, communicate, and negotiate can quickly create devastating financial situations which no hospital can tolerate today.

STORIES TO ESTABLISH CREDIBILITY

Another reason to tell stories is to establish one's credibility—an absolute must for leaders. What better way to demonstrate that credibility than by relating success stories! Recall the despondency seen in the patient having recently undergone a laryngectomy as he tries to relearn to communicate, eat, drink, or even care for himself. Then, arrange a visit by a member of the support group, a recovering patient, to show a newcomer the way. When the timing and personalities are a match, you have facilitated the "mentorship of a lifetime." Success stories like this spread quickly among those in need.

Without storytelling, oncology nurses would be at a loss when trying to create hope in patients newly diagnosed with cancer. The supportive relationships of nurses leading "I Can Cope" programs attest to their leadership ability. Oncology rehabilitation programs developed and implemented by nurses often use stories to enhance the quality of life of clients with cancer. Consider the powerful influence of the following story:

> Ms. James, a 47-year-old woman diagnosed with breast cancer, is at the height of her busy career, and is vital to the company's daily work. Cancer abruptly throws her from a 10- to 12-hour day devoted to her job into a wilderness filled with tests, procedures, drugs and activities. For 6 months, all her energies are devoted to "hanging on." (This is the time before the liquid

gold anti-nausea drugs.) At the end of 6 months, she is "bald, bloated" (increase in weight of 25 pounds), and "blue" (depressed). Her self-image is destroyed by a modified mastectomy compounded by the weight gain and a total loss of hair. Depleted and changed physically, mentally and spiritually, she completes her medical care and begins the task of rebuilding her life and returning to "normal." Her oncologist believes she will soon be back to normal and refers her to the local oncology rehabilitation program run by a clinical nurse specialist (CNS). "I thought I'd have to be taken by wheelchair to begin the program," she exclaims. Six months of inactivity, bouts of nausea and vomiting, and lowered blood counts leave her weak and fatigued. Then she met Margaret, the clinical nurse specialist. By being there and caring, identifying resources, and supporting Ms. James and her family, Margaret helped Ms. James reverse her life of devastation to one of meaning. Margaret's confidence and therapeutic caring helps Ms. James see the word *CAN* in *can*cer and restores her hope. By starting Ms. James in a support group led by the CNS and in a prescribed physical activity program on the treadmill, the program activities enhanced her strength and endurance, rebuilt and assisted her to positively cope with the stress of this disease and its treatment, as well as empowering her to take the best care of herself in restoring wellness. The entire interdisciplinary health care team delivered patient-focused care to provide both Ms. James and her family the support and resources they needed for complete rehabilitation. Margaret and Ms. James formed a therapeutic relationship with a very strong bond. Ms. James, restored to an improved level of health, now tells everyone, "If my oncologist and nurse had not believed I could, I'm not sure I could have made it." Today, Ms. James serves in the support activities of other patients to tell them the story of her remarkable recovery.

This story reinforces Kouzers and Postner's (1988) premise that credible leaders sustain hope by depicting positive images, role modeling, advising, counseling, and maintaining a caring relationship. Nursing leaders must teach this type of caring to practicing nurses and students. There seems no better way than by telling one's own credible stories and helping learners develop their own skill of storytelling.

STORYTELLING FOR TEACHING
LEADERSHIP CONCEPTS

Storytelling may be the best way to depict the paradigm shift occurring in health care. Individuals remember a good story. Nancy Austin (1995), coauthor of *In Search of Excellence,* recalls the parable of the gazelle versus the lion as told by managers at Nordstrom to remind them to stay competitive. "Every morning in Africa, a gazelle wakes up. It knows it must outrun the fastest lion or be killed. Every morning in Africa, a lion wakes up. It knows it must run faster than the slowest gazelle or it will starve. So it doesn't really matter whether you're the lion or the gazelle—when the sun comes up, start running" (p. 14). The message that "complacency is the enemy of success" is very clear in this parable. Nurses need to outrun the others, role model their behaviors, and lead others by telling their stories.

Most stories describe the best or worst times. Recent stories in the media reflect the dilemmas in hospitals when nurses delegate to unlicensed personnel. For example, Cowley in *Newsweek* (1995), relays the story of the nurse telling an unlicensed aide to respond to an alarm. Later when the nurse checked the patient, she found the sheets drenched with blood from a detached arterial line. The lesson of this story is that responsibility rests in the professional who must delegate according to the judgment skills of the person assigned. Such anecdotes serve to point out the responsibility of leadership. Nurses must be assured the aides have reasonable levels of judgment and assessment skills before entrusting various aspects of patient care to them. Each leader's stories can vividly make this point without detailed pedagogy.

Another concept taught in every leadership course and experienced by everyone almost daily is change. A parable told by N. Austin (1995) depicting how difficult change is, and the time it takes to acclimate to change, follows:

> Willie B., a majestic silverback gorilla, lived in isolation for 27 years in a dismal bunker at the Atlanta zoo. Having raised sufficient money for a new, state-of-the-art gorilla habitat, Willie B. would soon, for the first time in his captive life, be able to feel the sun and rain on his head. Willie B. took several days to fully explore his new surroundings. Taking a few small, tentative steps

at a time to explore his domain, the gorilla gingerly tested the grass with his toe. It took several days to coach the gorilla to leave the ugly, cramped space he knew so well for the light, spacious, clean surroundings of this new habitat.

Peter Senge in *The Fifth Discipline* (1990) relates several parables applicable to the change occurring in nursing today. The story of the "Boiled Frog" has a message for nursing leadership.

> If you place a frog in a pot of boiling water, it will immediately try to scramble out. But if you place the frog in room temperature water, and don't scare him, he'll stay put. Now, if the pot sits on a heat source, and if you gradually turn up the temperature, something very interesting happens. As the temperature rises from 70 to 80 degrees F, the frog will do nothing. In fact, he will show every sign of enjoying himself. As the temperature gradually increases, the frog will become groggier and groggier, until he is unable to climb out of the pot. Though there is nothing restraining him, the frog will sit there and boil. Why? (p. 22)

Change can be sudden, but more often in health care systems, it is slow and gradual. Learning to see gradual, subtle changes as well as the overt ones will help. Nurses need to be proactive and recognize the repetitive patterns and cycles of change. Cross-training or changing one's skills to those that many disciplines value are marketable skills that may be one way for nurses to survive in the health care system today. The time to change is now, not when one is the boiled frog.

Finally, power is taught as a concept of change. Yet power may appear lifeless in a didactic session. Gilbert (1995), as does Courtney in *Power of One* (1989), emphasizes the impact of power. This tale describes the historical basis of apartheid, as it relates to one person's ability and commitment to transform a nation. Concepts about power, such as its sources and types are evident in this story with the reader having to identify, extract, and analyze them. Such analysis, which causes the reader to critically think about what he/she is reading, stimulates the reader through many of the senses.

SUMMARY

Storytelling:

- is an effective way to teach leadership
- shows the influence health care providers have on their clients
- helps learners to market themselves and their product: professional nursing and their institutions
- instills hope
- communicates a message
- crosses cultural barriers

The outcomes of storytelling are that the principles and morals are passed on to others. Learners remember stories with powerful messages. As Kerfoot and Sarosi (1992) say, "In health care institutions, the quest for quality of experience and for healing to accompany technology is increasingly evident. Hospital cultures encourage shared governance, total quality management, and patient-focused care. Stories will transmit this new culture" (p. 107). Leaders in health care can improve humanistic behavior in health care systems by helping future leaders address the personal, cultural, and moral issues of health care delivery through storytelling.

REFERENCES

Austin, N. (1995). Managing by parable. *Working Woman*, pp. 14–16.

Armstrong, D. (1992). *Managing by storying around: A new method of leadership.* New York: Doubleday.

Barker, J. (1990). *Discovering the future: The business of paradigms.* Barnesville, MN: Charthouse International Learning Corporation.

Byham, W. (1988). *ZAPP: The lightning of empowerment.* New York: Fawcett Columbine.

Carlzon, J. (1987). *Moments of truth.* New York: Harper Collins Publishers.

Courtney, B. (1989). *Power of one.* New York: Random House.

Cowley, G. (1995, February 13). Intensive care on a budget. *Newsweek.*

Gilbert, T. (1995). Nursing: Empowerment and the problem of power. *Journal of Advanced Nursing, 21,* 865–871.

Greenleaf, R. K. (1991). *Servant leadership.* New York: Paulist Press.

Kerfoot, K., & Sarosi, G. (1992). Today's patient care unit manager. *Nursing Economics, 11*(2), 107–108.

Kirkpatrick, M., & Kirkpatrick, J. (1995). *Stories: A new approach to leadership.* [Poster, Nurse Educator Conference]. Baltimore, MD.

Kouzers, J., & Posner, B. (1988). Relating leadership and credibility. *Psychology Reports, 63*(2), 527.

National Association of Storytelling (1994). Jonesborough, TN.

Neuhauser, P. C. (1993). *Corporate legend and lore: The power of storytelling.* New York: Springer Publishing.

Rost, J. (1993). *Leadership for the 21st century.* Westport, CT: Praeger.

Sarosi, G. M., & O'Connor, P. (1987). The microsity pathway of executive nursing rounds: Storytelling as a management tool. *Nursing Administration Quarterly, 17*(2), 30–37.

Senge, P. M. (1990). *The fifth discipline.* New York: Doubleday.

CHAPTER 4

Preparing the Nurse Executive of the Future

Harriet R. Feldman

Health care reform is well underway, with hospitals merging, right-sizing, and closing, and health care systems merging into supersystems. Physicians are joining groups that are extending into supergroups. Managed care organizations are mushrooming and there is a tremendous expansion of home care services. Change is constant and the pace is accelerating. How should nursing education prepare students for this sort of world? More particularly, what should be the education of the nurse executive of the future? And what kinds of partnerships should educators develop with the health care system to achieve its goals?

The history of change in nursing education marks us as slow-moving, complex, and politicized by accreditation, professional organizations, and certifying bodies. In this changing health care environment, however, a great deal must be accomplished in a relatively short period of time. Three broad questions concerning educational preparation of the nurse executive of the future can direct our deliberations: What must they learn? How will they learn it? How will we know that they have learned it?

WHAT MUST THEY LEARN?

The preparation of nurse executives should focus on at least five essential skills required to survive and, indeed, thrive, in a rapidly chang-

Note: Originally published in *Nursing Leadership Forum*, Vol. 1, No. 1, 1995. New York: Springer Publishing Company.

ing environment: leadership, financial management, information management, service delivery, and strategic management.

Leadership

The nurse executive of today is very different from her/his counterpart of past decades. A shift in focus from administration to management to leadership has evolved to meet the needs of highly complex institutional settings. In his book entitled *A Briefing for Leaders*, Dilenschneider (1992) shows the evolution of power (Table 4.1) to the current decade of the visionary leader.

As leaders, "how *do* you match the right idea to the right problem, at the right time, and in the right way?" (Bolman & Deal, 1991). Too often our vision is truncated; we attack new challenges with old tools. Nurse executives must be agile in reframing their responses if they are to survive in dynamic, changing organizations. They must be aware that there is always more than one way to respond to any organizational problem. The ability to reframe with problems and solutions enriches and broadens one's repertoire. It expands choices. Leaders need multiple tools, the skill to use them, and the wisdom to match frames to individual situations. Bolman and Deal (1991) describe four such perspectives or schemata and corresponding personal "frames" that are used to "gather information, make judgments, and determine how best to get things done" (p. 11).

TABLE 4.1 The Evolution of Power

The 1950s and 1960s	The 1970s and 1980s	The 1990s
Power as administration	Power as management	Power as leadership
Conformist	Exception-driven	Visionary
Chain of command	Ad hoc	Instant
Stable	Turbulent	Sustaining
Introspective	Market-driven	Positioning
Apprenticeship	Mentoring	Collegial

From *A briefing for leaders* (p. 5) by R. L. Dilenschneider, 1992, New York: Harper Collins Publishers. Copyright 1992 by Harper Collins Publishers. Reprinted by permission.

The four perspectives are: structural, human resource, political, and symbolic. The structural frame draws on the discipline of sociology and emphasizes formal roles and relationships. The human resource frame uses the ideas of organizational social psychologists and is based on the premise that organizations are inhabited by individuals who have needs, feelings, and prejudices. The political frame, based on the work of political scientists, views organizations as arenas in which different interest groups compete for power and scarce resources. The symbolic frame draws on social and cultural anthropology, treating organizations as cultures propelled more by rituals than by rules.

Each frame has its own image of reality and each is appropriate at a given time and circumstance. Structural leaders are likely to believe strongly in the importance of clear structure and well-developed management systems. An effective structural leader is someone who thinks clearly, has good analytic skills, makes good decisions, and can design structures and systems that get the job done. Human resource leaders view the central task of management as developing a good fit between people and organizations, and believe in the importance of coaching, participation, motivation, teamwork, and good interpersonal relations. An effective human resource leader is a facilitator and participative manager who supports and empowers others. Political leaders believe that managers and leaders live in a world of conflict and scarce resources. They emphasize the importance of building a power base that includes allies, networks, and coalitions. An effective political leader is an advocate and negotiator who understands politics and is comfortable with conflict. Finally, symbolic leaders believe that the essential task of management is to provide vision and inspiration. An effective symbolic leader is a prophet and visionary who uses symbols, tells stories, and frames experiences in ways that give people hope and meaning (*Leadership Orientation Scoring*, 1988). The issue is whether the leader selects the right one (best one) in a given situation. These leadership orientations can be learned and applied to the organizational problems that nurse executives confront daily (Table 4.2).

Bringing the right tools to bear helps an executive create her/his vision, but problem-framing/solving strategies, no matter how important, cannot supplant the need for vision. The nurse executive must be visionary, and vision is both intellectual and intuitive. As Haas

(1992) said, vision must "draw simplicity out of complexity and clarity out of obscurity" (p. 19).

Today's response must be not only visionary, but quick. Haas (1992) tells the *boiled frog story*. A live frog placed in a pot of water at room temperature swims around. If the temperature of the water is raised 1 degree every 30 minutes, the frog stays in the water and swims around until it is boiled. Why? Because the frog cannot sense that the environment is changing. On the other hand, if you drop a frog into water already boiling, the frog will jump out immediately. Nursing education must prepare executives who relish change and who can build the kind of organizational culture that will respond in a timely fashion. No boiled frogs here!

FINANCIAL MANAGEMENT

Fiscal management is the next major criterion in preparing the nurse executive. The development and use of financial information in institutional decision-making and analysis are essential for making good qualitative judgments. The educator must identify the concepts and practices of financial management necessary for the nurse executive. What are the elements of an effective and efficient financial management system, including planning, budgeting, and ongoing cost variance management? How can the nurse executive recognize and respond to financial variances? What are the fiscal alternatives in managing declining resources and responding to retrenchment pressures? How can one contain costs, yet maintain productivity? How are profit centers held accountable?

While enrolled in a management development program at Harvard University, I participated in an exercise on allocating limited resources. Each group of 12 participants was given the same resources: *one can of Coca-Cola per person and one split of chilled champagne with three glasses per group*. Each group had to plan how it would allocate the resources. The exercise ended when the majority reached an agreement as to how the resources should be allocated. The recorded agreement had to state explicitly who got what and why. If agreement was not reached within 30 minutes, that group's resources were automatically confiscated for redistribution without any right to recourse or appeal. Participative strategies such as this stimulate critical thinking and

TABLE 4.2 Four Interpretations of Organizational Processes

Process	Structural Frame	Human Resource Frame	Political Frame	Symbolic Frame
Planning	Strategies to set objectives and coordinate resources	Gatherings to promote participation	Arenas to air conflict and realign power	Ritual to signal responsibility, produce symbols, negotiate meaning
Decision-making	Rational sequence to produce right decision	Open process to produce commitment	Opportunity to gain or exercise power	Ritual to provide comfort and support until decision happens
Reorganizing	Realign roles and responsibilities to fit tasks and environment	Maintain a balance between human needs and formal roles	Redistribute power and form new coalitions	Maintain an image of accountability and responsiveness; negotiate new social order
Evaluating	Way to distribute rewards or penalties and control performance	Process for helping individuals grows and improve	Opportunity to exercise power	Occasion to play roles in shared ritual

Approaching Conflict	Maintain organizational goals by having authorities resolve conflict	Develop relationships by having individuals confront conflict	Develop power by bargaining, forcing, or manipulating others to win	Develop shared values and use conflict to negotiate that meaning
Goal-setting	Keep organization headed in the right direction	Keep people involved and communication open	Provide opportunity for individuals and groups to make interest known	Develop symbols and shared values
Communication	Transmit facts and information	Exchange information, needs, and feelings	Vehicles for influencing or manipulating others	Telling stories
Meetings	Formal occasions for making decisions	Informal occasions for involvement, sharing feelings	Competitive occasions to win points	Sacred occasions to celebrate and transform culture
Motivation	Economic incentives	Growth and self-actualization	Coercion, manipulation, and seduction	Symbols and celebrations

From *Reframing organizations* (p. 323) by L. G. Bolman and T. E. Deal, 1991, San Francisco: Jossey-Bass. Copyright 1991 by Jossey-Bass. Reprinted by permission.

planning so necessary for effective fiscal management. These kinds of strategies can be used both in education and practice settings in dealing with declining resources.

Information Management

In a recent issue of *Harvard Business Review,* Davenport (1994) said that, ". . . effective information management must begin by thinking about how people use information—not with how people use machines" (p. 120). Since it is impossible to completely control information, and information is complex and ever-expanding, a human-centered approach is needed. In a changing technological system, it is important for the nurse executive to have excellent communication skills and to model appropriate information-sharing behaviors. Relationships must be developed between people and data, sensitive to maintaining a delicate balance between unlimited and limited sharing of information. Guidelines for how to use information must be created and applied. Information decisions determine how people use their time. Often there is far too much noninformation, e.g., junk mail, data that do not address problems or are too complex for easy interpretation, at the expense of useful information.

Service Delivery

In this era of customer service, one may ask, "Who are the customers of a health delivery system?" One customer/client is the individual who is restored to health, but so is the family who receives benefits from the client's recovery and the community that derives social and economic benefits from the client's return to productivity. For the nurse executive, the customer consists of frontline workers and other professionals and service providers. Support of all clients and their networks needs to be at the center of the nurse executive's concern. We can learn a lot from the private sector in this regard, for links in the service-profit chain (Heskett, 1987; Heskett, Jones, Loveman, Sasser, & Schlesinger, 1994) apply to the nonprofit, public sector as well. Employee satisfaction, evidenced by higher retention and productivity, and client satisfaction, evidenced in loyalty, referrals to others, and ultimately, increased revenue, are but a few indicators of satisfied customers.

A strategic service vision builds shared values and bonds people together. It develops relational and technical skills and integrates marketing and operations into the design and implementation of service delivery processes. Such a vision can be fostered in the educational as well as the work setting. Heskett, Jones, Loveman, Sasser, and Schlesinger (1994) present the example of *ServiceMaster*:

> ServiceMaster, a provider of a range of cleaning and maintenance services, aims to maximize the dignity of the individual service worker. Each year, it analyzes in depth a part of the maintenance process, such as cleaning a floor, in order to reduce the time and effort needed to complete the task. The 'importance of the mundane' is stressed repeatedly in ServiceMaster's management training—for example, in the 7-step process devised for cleaning a hospital room: from the first step, greeting the patient, to the last step, asking patients whether or not they need anything else done. Using this process, service workers develop communication skills and learn to interact with patients in ways that add depth and dimension to their jobs. (p. 168)

Strategic Management

The nurse executive needs to marshal and allocate resources to achieve goals and objectives in the face of changing competitive, environmental, and internal forces. Strategic management provides a framework for organizational analysis that can facilitate executive decision-making. It forces the executive to consider various critical dimensions of the organization and so is likely to improve organizational performance, both in providing services and in effectively using resources and controlling costs. Hatten (1982) provides a model of the strategic planning process in not-for-profit organizations (Figure 4.1). Past practice is a useful starting point in developing strategies to improve future performance in light of current and likely future reality. Once a strategy is determined, it is tested and evaluated, then reformulated as needed to respond to change.

In summary, the nurse executives of the future will need to be knowledgeable leaders and financial, strategic, and information managers; they will also need to have a strategic service orientation.

FIGURE 4.1 Strategic planning process in not-for-profit organizations.

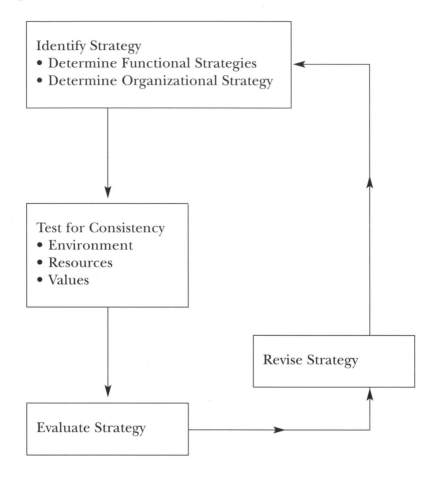

From "Strategic management in not-for-profit organizations," by M. L. Hatten, 1982. *Strategic Management Journal, 3*, pp. 89–104. Copyright 1982 by *Strategic Management Journal*. Reprinted by permission.

HOW WILL THEY LEARN IT?

Two educational modalities for preparing nurse executives are degree and continuing education, both of which are important in an era of change. Let's look first at degree education. I would like to propose a radical model of master's degree education for nurse executives. It is my belief that in order to be most effective in the health care arena, the nurse executive must be able to "walk the walk" and "talk the talk" characteristic of a broad spectrum of administrators of health care. The master's in nursing administration, as currently designed, just doesn't do it! I propose the creation of MBA and MPA models that include a concentration in nursing management, that is, programs specifically designed to apply broad concepts of administration to the nursing service setting rather than a degree geared solely to the nursing domain. Such a model is presented in Table 4.3, and addresses the five essential skills described in this chapter. In addition, research, public policy, and legal/ethical topics are covered.

I am not advocating traditional doctoral preparation in the discipline of nursing as the direction for nurse executives. Rather, I would suggest a doctoral degree, be it nursing or non-nursing, that focuses

TABLE 4.3 Model for an MPA or MBA With a Concentration in Nursing Management

Course	No. of Credits
Organizational Theory	3
Management of public and nonprofit organizations	3
Budgeting and financial management	3
Public policy analysis and formulation	3
Human resources management	3
Quantitative methods in decision-making	3
Management information systems	3
Strategic management in health delivery systems	3
Fiscal management of the nursing organization	3
Ethical and legal issues in nursing management	3
Managing change in nursing service (including practicum)	3
The culture of nursing management	3
Research project	0
Total credits	**36**

on such areas as public policy, public health or health administration. We cannot continue to be narrow in our thinking. We must be open to broadening our networks with other disciplines through the educational process. Nursing simply doesn't have all the answers!

Continuing education must be a mainstay for the nurse executive of the future, not something to be done "if time permits." Changes in environmental systems are accompanied by changing paradigms for leadership and management; the nurse executive must keep abreast of what is new in order to deal with the present and plan for the future. Continuing education programs offer opportunities to dialogue and form networks with colleagues in service and education to discuss such topics as management strategies, customer satisfaction, service/education initiatives, and transforming organizations to accommodate a reformed health care system.

In terms of "how" the learning takes place, educators must be flexible and creative. Strategies for degree and continuing education might include modular self-directed learning, distance learning to reach nurses in their work settings and homes, executive models that meet in cohort groups regularly for a specified time period, 2- to 3-day institutes, and unlimited opportunities for mentoring and colleagueship among nursing executives and other health care administrators.

Establishing a new generation of relationships within the health delivery system is essential to the survival of the education delivery system. More than ever before, educators need the guidance and participation of those in the health care setting. They need to learn: What are the real needs of the delivery system? And, how can educational institutions prepare students to meet these needs?

HOW WILL WE KNOW THAT THEY HAVE LEARNED IT?

There are a number of outcomes that bear testimony to excellence in the preparation of nurse executives. Ultimately, though, there are two challenges. First is the nurse executive's ability to reframe leadership behavior when confronted with multiple challenges on a daily basis. For example, what frames are relevant in setting goals and policies under conditions of uncertainty? What frames are relevant when the executive needs to achieve a "delicate balance" in allocating scarce resources? When keeping on top of a large, complex set of activities? When seeking support from corporate staff? When motivating, coordinating, and controlling a large, diverse group of employees?

Second is the nurse executive's ablility to generate customer satisfaction in various clients and employees. Today this must be achieved in ways that both contain costs and improve profits. We need to be creative in the way we generate satisfaction, and unbiased in our evaluation of satisfaction outcomes, many of which are imprecise at best.

SUMMARY

There is much work to be done to arrive at the kind of education that will prepare nurses to assume executive roles within and outside of nursing service. Nurse executives must be prepared to meet the challenges of shifting paradigms in health care and be able to comfortably move into leadership roles in a variety of health care delivery systems. In developing their leadership skills, nurse executives must learn to innovate, regulate, share power, and empower others. They need to be able to accommodate national, regional, and state forces, regulatory bodies, legal and ethical standards, and shifts in amounts and sources of funding. Educators can be effective in ensuring competence of the nurse executive by developing curricula that establish a sound knowledge base in leadership, financial management, information management, service delivery, and strategic management. It is only through intense, collaborative efforts between service and education that we can effectively answer the three questions posed: What must they learn? How will they learn it? How will we know that they have learned it?

REFERENCES

Bolman, L. G., & Deal, T. E. (1991). *Reframing organizations: Artistry choice, and leadership.* San Francisco: Jossey-Bass Publishers.

Davenport, T. H. (1994, March–April). Saving it's soul: Human-centered information management. *Harvard Business Review, 72,* 119–131.

Dilenschneider, R. L. (1992). *A briefing for leaders—Communication as the ultimate exercise of power.* New York: Harper Collins Publishers.

Haas, H. G. (1992). *The leader within: An empowering path of self-discovery.* New York: Harper Collins Publishers.

Hatten, M. L. (1982). Strategic management in not-for-profit organizations. *Strategic Management Journal, 3*, 89–104.

Heskett, J. L. (1987, March–April). Lessons in the service sector. *Harvard Business Review, 65*, 2.

Heskett, J. L., Jones, T. O., Loveman, G. W., Sasser, W. E., & Schlesinger, L. A. (1994, March–April). Putting the service-profit chain to work. *Harvard Business Review, 72*(2), 164–174.

Leadership Orientations Scoring. (1988). Brookline, MA: Leadership Frameworks.

CHAPTER 5

Reflections on Achieving Professional Leadership

Joyce J. Fitzpatrick

> *This inspirational message was prepared as the capstone speech for the 1999 Helene Fuld Health Trust Fellowship Program for Emerging Nurse Leaders. At the time, Dr. Fitzpatrick was President of the American Academy of Nursing. Key to her message is that future leaders should be encouraged to focus on development of a career perspective as they develop transformational leadership skills.*

As President of the American Academy of Nursing, I am often called upon to address groups within nursing concerned with our collective leadership challenges. On occasions such as the capstone celebration of the completion of the 1999 Fuld Fellowship Program, and other similar leadership development training sessions, it is most appropriate to deliver as simple and as meaningful a message as possible. The message from Dr. Seuss's 1990 book: "Oh, the places you'll go!" helps to frame the leadership challenges for the future:

> Congratulations!
> Today is your day.
> You're off to great places!
> You're off and away!
> You have brains in your head.
> You have feet in your shoes.
> You can steer yourself

Note: Originally published in *Nursing Leadership Forum*, Vol. 5, No. 1, 2000. New York: Springer Publishing Company.

Any direction you choose
You're on your own.
And you know what you know
And you are the guy who'll decide where to go.

               (Seuss, 1990, pp. 1–2)

Each future leader will choose how he/she will lead in the profession of nursing. In determining the particular avenue for excercising leadership skills, it may be helpful to reflect first on the nature of the nursing profession and the challenges inherent for leaders within professions such as nursing. The basic message that I want to share is one of shaping your own career as a leader.

REFLECTIONS ON NURSING AND NURSE LEADERS

In a recent Harris Poll regarding the public's view of the nursing profession, 85% of Americans said that they would be pleased if their son or daughter became a registered nurse. Ninety-two percent of the public trusts the information that registered nurses provide about health care (American Nurses Association, 1999, p. 6).

With the public's confidence and trust in nursing so high, together as nurses we must reaffirm our vision and values for the profession and for the patients we serve. I have always believed that the profession of nursing had as a foundation three "Cs": competence, commitment, and community. Nursing competence involves scholarship and professional skills; the many components of professional nursing competency are built into the basic nursing curricula that each of you knows so well. Cornerstones of professional nursing are compassion and passion, caring, and communication. Professional nursing commitment helps to distinguish us as professionals, dedicated to health care and nursing. It is reflected in the care that we provide for each individual patient and for the public good. And our commitment and competency are demonstrated through our community of action, for a profession serves the public and society, the community in the broadest sense of the term.

As nurse leaders you will be called upon to demonstrate these characteristics in everything that you do. You will be judged on your commitment and competence, and will be expected to give to the community of nurses, patients, health care professionals, and society. Nurse leaders of the past and the present have demonstrated these qualities. They are competent, committed professionals who serve others, whether their professional peers or their patients, for the greater good. Future leaders in nursing, and I count you among these, also will be expected to meet the standard of leadership within the broad health care arena.

ADVICE ON LEADERSHIP

Yet "leadership" is a somewhat elusive concept, having almost as many meanings as there are scholars defining it. Leadership has been formally defined in terms of traits, behaviors, power, politics, authority, charisma, vision, transformation, management, change, goal achievement, and influence. Leaders may be heroes and heroines, supermen and superwomen, spellbinders and dreamers, pathfinders and trailblazers. Leaders may be champions such as Isabella of Spain and Napoleon, saviors such as Moses and Nightingale, servants such as Mother Theresa, visionaries such as Joan of Arc and Martin Luther King, or revolutionaries such as Dorothea Dix, Lillian Wald, and Susan B. Anthony (Klenke, 1996).

Today most of us want, and often expect, our leaders to have charisma, a word derived from the Greek, which literally means "gift of grace." And, through the study of current leadership theories, we strive toward the ideal of "transformational leadership," a leadership style that is characterized by important personal characteristics, including self-confidence, dominance, and a strong conviction in the moral righteousness of one's beliefs or causes (Kuhnert & Lewis, 1987).

As future leaders who will be considering your role as transformational leaders in nursing, the skills imbedded in the four "Is" of transformational leaders described by Avolio and colleagues (Avolio, Waldman, & Yammarino, 1991) represent critical components for development. For future leaders the key aspects of leadership to consider include:

- How will you give individualized attention to your followers, attention that encourages personal growth of each individual?
- Can you offer intellectual stimulation, or new ways of looking at things, novel ideas, and creative solutions to problems?

- Can you provide inspirational motivation, helping others to derive meaning and challenge from their work?
- Do you have idealized influence, such that you can serve as a role model, a leader whom others wish to emulate?

Leaders are expected to lead, to influence, and to not only do things right, but to do the right things.

I am often asked, as I am sure many other nurse leaders also are asked . . . what do you think led you to a leadership position? Was it family life that in some way influenced you? Did you have a significant life experience that made you dedicate your talents and energies to nursing? Was there a particular mentor who influenced your career development?

Besides the easy and accurate answer that it was "all of the above," I firmly believe that it was the early adoption of a career perspective that has served as a driving force for me in my career. I have always had very structured and specific career goals. Beginning when I was an undergraduate student, I defined goals that were achievable and concrete, and then sought advice about how to accomplish the goals. In an editorial that I wrote for *Nursing and Health Care Perspectives*, published in the November/December, 1999 issue of the journal (Fitzpatrick, 1999), I reflected on what I consider a "defining moment" of my career. As I was learning the roles and responsibilities of leadership, while I was a student in the PhD program at NYU, Dr. Martha Rogers introduced me to one of the most powerful religious leaders of the time, Dr. Norman Vincent Peale. Dr. Peale's message, not only of the "power of positive thinking," but also of the creative use of self, tough-minded optimism, and the channeling of energy to positive results, has served as my professional leadership compass. I have had more than a few occasions in positions of professional leadership when I have had to consciously remind myself of the "unlimited power" that resides in the human spirit. And as discovered by Bennis (1990) in his years of research on leaders, every leader shares at least one characteristic: a concern with a guiding purpose, an overarching vision. As a leader you will be expected to have a vision, one that you can clearly articulate to others so as to guide them toward lofty and challenging goals.

There are many ways to learn leadership. One is to adopt the advice of a key leader as a compass to guide one's own development of skills.

The following examples of leadership quotes can be used as compasses to guide a lifetime of nursing work, whether this work occurs through leadership roles in patient care, in nursing organizations, or in the formation of health programs and policies.

First a quote from Margaret Mead: "Never doubt that a small group of committed citizens can change the world; indeed it is the only thing that ever has."

Second, from another great woman leader from this past century, Eleanor Roosevelt, who said: "You must do the things you think you cannot do."

Third, Marie Curie's advice: "We must have perseverance and above all confidence in ourselves. We must believe that we are gifted."

Fourth, from President Theodore Roosevelt: "Far and away the best prize that life offers is the chance to work hard at work worth doing."

Fifth, from George Eliot: "What do we live for, if it is not to make life less difficult for each other?"

And last, again from George Eliot: "It is never too late to be what you might have become" (Bartlett & Kaplan, 1992).

Because leaders come in many shapes, sizes, and dispositions, each of you as future leaders will choose your own way to lead. Thus, as a leader your guiding purpose and overarching vision can and should be your own. In the words of Dr. Seuss: "Your mountain is waiting . . . so get on your way" (Seuss, 1990, p. 42).

REFERENCES

American Nurses Association. (1999, September/October). *American Nurse.* (p. 6). Washington, DC: Author.

Avolio, B., Waldman, D., & Yammarino, F. (1991). Leading in the 1990s: The four I's of transformational leadership. *European Industrial Training, 15,* 9–16.

Bartlett, J., & Kaplan, J. (Eds.). (1992). *Bartlett's familiar quotations* (16th ed.). Boston: Little Brown.

Bennis, W. (1990). Managing the dream: Leadership in the 21st century. *Training: The Magazine of Human Resource Development, 27,* 43–48.

Fitzpatrick, J. J. (1999). The power of positive thinking and other new age ideas from the past [Editorial]. *Nursing and Health Care Perspectives, 20.*

Klenke, K. (1996). *Women and leadership: A contextual perspective.* New York: Springer Publishing.

Kuhnert, K., & Lewis, P. (1987).Transactional and transformational leadership: A constructive developmental analysis. *Academy of Management Review, 12,* 648–657.

Seuss, Dr. (1990). *Oh, the places you'll go.* New York: Random House.

This chapter was first presented at the Fuld Fellowship Capstone Retreat on Leadership for Student Leadership Development Project, New York University Division of Nursing and Wagner School of Public Policy, New York, NY, October 10, 1999.

PART II

Developing
Leadership Skills

CHAPTER 6

Business Plans: An Effective Tool for Making Decisions

Norma Ness Turini

In today's economic market the management and utilization of resources for the provision of health services is of the utmost importance and concern for nurse leaders. We must be knowledgeable of the various managerial and business modalities necessary to function in today's environment. We have an enormous opportunity to take the lead and participate in the business decisions being made concerning the expansion or elimination of existing services and the implementation of new ones. In order to meet this challenge nurse managers at all levels must be prepared to incorporate sound business practices into their decision-making processes.

Nursing already participates in many on-going general businesses, such as the business of education, or management, consultation, primary care, community health, nursing informatics, organizational development, occupational health, research, and continuous quality improvement, among others. Inherent in each business are the items or services it produces. Consequently, a carefully drawn, professionally written business plan is an effective business tool nurse leaders can develop when justifying their recommendations for products or services and/or raising of capital. The business plan can be the vehicle by which all those involved in developing the product will be included from the beginning, coordinate their actions, assess the financial viability of the plan, and produce a realistic appraisal of the venture. In addition, the process will enhance the professional development, business acumen, knowledge and skills of those involved.

Note: Originally published in *Nursing Leadership Forum*, Vol. 1, No. 4, 1995. New York: Springer Publishing Company.

A business plan has two basic functions. First, it is the *operating blueprint* for the business and is used as an internal document by management. Second, it functions as the *marketing document*, used to describe the different steps that will be taken and the anticipated results to persuade "the powers that be" that this venture will prosper and succeed and that both the Project Leader/Director and the business proposed, are a good choice.

The length, details, and format of the business plan can vary depending on the size, scope and nature of the project, but there are basic components with common elements that comprise each plan. The plan addresses the who, what, where, when and how of a new or different venture, and combines the components of a strategic plan, a written proposal, and a financial analysis. Input from all available resources should be utilized when preparing the plan so that it is as comprehensive and accurate as possible. Persons involved in the areas of Strategic Planning, Development, Human Resources, Finance, Materials Management, Systems Analysis, Facilities Planning, Community Relations, Public Relations, and Information Services are valuable contributors and can often assist when making the oral business presentation of the plan and/or in marketing it.

The design and format of the business plan is extremely important to its success. It should be well organized, flow logically, and attract and maintain the reader's attention and interest.

The plan itself should be organized into two sections: 1) The Plan of Business, 2) The Supporting Information and Documentation. It should be a comprehensive document with the first section no more than 60 double-spaced pages, no matter how complex the proposal. Documentation of the details should be located in the second section. Geared toward the reader, written in a positive and enthusiastic tone in a style that's interesting and realistic yet concise and complete, the business plan may be accompanied by photographs, videotapes, or other supporting materials useful to the presentation. (In most, but not all situations, the proposer has the opportunity to support the business plan with a presentation.)

COMPONENTS OF THE BUSINESS PLAN

The components of the Business Plan include: a Title Page, Table of Contents, Executive Summary, History or Introduction, Management

Team Description, Business Description, Market Analysis, Competition, Potential Risks and Problems, Marketing Goals/Strategy, Operational/ Organizational Plan, Financial Plan and Strategy, Evaluation and Control System, Implementation Plan and Timetable, and an Appendix containing the Supporting Information and Documentation.

Title Page

This page lists the organization's name and address, the title of the business plan, time frames addressed, and the name and telephone number of the nurse who is Project Director.

Table of Contents

This element should be comprehensive, listing major headings with their various components, so that readers can easily refer to any section. It should also include the appendix listing all supporting documents, illustrations, tables, and graphs.

Executive Summary

This section is an overview or abstract of the business plan. The summary sets the tone for the planning process. After a descriptive opening, the vision, mission, goals, and objectives of the organization should be related to the business plan. The business or product being proposed and the environment in which it will function, follows. One should include any unique features, whether the proposal is a new venture or an expansion of an existing one, why it is needed, as well as the cost and the results expected. The summary should be written clearly and succinctly, with no technical words unless absolutely necessary as the readers may be nonmedical. It should be no more than two double-spaced pages and should be able to stand alone, if necessary. *Remember that some readers may only read this section and then refer to the Appendix for back-up information without reviewing any other portion of the plan.*

History or Introduction

This section describes the organization's present status, organization and principal people such as the Board of Trustees, key executive staff, business, community, and government leaders. The introduction explains the organization's current position in relationship to its competition, new technologies, innovative approaches to healthcare, and the current environment. Projections of where the organization can go and why the project will be profitable are given here. Often a synopsis of the organization's history such as who founded it, when, and why are included. What were the original goals and objectives? How was it funded? What have been some of the major accomplishments?

Management Team Description

The management team should be described in terms of function and background relating to the business being proposed as well as in the context of the larger organization in which this team will function. The responsibilities, authority, accountability, and salary ranges for each key director, manager, employee, and consultant should be included, along with he number of employees involved. Applicable organizational charts should also be included. If an Advisory Team/Board is being utilized for this project, then a 2-3 paragraph description of each member's background and skills should be included. Explain each member's personal history, applicable qualifications, and related work experience (both operational and managerial). The resources that the person brings to the business should be spelled out.

Business Description

This is a critical part of the business plan because it is here that the business being proposed is defined and its marketability, salability and profitability will be projected and evaluated. The details have to be carefully chosen and organized so that they provide the reader with a comprehensive picture of the venture. It should be written completely, clearly and simply without medical terminology, so that it can be easily understood, beginning with a clear statement of what the business is and what its goals and objectives are. Details of the present and future services/products are given as well as why they will be attractive to consumers. This section describes how this service/product will be used as well as by whom, where, and why. Any secondary uses it may have (e.g., bringing maternity cases to the facility whose newborns will come back for primary care) should be included. Unique and proprietary features such as copyrights or patents are listed as well. The present state of development or any pilot or research projects done as a predecessor of this venture are given here. Also mentioned are the disadvantages or possibilities of obsolescence, especially in light of the current environment in the health care field. If these obstacles exist, one also tells what will be done to counter them. Opportunities for expansion of this service/product or development of related services/products are given in detail if they are central to this business plan, and in general terms, if not. Samples, illustrations, photos, and/or videos are included if it will make the presentation more effective. *This section will lay out the strategy planned so that the business will be a success and should be critically evaluated to see that it puts the business in its best light.*

Market Analysis

It is here that enough facts are presented to convince the reader that the proposed service/product can obtain a viable share of the market in a growing industry, despite the competition. (It is only the unique product that lacks such competition today.) Documented evidence about the market, its trends, and where the businesses services/products fit in, is presented. Both the internal (organizational) and external markets must be analyzed, for the success of the venture is dependent on the strengths and weakness of both the organization and the marketplace as well as a realistic assessment of both the organization's and the project's limitations. Visual aids such as charts, graphs and graphics can illustrate these points.

Externally, one describes the targeted market, its current size and potential, its segments, growth potential, trends, and the environment in which it is functioning. Also included are current prices and costs, if applicable. Next, one explains what need the service/product will fill, how it is being filled without the proposed business, and what the perceived market gap or niche is. In keeping with today's trends, it is important to look at the economic, regulatory, and legislative trends. How will government financial policies affect the venture? What are the regulatory actions and trends such as those of the Joint Commission on Accreditation of Healthcare Organizations?

How will the various regulatory demands impact on this business?

Internally, the history of the organization and its financial performance has to be examined. Who has utilized the facility in the past? Who will use it in the future? What are the operational and management resources that can be counted upon to assure the success of this business? How will the organization's direction, for example, its position in the integrated health systems and managed care environment, affect this venture? Is this venture in keeping with the current mission and goals of the facility? How well has the organization stood up to its competition? Will it be able to maintain a viable market share in the future?

Competition

Here one describes the competitive environment and who the competition is. Include details concerning the major competitors, direct and indirect, their strengths and weaknesses, history, and their ability to react should this project materialize. Also one examines the minor competitors and their prospects for becoming major ones. In the environment of integrated networks this must be scrutinized closely due to the prolific joining of many of the smaller community facilities with the major medical centers. These integrated networks can impact on various ventures in a target area. In addition one must study the home organization and see what has been learned from studying competitors in the past. What effect will their reactions have on the success of this venture?

Potential Risks and Problems

In this section it is important to demonstrate our management skill, integrity, thoroughness, and initiative by describing the risks in this business and the plans for minimizing risks. Usually the risks and problems are also seen by the reader, and it works better to be on the offensive rather than the defensive. It also opens up this area of discussion for informed, constructive discussion during the oral presentation. It is important also to describe past crises and how successfully they were resolved. One format for handling this section is a question and answer format. For example, the following questions might head the subsections:

- What vulnerabilities are there in the assumptions made in the proposal?
- What are the internal or external factors that might cause this business to fail?
- What effect would an increase in the competitive environment have on the business?
- What impact would proposed or anticipated health care legislation have on this business?
- What potentially unfavorable trends might affect the project?
- What would happen if the various projections were not met?
- What will be the impact on this venture if costs of materials, equipment and staff salaries rise over the anticipated projections?

What level of business would require additional capital to keep the venture alive?

What level of business would suggest that the venture be deactivated?

Another format for handling this section is called the SWOT format. SWOT stands for Strengths, Weaknesses, Opportunities and Threats. In this format one describes the relationship of the venture in the business proposal to the overall mission and goals of the organization in terms of its strengths, weaknesses, opportunities and threats. List as many of each as is appropriate for a constructive discussion during the oral presentation.

An example of each follows:

Strengths—Provides market leadership for a new concept in providing continuing education.

Weaknesses—High start-up costs for hardware and software.

Opportunities—Will be the first medical center in this area to use networked Computer Assisted Instruction (CAI) for mandated classes for continuing education.

Threats—May have to compete with nursing organizations that provide networked CAI for mandated classes.

Whatever format is used, every crisis can be turned into a problem-solving opportunity. The plan should be realistic, yet presented in the best light possible.

Marketing Goals and Strategy

This section explains in detail how the services/products are to be marketed. Although the needs of a particular target group are identified, one wants to deliver the product more effectively than the competition while meeting one's organization's goals and objectives.

Distribution channels are important here. Which are currently being utilized and how are they being set up? Then one looks at how to attract and expand the market. Plans for advertising, promotion, public and community relations, and publicity consider what customers are going to be targeted initially and which ones later. Determinations have to be made on how specific consumer groups are going to be identified and contacted and what features of the service/product are to be emphasized with each group. In addition, pricing has to be looked at from various standpoints such as initial market penetration and acceptance, market share, and profit. Plans have to be made for marketing management, training, organizational development, and staffing. Milestones (goals and objectives) have to be set with estimates made for shares of the market (for example, for 12, 24, and 36 months). Ongoing market evaluation is planned to assist in expanding and improving the venture.

Operational/Organizational Plan

This portion of the business plan follows the objectives of the plan and paints a picture of how the service/product is going to be researched, designed, developed and provided. Where applicable, a site has to be chosen, a facility planned and established, supplies, equipment and furniture have to be purchased, an organizational chart has to be formulated, staffing has to be determined, standards have to be set, policies and procedures have to be written, and costs and revenues have to be determined. An operational plan with a development schedule has to be formulated related to income and expense. Time frames have to be established for each category and subcategory. The ultimate plan is to establish and present schedules or timetables that are concise, complete and comprehensive. In order to give an overview of the time frames, and/or to assist in analyzing operations in relationship to scheduling, various charts can be utilized. Two examples are:

Gantt Chart—Gantt charts are used to depict a schedule graphically, in terms of blocks of time, representing the number of weeks or months required to complete each operational sub task. This chart displays all development data while indicating how the schedule will be monitored on an ongoing basis.

Program Evaluation Review Technique (PERT) Chart—This is a technique that was established to assist with operations analysis and project management tasks related to scheduling. It identifies critical paths (including those in which schedule slippage will have an adverse effect on successful completion of the total project by the targeted date) in schedule development. Although these charts can be done manually, software packages are available for both of these processes.

Once these time frames and tasks are established, they are related to income and expense, providing the basis for the financial plan.

Financial Plan/Strategy

When the financial plan is complete, a determination can be made as to whether or not this is a viable business plan. It will integrate and compile all the data, numerically, from the goals and objectives of the business plan. In order to prepare the financial section, in addition to knowing the business on a variety of levels, one must be knowledgeable in the use of the various financial tools used to measure performance, including knowledge of microcomputers and spreadsheets.

The finance department can be of valuable assistance while preparing this portion of the business plan. Summaries of tables of projected income and expenses, balance sheets, and cash flow projections on a quarterly basis, are some of the tables that should be included in the business plan. The major underlying assumptions for those projections are included. Working capital requirements, spreadsheets of accounts receivable and payable will be expected. Worst case/best case scenarios with the financial results and implications should also be prepared. Explanations of how much financing is desired, how the amount was calculated how and when it will be used (and if investors are involved, what they can expect for it), should be included.

Evaluation and Control System

An evaluation and control system, as well as a deactivation plan should be identified during the initial planning stage of the business plan. Goals, criteria and timelines for both the evaluation and control and the deactivation plan should be established. Depending on the nature of the venture, inputs, outputs, productivity, continuous quality improvement, income, expenses and budget are some of the items which should be monitored closely and continuously evaluated.

Implementation Plan and Timetable

A description of the plan for implementation and a month-to-month timetable that shows the interrelationships among the major events necessary to develop the business and to realize its marketing and financial objectives should be included in the business plan. Specific milestones that are expected to be met, together with the financing each would trigger, should be overlaid with the schedule. This should include, if applicable, structuring the business, legal and regulatory compliance, obtaining the facility or space, staff, furniture and equipment; developing a prototype, arranging for distribution, suppliers and advertising, starting operation and monitoring the workload for the first six months. Milestones for any long-term items that are listed in the business plan should also be included such as expansion, or increasing workload.

Supporting Information and Documentation

This material includes all back-up information for the first section such as reports, printouts, lists, documentation, and letters of support, etc. These data give insight to the information contained in the first section, and are read by the serious reader. Following are some examples:

Key Personnel Data
> Resumes of each key person in the plan are attached, listing detailed business expertise, emphasizing achievements. Letters of reference also are provided.

Job Descriptions, Personnel Policies, Training Programs

Complete organizational charts are provided along with job descriptions and salaries for each position. Employee incentives, rewards, benefits, and perquisites are described along with current training programs and plans for new programs.

Service/Product Information

The service/product should be made as tangible as possible with samples, transcripts, drawings, photographs, research reports, and pilot studies.

Marketing Information Detail

Articles, clippings, videos, publicity, and marketing analysis data are included here.

Competition

A table of competitors with comparative descriptions of their services, products and market share should be provided, including samples of their advertising and publicity.

Customers

Names of key customers, current or prospective are provided. If possible they should write letters of support saying they plan on using the products or services.

Operation

Details about sites, staffing, scheduling, and training classes are provided here.

Community Benefit

The potential economic and social benefits this venture can create for the community it serves is described. Local, regional and national leaders and investors will feel this is important. Included are such items as: new jobs generated; new opportunities for the unemployed or underserved; new skilled and higher paying jobs; training and development programs; purchase of goods and services from local suppliers; development of the community's physical assets; provision of needed or unsupplied services to the community; improvements in the living environment; new outlets for community pride, participation and support.

Financial Details

Computer printouts of projected income are placed here, along with balance sheets, cash flow sheets, and month-to-month calculations for the first three years, quarterly for the next two. Footnotes itemizing assumptions behind each major calculation should be complete to the last detail. Separate fixed and variable expenses are specified including reserve for bad debt and allowances for depreciation. A break-even analysis in graph form is accompanied by a description of the cost control and financial accounting system. *The financial section should be last so that the reader can flip to it easily.*

PRESENTATION

After preparing the business plan, the nurse leader who conceived the business venture and prepared the documentation, with the valuable input of many knowledgeable colleagues, will be able to make the oral presentation with the knowledge and expertise expected in the health care environment today. In presenting the plan, one must remember that the goal of the presentation is to convince the audience that this project is a worthy endeavor. The presentation should be carefully thought out, giving priority to areas such as: the nature of the audience that will be addressed, the best approach to use, the style and appearance of the presenters, and the effectiveness of the audiovisual materials.

The Audience

In order to produce a positive response, the presentation must address the concerns and interests of the audience. When formulating the plans for the presentation, the following questions should be addressed:

- How will I get the immediate attention of *this audience* at the beginning of the presentation?
- How will I keep *their* attention?
- How can I make the presentation meaningful *to them?*
- How will I address the *varying points of view of this audience?*
- How can I *get them to act* on my message?

The Approach

In determining what approach is to be used in making the presentation, one must look at what is the most effective method to use to have the audience "buy into" the message being given. In other words, what is the principle reason the audience will accept, approve and adopt what is being presented?

One method of initially drawing the audience into the presentation is validating that both the audience and the presenter have shared views. The items addressed here might include: the presenter's concern for and interest in seeing that the organization survives and thrives, that revenues are increased, and that employees and customers are satisfied. Once the audience sees that one's thinking is aligned with theirs, other "buying in" motives are addressed. This could include such items as mission, profit, power, prestige, and practicality.

Style

How successful the presenters are in reaching the audience and persuading them is dependent on how they are perceived. Many times perception is more powerful than fact and how one is perceived is reflective on one's style. One wants the audience to see that the *presenters are credible and competent* and the concepts, information and recommendations being given have been well thought out by knowledgeable, capable people who are qualified to speak on the subject. In addition they should *be confident and care about the subject*. The presenters should come across as self-assured, welcoming the opportunity to present the project to this audience.

Being energetic, enthusiastic and well organized is as important as the visual cues communicated through eye contact, facial expressions, gestures, movement and attire.

Appearance

Presenters will be well scrutinized by the audience from the moment they enter the room and their attire will be the most visible thing the audience sees throughout the presentation. Appropriate attire, accessories and grooming will enhance the audience's perception of the presenters, especially in a business presentation. Successful professionals usually follow these guidelines for a business presentation: A conservative business suit or dress should be worn with few accessories, neatly styled hair and nails, and polished conservative shoes. Dangling chains and earrings or hair falling across one's face is distracting during the presentation. The presenter's purpose is to deliver a message that will be taken seriously, not to make a fashion statement.

Audiovisual Materials

Audiovisual materials are included in the presentation to support the presentation, not to replace the presenter. They are used to clarify some of the concepts or data that are being presented, to highlight important points or to reinforce the verbal communication so that the information has a better chance of being retained. They can also be utilized in other ways such as to stimulate thought or inject humor. The audiovisual materials should be clear, concise, colorful, and creative so the audience will be interested in the message they are intended to convey. Effectively used, audiovisual materials complement a presentation.

Rehearsal

In preparation for the presentation of the business plan it is important to rehearse. Each participant should rehearse alone in front of a mirror in order to see what the audience sees. Then the group should practice together. Live performances should be given in front of an audience consisting of friends, co-workers or associates who will give honest constructive criticism. In addition, a videotape of the presentation should be made so the presenters can critique themselves, from the audience's point of view, evaluating what the presenter sees and hears.

These factors all play an important part in the successful presentation of a plan. By not underestimating their effectiveness, one will be placed in the best light.

By including the other members of the planning team in the presentation it gives the plan reviewer(s) the opportunity to speak with others and gain more knowledge from their insights. In addition, it will enhance the image of the nurse as the leader and hopefully provide the message that will influence those who make the final decision.

SUMMARY

In the current health care environment, health care organizations are functioning as businesses, adopting the tools and techniques utilized by businesses of varying sizes. The business plan is a standard tool for presenting changes in programs/products, and many healthcare organizations have begun to require that business plans be presented when preparing annual budgets. By expanding boundaries, nurse leaders on all levels will develop the skills, knowledge and ability to prepare, and successfully present a professionally written business plan and make an impact in this environment.

SUGGESTED READINGS

Arredondo, L. (1993). *The McGraw-Hill 36-hour course: Business presentations.* New York: McGraw-Hill, Inc.

Barnum, B. S., & Kerfoot, K. M. (1995). *The nurse as executive* (4th ed.). Gaithersburg, MD: Aspen Publishers, Inc.

Detz, J. (1992). *How to write and give a speech* (2nd ed.). New York: St. Martin's Press.

Droms, W. G. (1992). *Finance and accounting for nonfinancial managers* (3rd ed.). Reading, MA: Addison-Wesley Publishing Co.

Finkler, S., & Kovner, C. (1993). *Financial management for nurse managers and executives.* Philadelphia: W. B. Saunders.

Johnson, J. E. (Ed.). (1988). *The nurse executive's business plan manual.* Gaithersburg, MD: Aspen Publishers, Inc.

Marszalek-Gaucher, E., & Coffey, R. (1990). *Transforming healthcare organizations: How to achieve and sustain organizational excellence.* San Francisco: Josey-Bass Publishers.

CHAPTER 7

Making That Speech: What You'd Better Know Before You Go

Barry Jay Kaplan

More nurses are speaking in public today than ever before. They are participating in national conferences, panel discussions, seminars, and local union meetings, communicating with other nurses and health professionals via telephone and conference calls, leading staff meetings, providing patient education, lecturing to community health leaders, teaching students and peers, acting as management consultants, and dealing with various health workers, pharmaceutical salespeople, alumnae, and professional associations. As the role of the nurse within the health care system changes and grows, the issues on which nurses will communicate via speech will be as broad, varied, and dynamic as the health industry itself.

We tend to think of public speaking as a formal event, something other people do: professional speakers, politicians, celebrities, people working for a cause, raising money for charity, garnering publicity for a candidate or for the book they've just written. This view of public speaking is accurate but limited. Public speaking, in fact, affects every aspect of oral communication because, on its most basic level, it refers to the ways in which people get ideas and information across, educate people about something they didn't know, or persuade them of a particular point of view: all via the spoken word.

Note: Originally published in *Nursing Leadership Forum*, Vol. 2, No. 1, 1996. New York: Springer Publishing Company.

In the daily life of a nurse, there are countless times when she has to rely on her speaking abilities to communicate ideas and information: in staff meetings, on the telephone, when explaining complicated procedures to a new nurse, educating patients and families, or speaking to doctors, dietitians, lab workers, pharmacists, housekeeping staff, and technicians.

Yet many nurses separate lectern-style public speaking from the speaking they do in their many one-on-one meetings. In fact, they have a lot in common: Both require preparation, knowledge of the subject matter, clear thinking, and a structured, concise delivery. Both consider who is being spoken to, why the information is being delivered, and how the location affects the presentation. Many of the decisions that go into even the most routine delivery of spoken information are based on a combination of instinct and experience, which together have taught us that it is not enough just to give the information, taking it for granted that the other person will receive it. The information has to be presented in a way that compels the listeners' attention and makes it easy for them to understand and remember just what you want them to.

There are many forms of public speaking we'll consider in this chapter, including panel discussions, group discussions, interviews, telephone meetings, and conferences. They have many things in common. But let's begin by taking a look at the hardest case: you behind a lectern, on a podium, making a formal speech to a large group of people. Once you master this, the rest is simple.

Ready?

The President of the Head Nurses Council you used to belong to calls you at work and asks if you would like to give a talk at the fall members' meeting. The subject: making the transition from union to management. You certainly know the subject, having made just such a transition yourself. You know the pitfalls, the problems, and the rewards, and you've got some humorous anecdotes that would illustrate what you want to say. You're flattered she's thought of you. You check your calendar to see if you're free. You are. Yes, you say. I'll be glad to make the speech.

You hang up. Suddenly your hands are sweating and your heart is pounding. You have a vision of yourself standing in the Roman Coliseum, thousands of people looking at you, hands raised, ready to turn thumbs up or thumbs down on what you're about to say, only you're so paralyzed with fear you can't open your mouth.

What have I done, you think. Why did I say yes? I'm unprepared. My throat gets tight when I'm nervous and I'm nervous right now, so how am I going to be when I actually have to give the speech? I don't even know the location where I'll be speaking. I don't know how I let myself agree so readily. I don't know what to wear. Worst of all: What am I going to say?

Okay. Okay. Calm down. Back up. You're way ahead of yourself. Before you get to composing the speech and deciding whether to wear the black suit or the red dress, there's plenty of preparation you have to do and information you have to get. In fact, you'd better get a pencil and paper and start making a list of questions, then call back the person who offered the invitation to speak. There's a lot you need to ask her.

CHECK ON THE ENVIRONMENT

Location, Location, Location

Knowing as much as you can about where you're going to speak will help make your speech more effectively. You'll give a different kind of speech, speak in a different way, even use different gestures if you're speaking in a hotel conference room than in the training center of a large corporation or a university auditorium, a high-school classroom, a gymnasium, a restaurant dining room, or outdoors.

Learn all you can. Assume nothing.

The best thing to do is visit the site. If it's in the town where you live, great. If it's not, it might be worth a short trip. If that's not possible, call your host and have list of questions ready to ask. Can you get a floor plan of the room? No? Well, then, how big is it? How many people does it seat? Is there going to be a podium? Where is the audience? Are their chairs moveable? Is the floor banked like in a theater? Or is it flat? Is the audience seated around tables, in rows, or on folding chairs?

All of these things affect how you will speak, and the fewer surprises, the better you can deal with the situation.

If you can't get to the site to check it out before you speak, the next best thing is to have someone you know and trust check it out for you: a colleague who lives in the town where you'll be giving the speech, or someone who has access to the site.

There's a lot to check out beforehand.

You'll probably think of some things yourself. This is a beginning list of questions to ask of yourself, your host, and the technicians involved. Some of the items to follow are within your control: You can change them (or request that someone else change them) or accommodate yourself to them if they can't be changed. Some of the items are not within your power to control or change, in which case it is better to know about them beforehand than to arrive prepared to do one thing and discover that something about the physical properties of the room prevents you from doing it. If you can't get to the site beforehand, you can certainly get there an hour or two before the time you're scheduled to speak. There's plenty for you to do when you arrive.

Windows

Are there any? If there are, will the sun be in your eyes or the eyes of your audience? Will your speech be competing with a beautiful view (cherry blossoms blowing in the breeze) or a lot of distracting activities (people poolside, people skiing)? Can the windows be shaded against such distractions?

Lectern

Is there one? Does it have a light? Is the bulb burned out? What do you do if it is? Is there a shelf under the lectern for our purse, your cough drops, your handkerchief? Is there a lip on the surface that will keep your speech from sliding away? Is the lectern adjustable in terms of height? Failing that, is there a box to stand on?

Microphone

Do you need one? If one is available, does it work? Can you adjust the height? It should be chin level so it doesn't hide your face and so you don't have to bend over to speak into it.

Lighting

Does it glare in your eyes? Does it glare in the audience's eyes? Is it bright enough to read your speech by? Is it bright enough for you to make eye contact with people in the audience? Is it bright enough for them to read their program and take notes?

Seating Arrangements

Check this before the audience arrives. Once they're seated, they're not getting up. If there are 100 chairs spread out all over the room and you know only 50 people are coming, try to have some of the extra chairs removed and group the remaining ones close to the center. If the seats are fixed, rope off the rear area so the audience will be compelled to sit closer to you.

Ventilation

Make sure the air conditioning does not make the room too cold or the heating make it too stuffy. Check and listen for the noise the temperature controls make. You may want to turn them off for the duration of your speech or risk competing with a hissing radiator or a humming cooler.

Doors

Are they at the front and rear of the room? If there are doors on the same side of the room where you're speaking, make sure they are locked when you start. Otherwise, you run the risk of latecomers appearing "on-stage" during your speech.

Noise

Are other events going to be going on in adjacent rooms? Find out. Find out if they're going to be playing music or batting a ball around or cheering. In other words: Find out if the rooms are soundproof. Do this by going inside one and listening. Alert the management that you are aware of the potential dangers in the situation and this will increase their sensitivity.

Help

When you arrive, find out the name and phone number or beeper number of the manager, the maintenance engineer, the sound engineer, or whoever can change a light bulb, adjust the air conditioner, stop a leak, fix a fuse.

> I never accept an invitation unless I know the expectations of the people who've invited me. I listen to them. I ask them questions: What would help you? What are your goals? Why are you inviting me? I suggest my own ideas. They don't always know exactly what they want so you can suggest things. After I tell them my ideas I tell them to think about it for a week and get back to me. During that time I don't necessarily work on the speech but I will gather information. I prepare what I think fits the group. Then, 3–4 weeks before the event I put it all together. I also get a letter of agreement, not necessarily a formal contract, but something that outlines what I'm going to do and my fee. During this time I keep in close touch with them. They may start without knowing the number of guests. I even help them develop their brochure. I send them a sample. I never assume they know how to do it all. I am sure to learn their objectives and what they expect in their evaluations.

> Madeleine M. Leininger
> PhD, RN, FAAN

KNOW YOUR AUDIENCE

In the course of your work, you wouldn't place a telephone call and start talking without knowing whom you were speaking to. In the course of planning a speech, the same basic rules apply: Know whom you're talking to and why you're talking to them.

The person who asked you to speak may not have told you anything about your audience, or may have said something so general it doesn't offer you much help. Saying: "they're all nurses" or "they're all lab technicians" doesn't go a long way toward informing you of anything.

There are ways to find out about your audience. The first person who might be of help is the person who invited you. During your initial conversation, she may simply have neglected to mention what she knows about the audience or you may have neglected to ask for specifics. Now is the time to do that. Call her back and ask. If she doesn't know, there are other people to ask.

Call the public relations department of the organization and ask them for last year's annual report. If the organization publishes a newsletter, ask them to send you a copy. What you'll find out by reading this material is the interests of the organization, who their officers are, what kind of structure they have. You can also tell the public relations person who you are and that you'll be speaking at the next conference. You might also take advantage of this opportunity to suggest a little publicity be planned for the upcoming event. And ask for any literature that might be available from the organization's last conference that would be helpful to you in understanding the people you're going to be speaking to.

When this literature arrives, read it carefully. With a little investigation, you'll uncover the names of previous speakers. They're another source. Call and tell them you'll be speaking to the organization they addressed last year. Ask for their reading on the audience. What did and didn't work? You may even know someone who'll be in the audience, another good source of information.

Use common sense and your inherent creativity and you'll be able to find out about the audience. But before you start asking questions, decide what you need to know.

> I was once asked to go to a presentation with a group and the subject was empowerment of women. I prepared a speech on community health issues that were mainly led by women and brought a video on the subject. When I got there I was shocked to learn that the audience was a group of legislators from Washington, DC, and the subject was not empowerment of women but empowerment as a strategy in general. I had to think on my feet, and adapted my speech to a more general audience. By speaking in a more general way I was able to change the focus of the video, too, from women to community.
>
> Helen K. Grace, PhD, RN, FAAN

What does the audience know?

Knowing the educational background of a group will tell you a lot about how much they probably already know about the subject you may have in mind. The more sophisticated they are, the more sophisticated your speech will have to be. You don't want to give a speech on basic pain medication to seasoned oncology nurses. Unless, of course, you believe they need it. On the other hand, the very fact that they're sophisticated means you can tell them something you're pretty sure they don't know. If you've uncovered some little known piece of scholarship or have the inside track on a new technique that's just being developed, a group of nurses who consider themselves up on the latest issues in their specialty will be very appreciative of hearing the last word on a cutting-edge technique.

Why has this audience come to hear you speak?

In other words: Do you have a captive audience, eager to hear what you have to say, regardless of whether or not they agree? Or is attendance mandatory? An audience that has come to hear you speak whether or not they are interested in what you have to say is a tougher crowd to please. You may want to acknowledge this situation right away in your speech: "I know some of you would rather be on the golf course/ski slope/horseback trail right now than have to listen to me but I think that when I'm finished . . . in exactly 20 minutes, by the way . . . you'll be glad you were here."

Does this audience know you?

If they do, is it by name or reputation? If you've spoken on this subject before or written articles on it, your audience is likely to have opinions about you as soon as they see your name. It helps if you know their expectations. Whether or not you decide to fulfill their expectations is another matter. You may use the fact that you are a known quantity to startle them with some facts or opinions they weren't expecting. Or take them in a different direction than they thought you would go.

> I presented a very scholarly speech to a group of nurses, not knowing that I had been recommended by a member of the group who had heard me make a humorous presentation on another topic. All through the speech I felt that something was wrong. Only later did I find out they had expected to be entertained more than educated.
>
> Barbara Stevens Barnum
> RN, PhD, FAAN

Is this audience interested in you? In your subject?

Will the audience be informed beforehand as to the subject of your speech or will they find out only when they sit down at the event and read the program? How much do they know about the subject? Where did they get this information? How much more do they need or want to know? Does this group have preconceived ideas about you or your subject? If they do, you may want to reassure them that their perception is safe in your hands. Or you may want to shake them up by revealing some new or contradictory ideas.

Is this audience with you or against you?

If you're going to be speaking to a group of doctors on the role of the nurse practitioner in a rural setting, it helps to know that you may be facing a hostile or suspicious audience. Although it can be very soothing to address a roomful of people who already agree with you, it can be an exciting challenge to attempt to convert people who are not on your side to your way of thinking or at least to open the door for a spirited discussion.

Who is this audience?

Are they pharmaceutical salespeople, medical suppliers, doctors, lawyers, technicians, specialists? If they are other nurses, at what level of education or which specialty are they?

How many people will there be?

Group dynamics is an interesting phenomenon. The way people behave in groups changes according to many variables. Do they know each other? Do they work together? Do they have similar jobs or the same professional interests? Not so obvious, but equally important, is the way in which the size of a group affects audience behavior.

People in small groups probably know each other and probably will pay closer attention to what you say, basically because it's too risky to daydream: it's likely that someone is going to ask them their opinion. Because they know each other—and are likely to have certain experiences in common—they frequently anticipate each other's reactions to new ideas. You know this is happening when you say something they haven't heard before, and all around the room people are turning to look at each other in agreement or disagreement. Not necessarily with you but with each other.

People in large audiences, on the other hand, are more likely to be anonymous, both to you and to each other. As a result, they feel less pressure to listen. It's easier to daydream; it is unlikely that anyone is going to quiz them on what they've heard. Therefore, your speech needs to be more dramatic, more entertaining, more inspiring. You need to get them to react by challenging them, startling them, surprising them, and compelling them to participate by asking questions that make them think.

KNOW THE OCCASION

Here are some of the basic questions you'll want answered.

Why does this group meet?

Is this a regular meeting? Is it a group that convenes every Thursday from 7 to 9? Is it a regular practice of this group to have people come in and speak to them? Do they already know you, either by name or title or association?

Is this occasion a special event?

A celebration, an anniversary, a sales conference, a seminar, a continuing education lecture?

Is it formal?

Will the leaders of the organizations be there, which means everyone is on their best behavior? Or is it for middle management, a group of equals, so that the mood is more casual?

Is food going to be served?

Is a meal going to be served before you speak? People who've just eaten a big meal tend to stay in a social, casual mood for a while, so if your speech is very serious, you'll need to lighten it up at the beginning to draw them in. Is a meal going to be served while you're speaking? This is a tough situation because your competition is a person's appetite, and if that person is hungry, you're in trouble. If this is the case, it's best to acknowledge the situation good-naturedly rather than pretend it isn't happening.

What about noise?

Consider that the noise level in the audience will be higher during a meal: the sound of silverware, plateware, and glasses. Expect that at least one of the waiters is going to drop a tray of chicken à la king just when you've reached a climactic moment in your speech. It's best to be prepared for this with a joke: "I didn't expect such an explosive reaction to my speech!"

Will drinks be served?

If they are, you can expect to face an audience that is at best relaxed, at worst inattentive.

OTHER THINGS TO KNOW

What is the ratio of men and women in the audience?

An audience of male nurses has different interests, different needs, and a different perspective on the role of the nurse than female nurses do.

What is the economic status of the group?

If the group is known to you to be low-paid, this can predict their point of view if you're giving a talk on hospital costs or layoffs or cutbacks. They may have different needs, different resentments and different values than an audience of well-paid managers.

When will you be speaking?

Think about what the time of day means to the audience.

Breakfast: They had to get up earlier than usual. They still face a whole day of work. Be brief.

Midmorning/just before lunch: They've had a tough morning. They're hungry. Avoid a darkened room at this time of the day. Your audience might nod out.

Midafternoon: The day is almost over. The 3:00 p.m. blahs are setting in. Try not to be the last speaker of the afternoon. If you are, keep it short and energetic.

Early evening: Have they just eaten? A full stomach is not conducive to rapt attention. You'll have to be lively or they'll drift.

Late evening: They've had time to refresh themselves after a day's work, a shower, and a good meal. Take advantage of their good mood but don't ruin it with a long or overly serious speech.

The worst case is when the audience is dozing, especially after lunch. I once gave a talk in Japan. They wanted the written paper beforehand so they could translate it. The way it worked was that I would speak a paragraph and the translator would then speak it in Japanese. And this was after lunch! The audience just conked out, though I was told that it is not considered rude in Japan to close your eyes and nod during someone's speech.

Chris Tanner, PhD, RN, FAAN

How long do you have?

People speak at 150 words a minute, so 3 double-spaced typewritten pages take 5 minutes to deliver. Calculate your time. Don't leave it to chance.

Who else is speaking and what are they going to say?

Ask for a copy of the other speakers' speeches; at least find out the topic of their speech. You certainly don't want to find yourself in the position of following someone who has just said exactly what you're about to say. And if they've said the opposite of what you're about to say, you want to know about it beforehand so you prepare an appropriate response.

If you can't get advance copies of the speeches, ask for the speakers' telephone numbers. Call and confer with them. You'll all be better off if you know what the other is going to speak about. And the occasion will go better too.

Know the remunerative arrangements.

Ask if there is a fee involved. Don't be embarrassed to do this. Asking is not demanding. Asking does not mean that you won't accept the invitation if you're not paid. But don't assume that you'll be paid, only to discover later that such was never the organization's intention. Prevent any hard feelings by discussing this up front. Many people will ask you in advance what your fee will be. Be prepared with a figure. Ask friends whom you consider to be comparable to yourself in experience and background what they charge for similar presentations.

If there is no fee for this engagement, you will want to know if the organization provides transportation, a room, and meals, or how these items will be arranged. Don't assume that because you're going to have to travel and spend the night, that they're going to pay for it. Ask about the arrangements. Are you expected to lay out the money for everything and submit receipts for reimbursement?

If you're on your own in terms of travel, accommodations, and meals, you may not want to accept the invitation. You'd certainly be within the boundaries of good sense and politeness to say so. You may even indicate that you would be happy to come if they would pay for your expenses.

On the other hand, you may feel that this occasion is worth footing the bills yourself because of what it may do for you, namely, give you a chance to meet significant people in your field, provide the opportunity to present your ideas to an audience that most needs to hear them, and avail yourself of the opportunity for visibility to your peers and the nursing leadership. In fact, the speech may be giving you more than you are giving it.

"My biggest fear about public speaking is not getting paid."

(Barbara Stevens Barnum)

CHAPTER 8

Succession Planning: A Strategy for Taking Charge

Fay L. Bower

> Without leadership, an organization is like a lifeboat adrift in turbulent seas with no oars, no compass, no maps—and no hope.
>
> Burt Nanu

Planning is a major part of our lives. We plan for each day, each vacation, for major events like weddings and births, and even for the memorial of a friend or relative. We read about and do strategic and operational planning and we prepare work, business, and care plans. Hardly a moment goes by when we are not planning something. A kind of planning that has not been given a lot of attention, however, is succession planning. Yet no organization, division, or department can succeed without it.

Succession planning is planning for the future by assuring there is leadership for the future. Given the rapid changes of today, no organization can remain healthy if there is not some time spent in seeing that the leadership for the future is identified, mentored, and prepared when there are openings, retirements or resignations. We can no longer afford to search for replacements never really knowing whether the person selected will fit or be able to carry forth the operation successfully. Mentored and prepared leadership is necessary for carrying forth the goals of the institution. It is also a way of assuring continued influence for a particular direction long after the current leadership is gone.

Note: Originally published in *Nursing Leadership Forum*, Vol. 4, No. 4, 2000. New York: Springer Publishing Company.

Succession planning does not mean that creativity or new ideas are stifled. Also, the identification of potential leadership does not necessarily mean the leaders must come from inside the organization. To the contrary, succession planning may mean reaching to the outside. Where the talent is found is not the issue. What is important is that an effort is made to locate talent before the need is evident. It is time well spent in preparing future leaders by mentoring or schooling them or both.

Since it is an effort to think about the leadership for tomorrow before tomorrow becomes today, it is important to plan for succession. We know that although people may be groomed for leadership positions, these efforts are often sporadic or dependent on individual initiative. They usually are not a planned activity or part of the ongoing activity of an organization. Succession planning means that the leadership of the institution (CEO, VPs, directors, and unit managers) makes a deliberate attempt to select and prepare the leadership for tomorrow and do it as an ongoing activity.

Succession planning goes on at all levels of an organization. An organization can plan for the succession of its CEO, division directors, department heads, or unit chairmen. An educational institution can plan for the succession of its president, vice presidents, deans, and directors. Succession planning is appropriate in educational, health care, corporate, or voluntary organizations alike. As with the need for operational plans, every organization should have a succession planning process.

There are several reasons that succession planning is critical to an organization. For example, succession planning:

- creates a pool of leadership that is ready to assume responsibility and carry forth the business of the institution when the need arises
- assures continuity of the operations and a sense of security for the employees
- creates a link between today and tomorrow
- is a good way to be proactive rather than reactive when attempting to assure quality leadership
- is a wise use of resources.

Talented persons are often ignored, and instead, too much time and money is spent on searching for replacements from outside an organization when talent is readily available from within. Frequently, someone is just waiting to be discovered but is not. If succession planning were in place, talented persons would be identified and mentored so that when a position opens, a qualified and prepared person would be ready to assume the position.

COMPONENTS OF SUCCESSION PLANNING

There are three components to succession planning:

1. vision
2. networking
3. mentoring

First, the person looking for a successor must have a vision, must be someone who knows what is needed and where the organization needs to go. Second, in looking for a successor an excellent strategy is to use a network to locate potential candidates. Third, there must be adequate resources to groom candidates for succession so that the mentoring process is successful. It is these three processes, used together, that make up succession planning. One of these alone or even two will not create a succession plan. Further, all of these activities must be written down so they can be evaluated for their effectiveness for future use.

Vision

Having vision means we must to able to see beyond today and the issues affecting today and to predict what the future will be like. That future could be possible, probable, plausible or preferred. If the future is possible it means it is a future that may happen. According to Bezold, Hancock, and Sullivan (1999), the future includes everything that one can possibly imagine, no matter how unlikely, and includes "science fiction" futures that transgress presently accepted laws of science. For example, one possible future for an organization looking for a CEO could be found in a person who could lead the organization forward to capture 50% of the available market. On the other hand, the future could be seen as a plausible one, a future of what could happen. This is a narrower view, emphasizing those possible futures that seem to make sense given what we know today. Plausible futures can be discrete forecasts of individual trends or a set of scenarios, each combining different trends. Examples of plausible futures are a high-technology growth scenario, a scenario of environmental, economic, social decline, and/or a more controlled society (Bezold & Hancock, 1996).

A probable future is what is likely to happen and is based on our current situation and an appraisal of likely trends. It is sometimes referred to as "business as usual" or the official future. Until recently, predicting probable futures worked. The health care system was viewed as hospital-based and physician-dominated. Who could have predicted it would suddenly and so dramatically shift? Forecasts based solely on recent trends can preclude futures that are different and they can be the future we do not want. As futurist Dator (1993) has said, trends can take us with unerring accuracy to where we don't want to be!

Sometimes referred to as the prescriptive future or normative forecasting, a preferred future is what we want to have happen. According to Bezold and Hancock (1996), preferable futures are visions that generally begin by identifying and trying to create a future that does not yet exist. Vision moves reality beyond the present toward the best that can be.

Succession planners know the kind of future they want, locate the talent to make it happen, and see that they are prepared to create that future. Historically little effort has been expended on planning for the future because most leaders have not been prepared to do so. We have simply responded to what happens along the way. No longer will this approach work. Current leaders must think seriously about the future and be willing to create succession plans by locating and preparing leaders to move the organization toward the desired outcome.

Networking

Networking is the second element of succession planning. Networking is the ability to reach out to colleagues for the referral of a potential leader. Knowing who has potential leadership skills, and where to develop those skills are important aspects of succession planning. It just is not enough to provide good leadership; leaders need to know what kind of person will be needed when they are ready to move on, where to find that person, and how to cultivate his/her potential.

Networks are not quickly arranged. In fact, networks take a long time to build, so it is essential that they be initiated early. Networks should include persons who know your business, are influential, and are willing to help you locate talented people. While it would be nice if they were good mentors too, they do not need to have that talent as long as they can point to those that do.

Developing a network is a process where people establish relationships because of mutual interest and trust. The persons in the network trust one another and use that basic trust as a springboard for many kinds of activities. Having a competitor as a member of the network might not work, as it would undoubtedly create a "conflict of interest" if both parties were looking for the same kinds of people.

Besides trust, networks involve exchanges. These exchanges must provide, over time, benefits for all parties involved. This means that we must be willing to give in order to get. O'Connor (1982) contends that network members must periodically identify mutual gains, direct or indirect, for all parties. The exchange must be equivalent, even if reciprocity is delayed.

Networks often begin in the workplace as a helping relationship. They sometimes begin at conferences, workshops, or at other professional functions where individuals discover they have something in common. Networks have even been established by persons who have read about someone and called that person to talk about something of common interest. Social events and school and committee assignments are also good places to learn about individuals and whether they might become a part of a network.

Networks should be diverse. They should include people from a variety of organizational levels and geographic locations with age and gender differences. Having persons with diverse experiences and perspectives provides the network with the "broad picture," so the membership has access to many kinds of advice and referrals.

Bower (1999) summed up the value of diverse networks by saying, "networking is a process of creating a select group of individuals who can supply information about contacts, referrals, or opportunities so the best vision of what is happening beyond the immediate situation is available"(p. 71).

Mentoring

It is likely that all successful leaders have had mentors, individuals whom they could confide in and seek advice and help from. Being influential and making a difference is often the result of learning leadership skills from a successful leader. Gaining recognition and power and being able to influence others is often learned from those who have recognition, power, and influence. Mentors often have positions and titles but they can be without both and still be influential and able to mentor others.

Mentors are role models and facilitators of career development; they can open doors to opportunity and teach by modeling. Mentors have specific characteristics that allow them to facilitate the development of others. According to Taylor (1992), a mentor is one who takes a personal interest in assisting someone to develop the knowledge and skills needed to meet specific career goals. Williams and Blackburn (1988) believe that a direct working relationship is most beneficial in developing others. Several authors, for example, Bower (1993), Moore (1982), Kanter (1977), and Levinson (1977), believe that the best way to mentor someone is to follow the tutorial model, where the selection of the protégé is specific and the relationship is close and supervised, with the mentor guiding the activities of the protégé. Vance and Olson (1998) believe that mentoring is a developmental, empowering, and nurturing relationship extending over time in which mutual sharing, learning, and growth occur in an atmosphere of respect, collegiality, and affirmation. The mentoring relationship can also be viewed as a gift-exchange (Gehrke, 1988) or as a collaborative learning experience for both parties (Kaye & Jacobson, 1995). While most mentoring occurs between two persons in the same environment, there are mentor relationships that have worked for persons who are at a distance.

The characteristics of mentoring relationships vary somewhat according to the literature. Taylor (1992), for example, claims that a mentor relationship includes valuing the protégé and believing in the individual's potential for success. The mentor is the role model, guide, teacher, coach, or confidant. Hockenberry-Eaton and Kline (1995) see the characteristics of an effective mentoring environment as: (a) providing leadership, (b) showing patience, (c) demonstrating caring, and (d) maintaining loyalty. They point out that building trust in the mentoring relationship is an essential component for creating a nurturing environment, and that the socialization process experienced during a mentor relationship should be effortless. Levinson (1977) suggests that there are several roles mentors must play at different times: teacher, sponsor, guidance counselor, exemplar role model, and initiator. Mentors also must provide moral support and indoctrination into the institution's values. Vance (1999) states the mentor guides, models, encourages, and inspires the protégé and that a key role of the mentor is to create an environment that supports the development of both an individual and collective mentor relationship. Ultimately, regardless of the mentor model, the relationship advances from a helping/learning one to a cohort relationship.

The impact of mentoring is supported by the literature. In a study by White (1988) where 300 academic nurse administrators were evaluated, mentors gave their protégés confidence and inspiration and encouraged achievement and intellectual development. Spengler (1982) evaluated 501 mentored doctorally prepared nurses and found them to have more definite career plans, more satisfaction with their career progression, and a greater sense of accomplishment than usual. Hamilton and associates (1989), in a study that evaluated mentoring and new graduate nurses, found that new nurses with mentors showed increased job satisfaction and leadership behavior. Clearly persons with strong mentors experience both professional and personal growth (Butts & Wither, 1992; Carey & Campbell, 1994; Martin, Tolleson, Lakey, & Moeller, 1995; Nayak, 1991).

INTRODUCING SUCCESSION PLANNING

All new employees in leadership positions should be introduced to succession planning during their orientation period. Succession planning should be part of the strategic and operational plans of the organization and the work plans developed by the unit. Those in leadership positions should know at the beginning of their employment that they are responsible for locating and preparing their successors. While there may be some apprehension about this process because it may look as though one would be replaced at any time, if presented properly succession planning should be viewed simply as another part of being in a leadership position.

All those in leadership positions need to accept the concept, process, and responsibility of mentoring. While mentoring often occurs incidentally rather than deliberately, it should be a formal, organized, and expected activity of everyone in a leadership position, especially as it relates to succession planning. Mentor programs should be an integral part of the ongoing work of every human resources department. Even though we are bound to adhere to affirmative action and labor law requirements, there is no reason why mentoring could not occur with employees inside organizations as well as with those outside of it.

HOW TO MEASURE WHETHER SUCCESSION PLANNING IS WORKING

Succession planning, as any other development program, must be evaluated. In terms of outcomes, there are several questions to be answered that will determine if succession planning is effective. The following questions should be considered:

- Has a pool of talented persons who could fill openings in leadership been identified?
- Do these persons have the qualifications necessary to chart the future direction of the organization, division, unit, or department? If not, would attending a management development program or a conference on executive development be appropriate?
- Have the CEO, vice presidents, or directors within the organization taken responsibility for mentoring the succession talent?
- Are the persons being mentored satisfied with the mentoring experiences?
- Are the mentors satisfied with the progress of the protégés?
- Have contingency plans been developed if mentored persons move on to other positions/places?
- Have the mentored persons who were hired been satisfactory? That is, have they assumed leadership and moved the organization forward?

If the answers to these questions are "yes," then the program is working and should continue. If there are any "no" responses, it is clear what needs to be changed.

One of the reasons it is important to have a pool of talented persons ready for future leadership positions is that there are always opportunities available for talented persons. Someone else may identify the same talent and be able to lure them away. If the pool is adequate, then losing a potential leader may not be a problem.

SUMMARY

The value of succession planning is that it provides a constant pool of ready-made leadership when there is a need for replacement or expansion of employees/members. It provides the organization with individuals who are ready to advance the strategic plans and mission of the organization because they understand what the organization is all about and what is needed to assure its further success. Most searches for leadership discover excellent candidates but they often must learn about the institution before they can provide the needed leadership. This is lost time that could be costly. With succession planning, candidates are already identified and prepared for the job.

Although succession planning is a process, to be most effectively used the plan should be written. It should contain the long-term strategic goals of the organization, a list of network members, a list of candidates, and a list of mentors with comments about each. The plan should be updated periodically so that it stays relevant. Ongoing succession planning of this kind provides the organization and the leadership with a current vision, with networks available for finding a successor, and with mentors who will hone the skills of the successor so that time and resources are used wisely and the direction of the organization stays on track.

REFERENCES

Bezold, C., & Hancock, T. (1996). Health futures: Tools for wiser decision making. In C. Bezold & E. Mayer (Eds.), *Future care: Responding to the demand for change.* New York: Faulkner & Gray.

Bezold, C., Hancock, T., & Sullivan, E. (1999). Examining nursing from a futures perspective. In E. Sullivan (Ed.), *Creating nursings' future: Issues, opportunities and challenges.* St. Louis, MO: Mosby.

Bower, F. (1999). *Nurses taking the lead: Personal qualities of effective leaders.* Philadelphia, PA: Saunders.

Bower, F. (1993). Women and mentoring in higher education. In P. T. Mitchell (Ed.), *Cracking the wall: Women in higher education administration.* Washington, DC: College and University Personnel Association.

Butts, B. J., & Wither, D. M. (1992). New graduates: What does my manager expect? *Nursing Management, 23*(8), 46–48.

Carey, S. J., & Campbell, S. T. (1994). Preceptor, mentor, and sponsor roles: Creative strategies for nurse retention. *Journal of Nursing Administration, 24*(12), 39–48.

Dator, J. (1993). *Health futures symposium.* Geneva: World Health Organization.

Eastman, L. J. (1995). *Succession planning: An annotated bibliography and summary of commonly reported organizational practices.* Greensboro, NC: Center for Creative Leadership.

Gehrke, N. (1988). Toward a definition of mentoring. *Theory Into Practice, 27*(3), 190–194.

Hamilton, E. M., Murray, M. K., Lindholm, L. H., & Myers, R. E. (1989). Effects of mentoring on job satisfaction, leadership behaviors, and job retention of new graduate nurses. *Journal of Staff Development, 5*, 159–165.

Hockenberry-Eaton, M., & Kline, N. E. (1995). Professional insights: Who is mentoring the nurse practitioner? *Journal of Pediatric Health Care, 9*(2), 94–95.

Hudson, T. (1993). Smart move: CEOs say succession planning up. *Hospitals, 67*(7), 42.

Kanter, R. M. (1977). *Men and women of the corporation.* New York: Basic Books.

Kaye, B., & Jacobson, B. (1995). Mentoring: A group guide. *Training and Development*, 23–27.

Levinson, D. (1977). *The seasons of a man's life.* New York: Alfred A. Knopf.

Maliszewski, S. (Ed.). (1988). Special issue: Succession planning. *Career Planning and Adult Development Journal, 4*(1), 3–27.

Martin, M. L., Tolleson, J., Lakey, K. I., & Moeller, E. (1995). VALUE students: A creative type of preceptorship. *Federal Practitioner, 12*(4), 47–50.

McConnell, C. R. (1996). Succeeding with succession planning. *Health Care Supervisor, 15*(2), 69–78.

Moore, K. M. (1982). The role of mentors in developing leaders for academe. *Educational Record, 63,* 22–28.

Nayak, S. (1991). Strategies to support the new nurse in practice. *Journal of Nursing Staff Development, 7*(39), 64–66.

O'Connor, A. B. (1982). Ingredients for successful networking. *Nurse Educator, 7*(6), 40–43.

Poteet, G. W. (1987). Succession planning in nursing administration. *Journal of Pediatric Nursing: Nursing Care of Children and Families, 2,* 342–347.

Pulcini, J. (1997). Succession planning: From leaders to mentors. *Clinical Excellence for Nursing Practitioners, 1,* 405–406.

Spengler, C. D. (1982). Mentor-protégé relationships: A study of career development among female nurse doctorates. (Doctoral dissertation, University of Missouri, Columbus, 1982). *Dissertation Abstracts International, 44,* 213 B.

Taylor, L. J. (1992). A survey of mentor-protégé relationships in academe. *Journal of Professional Nursing, 8,* 48–55.

Vance, C. (1999). Mentoring—The nurse leader and mentor's perspective. In C. F. Anderson (Ed.), *Nursing student to nursing leader.* Albany, NY: Delmar.

Vance, C., & Olson, F. (1998). *The mentor connection in nursing.* New York: Springer Publishing.

White, J. F. (1988). The perceived role of mentoring in the career development and success of academic nurse administrators. *Journal of Professional Nursing, 4,* 178–185.

Williams, R., & Blackburn, R. (1988). Mentoring and junior faculty productivity. *Journal of Nursing Education, 27*(5), 204–209.

CHAPTER 9

Ethical Leadership in Managed Care: Creating A New Vision

Virginia R. Cassidy

Changes in the structure and financing of health care require a new perspective on ethics in health care organizations. The organizational ethics model has been proposed as an approach for melding clinical and business ethics to enable health care organizations to improve their ability to achieve their stated mission, anticipate unethical outcomes, and correct unethical actions once they occur. Nursing leaders play a pivotal role in implementing the mechanisms, designing the strategies, and addressing the issues that arise in the creation of this new vision of ethics in the managed care environment.

The changes in health care financing that serve as the basis for managed care pose numerous challenges for nursing leaders. Changes in skill mix, overall staffing levels, the diversification of services, and the restructuring of existing services are but a few of the areas in which new modes of thinking, planning, and evaluating have been needed. Concomitant with the need for new approaches to financing and defining patient care services is the need for increased attention to and a new perspective or vision of the ethics of managed care. This vision for ethics in the current climate of health care has implications for health care organizations, the leadership of those organizations, direct health care providers, and the patients cared for in managed care agencies.

Note: Originally published in *Nursing Leadership Forum*, Vol. 3, No. 2, 1998. New York: Springer Publishing Company.

This chapter addresses the issues, strategies, and mechanisms for creating a new vision of ethics in health care organizations. Starting with a historical perspective of the ethical roots of health care ethics, clinical ethics and organizational ethics are compared and contrasted and the implications of a paradigm shift in thinking about ethics in managed care are presented within the context of nursing leadership.

HISTORICAL PERSPECTIVES ON ETHICS IN HEALTH CARE

Concern about the ethics of health care is not a new concept. Physicians can trace the ethical basis for their practice to the Hippocratic oath from the third century BC and nurses adopted the ethos of Florence Nightingale in the mid-1800s (Schyve, 1996). Since that time, professional organizations in nursing and medicine have created codes of ethics that serve as practice guides.

Attention to the ethical aspects of care is also reflected in health care organizations. In the 1960s special committees were created to make determinations about the acceptability of candidates for renal dialysis and kidney transplantation in the allocation of these new and scarce resources (Kotin, 1996). Additionally, a statement on patients' rights was included in the 1971 *Accreditation Manual for Hospitals* published by the Joint Commission on Accreditation of Healthcare Organizations (JCAHO) and the American Hospital Association (AHA) promulgated the *Patients' Bill of Rights* in 1972 (R. Potter, 1996; Schyve, 1996). In more recent years, many hospitals have adopted a model for ethical deliberations by creating ethics committees to provide a forum for case consultation in difficult and troubling patient care situations, clinical policy formation, and staff and community education (Fost & Cranford, 1985; Oddi & Cassidy, 1990). In 1991 the Patient Self-Determination Act was passed with the intent of raising public consciousness about advanced directives such as living wills and durable powers of attorney (Hassmiller, 1991).

The common theme of these ethical roots is attention to the clinical aspects of health care. Practice codes address the relationships between practitioners and the patients for whom they provide care. Policy statements address the rights of patients as the recipients of care in clinical agencies, and entities such as ethics committees direct their attention to clinical matters. The question arises, however, about the adequacy of this clinical focus on ethical matters in a managed care environment: Is it sufficient for the leaders in health care organizations to limit their ethical concerns solely to the clinical aspects of care or should the focus of attention to ethics be broadened?

Some early evidence of attention to nonclinically focused ethical concerns in health care can be seen in the 1978 JCAHO standard for hospitals to provide itemized bills to patients, thus acknowledging the rights of patients as customers or consumers. Additional JCAHO standards concerning marketing and billing practices were added later (Schyve, 1996). The 1970s and 1980s were an era in which health care corporations were formed in large numbers and additional governmental regulations of health care organizations were enacted (R. Potter, 1996). The change to a prospective payment system for health care services further emphasized the "business" of health care, as decision making shifted from being clinically based to organizationally based, creating a new order in which the best interest of the patient is only one of many considerations (Renz & Eddy, 1996). This attention to the business aspects of health care presages the need for the leaders in health care to broaden their thinking about health care ethics from that of clinical ethics, as we know it, to that of health care organizational ethics (R. Potter, 1996). And herein lie numerous challenges for nursing leaders.

CLINICAL VERSUS ORGANIZATIONAL ETHICS

"Ethics is a systematic process of reflection in which issues of what one morally ought to do are analyzed, decided, and evaluated through moral reasoning that encompasses, but is not limited to, ethical principles and theories" (Silva, 1990, p. 4). This definition of ethics exemplifies three important elements in understanding the requirements of "being ethical"; that, ethics: 1) is a process; 2) is based on knowledge of certain principles and rules; and 3) requires recognition, deliberation, and action on matters of right and wrong or good and bad.

Biomedical ethics is a specialized field of ethics that is concerned with the application of process, knowledge, and deliberation on what is right or wrong in health care; this term is sometimes used interchangeably with the terms "medical," "nursing," or "clinical" ethics. With a clear understanding of these elements, nursing leaders can apply their knowledge and skills in the transition of their thinking from clinical ethics to organizational ethics.

The cardiology group wants a community-based CPR program instituted while the pediatricians want programs to address gang activity and teenage smoking and drinking. The chief of surgery requests new fiber-optic equipment and the vice president for patient care services submits a proposal for hand-held computers on all of the in-patient units. The administrators of the organization have a commitment to providing care for the indigent, but the shareholders are interested in profits. What is the basis for decision making in the consideration of all of these legitimate claims? Who makes these decisions and how are these decisions evaluated in light of the mission of the organization?

Organizational ethics embodies clinical ethics but requires a paradigm shift from thinking about "issues concerning the individual patient to a wider sociological context" (R. Potter, 1996, p. 3). Robert Potter (1996) further defines organizational ethics as the use of values to guide the decisions of a health care system in a deliberate way. Organizational ethics, then, refers to the development of a set of values, defined by an organization, which become the normative basis for all decision making and action at every level within that particular organization (R. Potter, 1996). The advantage to this approach is that it elevates the importance of ethics in decision making within the organization to a level comparable with that of other elements of decision making, including those of financial and legal considerations and the diagnostic and prognostic data used in making clinical decisions about patient care (R. Potter, 1996). Organizational ethics can be viewed as the melding of "clinical" ethics and "business" ethics, giving recognition to their interdependence in providing quality health care services (Schyve, 1996). The goals of using an organizational ethics approach are to enable health care organizations to improve their ability to do good in achieving their stated mission, anticipate unethical outcomes, and have a mechanism to correct unethical actions once they have occurred (V. Potter, 1996).

MECHANISMS FOR IMPLEMENTING ORGANIZATIONAL ETHICS

Specific mechanisms for implementing an organizational ethics model have been proposed. These mechanisms already exist in health care organizations; what is needed is a set of processes to employ them in the development of the new ethical infrastructure. A brief discussion of three mechanisms is provided below.

The important role of the ethics committee in making the transition to organizational ethics has been identified by several authors (Christopher, 1994; R. Potter, 1996; Renz & Eddy, 1996; Schyve, 1996). The redefinition of the role of the ethics committee can be built upon its existing structure and responsibilities (R. Potter, 1996), codifying the stated organizational values. The focus of the committee's responsibilities must be broadened from case-level ethical issues and decision making to a more comprehensive strategy to address ethical concerns at all levels of the organization from the community that it serves to the board of directors to individual patients and their families (Renz & Eddy, 1996). The ethics committee also plays an important role in ensuring that ethical concerns are addressed at all levels of decision making (R. Potter, 1996) and for taking preventive action on such ethical matters as conflicts of interest and conflict resolution (Christopher, 1994; R. Potter, 1996). These changes in the perspective of the committee will necessitate the expansion of membership of the committee, greater emphasis on its educative and policy-making roles in the organization, and the education of its members to fulfill its expanded roles (R. Potter, 1996). In addition, these changes need to be supported at all levels of the organization in order to be effective in an organizational ethics model (Felder, 1996).

> Example: In an organizational ethics model, the scope of the ethics committee's educational responsibilities may be expanded to the community. Issues that might be addressed in community-based programs include the managed care philosophy of the organization and how incentives for physicians to control costs are related to ordering diagnostic tests, making referrals for consultations with specialists, and selecting treatment options.

A second mechanism for implementing an organizational ethics model is found in the quality management system of the organization. Based upon the values defined by the organization, changes in the existing quality management system need to be made to incorporate those values into the standards of care. The changes may even include the creation of ethics audits to determine if the organization is meeting its ethical standards. Overall, this mechanism offers the advantages of defining quality within the stated values of the organization, assessing the ethical aspects of the desired outcomes, helping to reduce the number of issues that produce crises, and providing a feedback mechanism for assessing the extent to which the stated values are accepted, put into operation, and sustained within the organization (Renz & Eddy, 1996).

> Example: A criterion related to ethical concerns may be incorporated into clinical pathways or care maps. The extent of patients' participation in decision making related to their care, their quality of life, the adequacy of their support systems, and their satisfaction with the quality of care received are some aspects that can be integrated into the evaluation of patient outcomes and the extent to which the organization is meeting its stated ethical standards.

The third mechanism in the implementation process is related to performance evaluation of the staff and management personnel. Integration of the ethical standards into this aspect of the organization further emphasizes ethics in decision making. It can foster the development of ethical behavior, reinforce the importance of ethics in performance, reward performance that represents high ethical standards, and provide a feedback mechanism for the evaluators and the individuals being evaluated (Renz & Eddy, 1996).

> Example: Respect for patients' rights is a criterion that could be added to the performance evaluation of staff nurses. Examples of having met this criterion can be found in activities such as requesting translators for patients who are non-English speaking, explaining treatments and procedures using terminology that patients can comprehend, seeking out family members to report patients' progress, making appropriate referrals to the ethics committee and pastoral care, and maintaining the confidentiality of patient-related information.

STRATEGIES FOR IMPLEMENTING ORGANIZATIONAL ETHICS

The changes in the mechanisms identified above require carefully thought out strategies for the implementation and maintenance of an organizational ethics model. As with all other changes, these proposed changes will be most effective if they are strategic and systematic and a participatory process is used in designing, implementing, and evaluating them. Renz and Eddy (1996, p. 33) suggest four general strategies to help ensure a successful change: define and articulate the values of the organization and clearly relate them to the mission; facilitate communication and learning about ethics and ethical issues and their relationship to practice; build structures to support the changes; and create monitoring and feedback mechanisms.

A variety of processes can be employed to achieve the organizational goals; the appropriateness of these processes should be determined within each organization. Among the processes suggested by several authors are those that range from retreats and workshops to the creation of task forces to team-building activities and small group discussions among all constituencies, including community members (Biblo, Christopher, Johnson, & Potter, 1996; Hofmann, 1996; Renz & Eddy, 1996; Schyve, 1996). A model that can be applied to the implementation of the four strategies identified above is provided in Table 9.1, although Renz and Eddy (1996) describe it specifically as it relates to the communication and learning aspect. In this model, awareness relates to raising consciousness about the changes; trial and experimentation refers to opportunities to discuss and practice

TABLE 9.1 Processes for the Development of an Organizational Ethics Model (*From* Renz & Eddy, 1996)

Awareness	←	←	F
↓			E
Trial and Experimentation			E
↓			D
Adoption			B
↓			A
Institutionalization			C
			K
↓ →	→	→	↑

new approaches; adoption involves embracing the changes; and institutionalization reflects the integration and acceptance of the changes within the organizational culture. The feedback loop ensures that the strategies designed to support the changes to the new ethics model are evaluated and modified, as needed.

CHARACTERISTICS OF NURSING LEADERS NECESSARY FOR CREATING A NEW ETHICAL INFRASTRUCTURE

The characteristics of leaders involved in the creation of an organizational ethics model do not differ from the characteristics for ethical leadership in any organization. Leaders always bear the responsibility for creating and communicating the ethical standards of their organizations (V. Potter, 1996) and for developing the processes for implementing those standards (Renz & Eddy, 1996). These responsibilities take on added importance in redesigning the ethical culture of an organization.

> The nurses in the critical care division raise two issues that have intensified for them since changes in staffing levels have occurred and the nurse-patient ratio has been increased from 1:1 to 1:2. One issue relates to the research being conducted in the critical care units in which the staff nurses assigned to care for patients who meet the criteria for the research protocols are responsible for collecting and recording data. The second issue concerns the nursing students who are either assigned to critical care patients or rotate to the intensive care areas. The question they raise is: What are their priorities to be—patient care, data collection, or teaching and working with the students? The broader issue for the organization is—how do the goals of patient care, research, and education "fit" with the organizational mission and its ethical standards?

Among the characteristics for ethical leadership consistently cited in the literature are integrity (Cassidy & Koroll, 1994; Jenkins, 1989; Morath & Manthey, 1993) and courage (Bruderle, 1994; Jenkins, 1989). Integrity refers to a goodness of character, a "wholeness, . . . uprightness, honesty, and sincerity" (*Webster's*, 1986, p. 732). Courage is defined as the "quality of being fearless or brave; valor" (*Webster's*, 1986, p. 325). Not surprisingly, these characteristics have been identified as essential for leaders creating the change to an organizational ethics model (Hofmann, 1996; R. Potter, 1996; V. Potter, 1996; Renz & Eddy, 1996) along with the characteristic of persistence (R. Potter, 1996; V. Potter, 1996) or "enduring continuance . . . tenacity" (*Webster's*, 1986, p. 1061).

Several other characteristics reflective of leadership, in general, that are needed to move to an organizational ethics model are worthy of comment. A vision of the future and the organization (Bruderle, 1994; Cassidy & Koroll, 1994; Kotin, 1996; Manfredi, 1994, 1995; Valiga, 1994; Warfel, Allen, McGoldrick, McLane, & Martin, 1994) is crucial in developing the foundation of the ethical infrastructure of organizational ethics. The success of the change must be based on a clearly defined, shared vision of how the organization wants to define itself to its administrators, staff, patients, and community.

The four "Cs" of effective leadership are also inherent in the mechanisms and strategies describe above. *Communication* (Bruderle, 1994; Valiga, 1994) at all stages of the process is central to raising awareness, learning new ways of thinking about, adopting and then integrating the model into the organizational culture. Being an effective *change agent* (Bruderle, 1994; Manfredi, 1995; Valiga, 1994) whose self-confidence, knowledge, and skills (Huber, 1996) facilitate adoption of the innovation by all constituencies is also pivotal to a successful transformation. *Collaboration* (Valiga, 1994) is essential to create an environment in which power is shared and, thereby, strengthens the organization, fosters the growth of those involved in the process, and develops a sense of pride and ownership that supports an enduring change. Comfort with *conflict* (Manfredi, 1994, 1995; Valiga, 1994) is the final element of leadership necessary for the creation of an organizational ethics model. In generating an environment in which existing ideas, structures, and processes are challenged, nursing leaders recognize that conflicts can occur. Managing these conflicts and viewing them as an opportunity to produce innovations in the organization (Manfredi, 1995) will contribute to the successful transformation of the ethical culture of the organization.

ISSUES FOR NURSING LEADERS IN AN
ORGANIZATIONAL ETHICS MODEL

Addressing the ethical issues in health care has never been an easy task. Even within the traditional perspective of clinical ethics, the dilemmas surrounding patient care issues have created conflicts and distress. These conflicts have involved balancing the rights of patients in making decisions about treatment options and care at the end of life, among others, with the legal responsibilities of health care providers and health care organizations, the advocacy role of nurses, and the allocation of resources. The Study to Understand Prognoses and Preferences for Outcomes and Risks of Treatment (SUPPORT) (The SUPPORT Principal Investigators, 1995), which serves to highlight the clinical issues related to the care of the critically ill and dying in the areas of patients' preferences for treatment, pain management, and the use of hospital resources, is just one example of the myriad of ethical issues found in contemporary health care.

Nursing leaders, by virtue of their membership on ethics committees (Oddi & Cassidy, 1990) and their leadership roles and responsibilities in health care organizations, have been intimately involved in these clinical ethical issues. Studies (Camunas, 1991; Sietsema & Spradley, 1987; Silva, 1994; Silva & Lewis, 1991) of the ethical dilemmas encountered by nurse executives demonstrate consistently, not only the variety of ethical issues encountered by the nursing leaders in health care organizations, but also the frequency of their occurrence. It is not surprising that many of the ethical issues identified in these studies are related directly to the managed care environment; namely, the allocation of resources related to the services provided within the organization, access to care, staffing levels and skill mix, the use of technology in patient care, and the quality of care provided.

Past experience in addressing ethical issues will serve nursing leaders well in the change to an organizational ethics model. Many of the ethical issues identified above reflect the conflict between the interests of patients versus organizational longevity and/or doing good for individual patients versus doing good for the aggregate (Schyve, 1996). By virtue of their knowledge of these matters, nursing leaders are poised to provide the direction needed to consider these matters within the framework of organizational ethics. Nursing leaders at the executive level may be the ones who initiate the process of change to an organizational ethics model and/or participate in the design of the new ethical infrastructure for their health care organization with other executives. Nursing leaders at all levels of the organization must be committed to the concept and play an active role in its inception, development, implementation, and evaluation. Further, as more nurse executives take on responsibilities for the administration of patient care services, of which nursing services are only a part, and move into chief operating officer positions, their power and authority within health care organizations position them to be indispensable leaders in moving to an organizational ethics model.

A special concern raised in the change to an organizational ethics model is that of the rights of individual patients that are being "lost." In a model where patients' rights are only one of many considerations in decision-making processes, this concern is a valid one. Some authors argue, however, that patients' rights may be better protected in this model because this concern should be incorporated into the overall values of the organization and reflected in the policies and procedures that make the model operational (R. Potter, 1996; Schyve, 1996). It is critical, therefore, for this concern to be a high priority in the development of the model and for nursing leaders to ensure that the rights of patients are protected. Will this model eliminate the conflicts that surround ethical decision making? In all likelihood, it will not, but it does provide a multifaceted structure that can result in more congruity in deliberations on ethical matters. If the model is prepared thoughtfully and implemented consistently, the rights of patients should be valued, preserved, and better protected.

CONCLUSIONS

Leadership can be viewed as both a process and an outcome (Manfredi & Valiga, 1994). In the change to an organizational ethics model, nursing leaders have the opportunity to experience leadership in both of these ways. Through the use of leadership processes, nursing leaders can create and shape a new vision for ethical reflection and action (R. Potter, 1996) in health care organizations. They can also ensure that that vision becomes a reality and produces the outcomes desired for the preferred future of health care.

REFERENCES

Biblo, J. D., Christopher, M. J., Johnson, L., & Potter, R. L. (1996). Ethical issues in managed care: Guidelines for clinicians and recommendations to accrediting organizations. *Bioethics Forum, 12*(1), MC3–MC24.

Bruderle, E. R. (1994). The arts and humanities: A creative approach to developing nursing leaders. *Holistic Nursing Practice, 9*(1), 68–74.

Camunas, C. E. (1991). *Ethical dilemmas of nurse executives: A descriptive study* [CD-ROM]. Abstract from: SilverPlatter File: Dissertation Abstracts Item: 155448.

Cassidy, V. R., & Koroll, C. J. (1994). Ethical aspects of transformational leadership. *Holistic Nursing Practice, 9*(1), 41–47.

Christopher, M. J. (1994). Integrated ethics programs: A new mission for ethics committees. *Bioethics Forum, 10*(4), 19–21.

Felder, M. (1996). Can ethics committees work in managed care plans? *Bioethics Forum, 12*(1), 10–15.

Fost, N., & Cranford, R. E. (1985). Hospital ethics committees: Administrative aspects. *Journal of the American Medical Association, 253*, 2687–2692.

Hassmiller, S. (1991). Bringing the patient self-determination act into practice. *Nursing Management, 22*(12), 29–32.

Hofmann, P. B. (1996). Hospitals mergers and acquisitions: A new catalyst for examining organizational ethics. *Bioethics Forum, 12*(2), 45–48.

Huber, D. (1996). *Leadership and Nursing Care Management.* Philadelphia, PA: Saunders.

Jenkins, H. M. (1989). Ethical dimensions of leadership in community health nursing. *Journal of Community Health Nursing, 6*(2), 103–112.

Kotin, A. M. (1996). Do no harm. *Bioethics Forum, 12*(2), 21–26.

Manfredi, C. M. (1994). Leadership preparation: An examination of master's degree programs in nursing. *Holistic Nursing Practice, 9*(1), 48–57.

Manfredi, C. (1995). The art of legendary leadership. *Nursing Leadership Forum, 1*(2), 62–64.

Manfredi, C. M., & Valiga, T. M. (1994). Forward. *Holistic Nursing Practice, 9*(1), vi.

Morath, J. M., & Manthey, M. (1993). An environment for care and service leadership: The nurse administrator's impact. *Nursing Administration Quarterly, 17,* 75–80.

Oddi, L. F., & Cassidy, V. R. (1990). Participation and perception of nurse members on the hospital ethics committee. *Western Journal of Nursing Research, 12*(3), 307–317.

Potter, R. L. (1996). From clinical ethics to organizational ethics: The second stage of the evolution of bioethics. *Bioethics Forum, 12*(2), 3–12.

Potter, V. R. (1996). Individuals bear responsibility. *Bioethics Forum, 12*(2), 27–28.

Renz, D. O., & Eddy, W. B. (1996). Organizations, ethics, and health care: Building an ethics infrastructure for a new era. *Bioethics Forum, 12*(2), 29–39.

Schyve, P. M. (1996). Patient rights and organizational ethics: The Joint Commission perspective. *Bioethics Forum, 12*(2), 13–20.

Sietsema, M. R., & Spradley, B. W. (1987). Ethics and administrative decision making. *Journal of Nursing Administration, 17*(4), 28–32,

Silva, M. C. (1990). *Ethical decision making in nursing administration.* Norwalk, CT: Appleton & Lange.

Silva, M. C. (1994). Nurse executives' responses to ethical concerns and policy formulation for allocation of scarce resources. *Nursing Connections, 7*(1), 59–64.

Silva, M. C., & Lewis, C. K. (1991). Ethics, policy, and allocation of scarce resources in nursing service administration: A pilot study. *Nursing Connections, 4*(2), 44–52.

SUPPORT Principal Investigators. (1995). A controlled trial to improve care for seriously ill hospitalized patients. The study to understand prognoses and preferences for outcomes and risk of treatment (SUPPORT). *Journal of the American Medical Association, 274*(20), 1591–1598.

Valiga, T. M. (1994). Leadership for the future. *Holistic Nursing Practice, 9*(1), 83–90.

Warfel, W. M., Allen, R. A., McGoldrick, T., McLane, S., & Martin, S. G. (1994). Organizational innovations that nourish staff leadership. *Holistic Nursing Practice, 9*(1), 58–67.

Webster's New world dictionary of the American language (2nd College Ed.). (1986). New York: Prentice Hall Press.

This manuscript was completed as part of a sabbatical leave granted to the author by Northern Illinois University.

CHAPTER *10*

Maintaining the Balance . . . and Thriving as a Leader

Kathleen D. Sanford

According to consultants, "burn-out and work-related stress are becoming the bad backs and carpal tunnel syndrome of the 90s" (CCH Inc., 1997). Nursing leaders would probably agree that these maladies will be the phenomena of the workplace that will continue into the next century as well. Downsizing, restructuring, and budgetary constraints have complicated the hospital world that Peter Drucker (1977) described already decades ago as a "two-headed monster," not easily compared to other industries. In the last decade of the 20th century, Drucker still believed that, "we have never in human history built anything as complex as the modern hospital" (Flower, 1991).

Management has never been without its challenges, but few would disagree that nursing leaders today face unprecedented change whether they practice in an inpatient, outpatient, home health or university setting. Employee associates, administrators, board members, physicians, and patients are insistently vocal in their demands of managers. Solutions to all of their real or perceived problems often call for dramatically opposite actions. No wonder Robert Samuelson (1999) says he'd never be a manager, because "their almost universal task is to serve twin masters, each of whom has grown more demanding. There's the Organization with its imperatives; and there's the Individual—each with 'needs.'" Some authors and theorists have contrasted "Management" with "Leadership." According to Neis and Kingdon (1990), "traditional management systems have been devised

Note: Originally published in *Nursing Leadership Forum*, Vol. 4, No. 3, 2000. New York: Springer Publishing Company.

to achieve control and maintain direction. Leadership draws its followers along by developing rather than directing." To be competent in their roles, nurses who supervise others must blend management skills with leadership abilities. They develop others but sometimes must direct.

Nursing leaders are challenged to manage productivity and also to bridge traditional management/front line clinical gulfs. They are supposed to improve employee morale while cutting costs and increasing patient satisfaction. The enormity of these expectations threatens to overwhelm even the most competent leader unless s/he can learn to balance the needs of all the organization's stakeholders.

The successful nurse leaders of the next century will understand and emphasize customer service. They'll develop an appreciation for finance and profitability. They'll encourage the growth and development of others and actively work to improve their communities. They will learn to take care of themselves and other managers. Sound impossible? It is, unless a conscious decision is made to balance the needs of all. It's when the organization or its leaders get out of balance that organizations and individuals falter, slip into mediocrity, and even fail. Examples of the out-of-balance health care facility are when: (1) financial needs become *more* important than patient care needs, (2) physician needs become *more* important than nurses' welfare, or (3) today's company success becomes *more* important than tomorrow's organizational survival.

Leaders who can balance the needs of various individuals while working for the good of the whole system are true value-added managers. They make choices that lead to long-term success for all, because they consider the whole system along with its parts. They can only accomplish this if they lead with a genuine concern for the well-being of the organization, customers, employees, and leaders. As nurses, it should be easy to identify this concern as love or at least as one of Webster's definitions of love: "an unselfish, loyal, and benevolent concern for the good of another" (Mish, 1988).

LOVING THE ORGANIZATION

Love for the organization starts with knowing and believing in its mission and understanding its vision and goals. If personal values do not correspond to the institution's values, there can be no real bond, which makes it unhealthy for managers (and all employees) to continue their relationship with the organization. Leaders can love the company only when they admire it, identify with it, want to protect it, and desire its success. Loving leaders do not meet personal goals at the expense of the company. They see their work as more than "just a job" and feel a loyalty that is made visible by their consideration of the organization's long-term success in every decision they make. That includes understanding fiscal realities.

Nursing leaders have been suspected by nonclinical administrators of being more loyal to their profession than to the organization that employs them. Raulin (1989) stated that there is a need for professionals entering management positions to understand that allegiance to their profession cannot take precedence over corporate loyalty because corporate efficiency and business success could be negatively impacted. While maintaining professional identity and standards, the leaders who will thrive and who will be best able to represent their profession are those who are equally loyal to their workplace. They ensure continuity of leadership through succession planning and development of younger leaders. They insist on a competent workforce and ethical behavior in both clinical and business decisions. They want to ensure the long-term financial health of their workplace. They want their customers, whether they are patients, families or physicians, to appreciate and admire their services.

Examples of choices that indicate a valuing of the organization are:

- Rewarding teamwork and being intolerant of turf-building within the company.
- Celebrating and rewarding growth in others (e.g., educational accomplishments, the completion of a difficult new task).
- Rewarding quality work and being intolerant of shoddiness or lack of quality.
- Making decisions for the good of the entire organization rather than just for one's own department.
- Making decisions for the long-term success of the company rather than for short-term, quick wins.
- Encouraging, rewarding, protecting, and recognizing the creativity of associates.

LOVING THE CUSTOMER

"Eye on Patients," a report from the American Hospital Association and the Picker Institute (1996), showed that patients generally feel they are treated with respect and their basic physical needs are met in our current system. But, they also feel that the health care system is a "nightmare to navigate," and that caregivers don't provide enough information and are not emotionally supportive. Organizations may suffer from any of five major impediments to superior customer service: (1) a high Self-Importance Quotient (SIQ); (2) high dependence on rules; (3) a low level of esteem for customers; (4) incompetence; and, (5) a low level of love for the employees. Health care institutions are susceptible to any or all of these challenges.

Some health care providers appear to suffer from self-importance, perhaps because health care is so important to people. Customers are expected to wait beyond their appointment times because the provider's time is so important. They're admitted to hospitals, dressed in revealing gowns and told they can't see their families outside of visiting hours. They're called "patients," which implies they are "different" from customers, so they are perceived to have a diminished need for customer service. After all, they need us!

Loving leaders question practices like these. They pay attention to the needs and complaints of individual customers, and then encourage all hospital employees to use creativity in solving them. They apologize for errors and then work to correct them. They ensure that the patient care team is competent as well as polite. They also don't limit their service to patients, understanding that physicians, too, are major customers.

Studies such as the Picker Institute's "Eye on Patients" show that customers want to believe providers care about them. Caring means listening to what people say they need. It means giving good service because you want to. It means considering that the welfare of customers is just as important as your own. It means consistent interactions filled with honesty, respect, and concern.

Of course, no matter how polite and kind the nurse is when giving an injection, patients want the nurse to know what she's doing. Part of caring for customers is ensuring that the people who will serve them are qualified, educated, and capable. Loving managers make it a priority to maintain a competent work team. They provide appropriate education and enforce high standards.

Finally, loving customers includes loving the employee. The relationship between employee satisfaction and customer services is so direct that the one cannot truly occur without the other. There is a saying, "You can't give from an empty basket," and it applies directly to those who serve others. Patient care staff can't continue to care long term for the needs of customers if their own needs are being neglected. A study of Sears, Roebuck and Co. workers, reported in 1997 by the CFI Group of Ann Arbor, Michigan (Sherman, 1997), found that a 5% increase in measured employee job satisfaction translates into a 2% measurable improvement in customer satisfaction. A leader who truly cares for customers must also love the employee team.

Examples of choices that indicate a valuing of customers are:

- Eliciting feedback from customers about what they want, and then acting on that feedback.
- Rewarding customer service and being intolerant of less than exceptional service.
- Providing a service or product that is of value to the customer, and refusing to make profit more important than safe, ethical, high-quality products.
- Being honest in advertising and marketing and not promising more than can be delivered.
- Employing only a competent team, correcting incompetence with education, enforcement of standards, and if necessary, discipline (including termination).

LOVING THE EMPLOYEE TEAM

Scientists in the field of human studies have documented that infants who receive adequate food and attention to physical needs, but who do not receive individualized loving attention, suffer and die from nonorganic failure to thrive, or marasmus (Whaley & Wong, 1991). Without loving leadership, individuals in institutions can suffer from a workplace "marasmus" in which their spirits, talents, and abilities do not develop, even if they are receiving adequate wages and benefits. Caring for employees does not mean controlling them. It means helping them—every one of them—develop their own abilities and pursue their own successes.

Loving leadership includes being a mentor (for all employees, not just for a selected, favored few), cheerleader, advocate, disciplinarian, ethicist, and futurist. As cheer-leaders, leaders encourage their associates when they're winning . . . and also when they're trying to play the game, even if they're not as successful as they'd like to be. Cheerleading managers aren't shy with praise. They inspire others by supporting them publicly.

As advocates, loving leaders champion the staff's needs and ideas. They ensure resources are available so jobs can get done. As ethicists, they set high personal standards and treat all employees with integrity and honesty. As futurists they manage proactively, making changes that solve potential problems before they even occur. As disciplinarians they care enough to confront problems.

The best loving leaders give feedback for the sake of another's growth and for the good of the company, not to meet their own needs for power or control. They use corrective action that is fair, logical, and free of favoritism and bias. They're consistent and make as few rules as possible, but then hold everyone in the organization to the same rules.

Examples that indicate a valuing of work associates are:

- To encourage, provide opportunities for, and invest in programs for lifelong learning—for every employee.
- To share information with associates, including trusting them with financial numbers.
- To help employees lead a balanced life by not expecting mandatory overtime, and by offering such things as exercise classes, flexible scheduling, on-site child and elder care, classes on stress reduction, parenting, time management, and an on-site occupational health nurse.
- To promote from within (even if an internal candidate will need additional training that an external candidate may already have).
- To openly address current problems, such as violence in the workplace, with plans to detect potential problems and prevent or be protected from them.
- To empower associates by giving them the necessary work tools and then getting out of the way so that others can do their jobs without bureaucratic interference.

LOVING THE LEADER

Few management theories address the need for managers to take care of themselves and other managers. Yet none can thrive if they continually give to everyone but themselves. It seems like common sense that you cannot give from an empty basket.

People with strong needs for positive affirmations from others don't do well as loving leaders. They're not going to have their adulation needs met because management is not a popularity contest (decisions that have to be made will not please everyone). Also, people who have the good fortune to work with caring leaders often develop a sense of entitlement that causes them to expect and demand more from these leaders.

Managers who thrive in their roles understand that concerned and loving behavior may not be reciprocated but they choose to behave with love anyway. They are able to forgive themselves when they make mistakes and they forgive their bosses when they make mistakes.

The best leaders lead a balanced life by dividing time and energy between work and home life. They take care of their own health with a good diet, exercise, and rest. They appreciate themselves and treat and support their bosses the way they want to be treated and supported.

Examples that indicate a valuing of self are:

- To invest in continuing education and lifelong learning for yourself.
- Not to work excessively long hours but to balance work with the rest of life: family, friends, hobbies, and leisure time.
- To maintain good health through diet, exercise, medical check-ups, and keeping an appropriate weight.
- Not to stay in a "toxic" environment or in an organization where the culture and ethics don't match your own.
- Reward yourself and celebrate when goals have been met and successes experienced.

THE CHALLENGES AHEAD FOR LOVING LEADERSHIP

Loving leadership is hard work. It calls for unconditional love, which means continuing to understand with no guarantee of being understood. It cannot be practiced by those who need to be universally liked or by those with strong codependence needs. Loving leadership requires consistent role modeling of integrity, competence, and superior interpersonal skills. It takes ability, knowledge, ethics, humor, and courage.

Courage is required because, however skillful the manager, his or her decisions lead to criticism. Loving leaders run the risk of seeming "too soft." They are not "believable" to suspicious workers whose acculturation has convinced them that whatever the manager does is yet another form of subordinate manipulation.

Peers may see successful managers as easy targets for turf takeover. It's believed they are so concerned with doing the right thing for the organization, patients, and staff that they can be surpassed and undermined by those whose sole goal is self-promotion.

Although caring managers may be seen as weak, frauds, or pushovers, they are actually exceptionally strong. Weaker leaders choose the easier, well-worn path of bosses before them by falling into step with "the big boys" and traditional styles of management. Superior leaders practice leadership because they care, not from a need to manipulate. They will make choices in the next millennium that will mirror a valuing of their organizations, employees, customers, and themselves. In making these choices, they will balance the needs of all, so that all will have the opportunity to thrive.

REFERENCES

American Hospital Association and the Picker Institute. (1996). *Eye on patients.* Chicago, IL: Author.

CCH Inc. (1997, March 26). Employers may benefit from nurturing employee's emotional well-being. *Human Resources Management, 402,* 46.

Drucker, P. (1977, June). Peter Drucker on hospitals and management. *Hospital Financial Management, 31*(6), 30–33.

Flower, J. (1991, July/August). It's late in the day: Some thoughts on the future of health-care. *Healthcare Forum Journal, 34*(4), 60.

Mish, F. (Ed.). (1988). *Webster's 9th new collegiate dictionary* (p. 707). Springfield, MA: Merriam-Webster Inc.

Neis, M., & Kingdon, R. (1990). *Leadership in transition* (p. 23). Schaumburg, IL: Nova.

Raulin, J. (1989, August). An anatomy of autonomy: Managing professionals. *Academy of Management Executive, 3*(3), 216–228.

Samuelson, R. (1999, March 22). Why I am not a manager. *Newsweek, CXXXIII,* 47.

Sherman, S. (1997, October 13). Bringing Sears into the new world. *Fortune, 138*(8), 183–184.

Whaley, L., & Wong, D. (1991). *Nursing care of infants and children* (p. 608). St. Louis, MO: Mosby.

CHAPTER 11

Primer for Philanthropy: The ABCs of Fundraising

Sandra S. Deller and Joyce J. Fitzpatrick

A – a broad-based development program
B – background research and preparation
C – cultivation and solicitation
  = DOLLARS

Development is a people business. Philanthropy is the application of interpersonal skills, leadership, management, and listening skills. Concepts are as basic as the ABCs. It is the application and individualization that translate to donor involvement and, subsequently, dollars. This "primer" addresses key components of a successful program of fundraising, including annual funds, major gifts, and endowments, and presents strategies that have been proven effective.

THE ANNUAL FUND

Development includes a broad-based program beginning with a well-developed annual fund as foundation. The Annual Fund is a yearly campaign for unrestricted operating dollars. Most often, it is this vehicle that provides an opportunity to become close to potential donors. Individuals who have been consistent donors, or those who increase or decrease support, should receive special attention.

Response to the Annual Fund drive is an indicator of your constituents' interests and commitment. If the Annual Fund is solicited

Note: Originally published in *Nursing Leadership Forum*, Vol. 3, No. 3, 1998. New York: Springer Publishing Company.

by direct mail and meets with a good response rate, it indicates a very invested group of alumni/ae and friends; however, direct mail is generally the least effective form of solicitation. The high volume of unsolicited appeals is staggering and competition is fierce. A combination of direct mail and telemarketing is more effective. Phone contact (telemarketing) elicits more personal information about supporters. Most effective is the combination of some direct solicitation, telemarketing, and direct mail. The mechanism is determined by the potential of the donor. If an individual has been a regular donor over several years, consider the advantage of a personal visit in generating increased support. Donor lists should be segmented according to giving potential and staff resources. The time commitment for individual visits will be well worth the effort, both in immediate gains and in building knowledge of the individual, developing relationships, and setting the stage for more significant future contributions.

There is a plethora of gift options suitable for an Annual Fund. These include the following:

- Anniversary Gifts—anniversary or reunion gifts are the easiest to secure. The request is based on the year of graduation with special attention to 5-year periods.
- Challenge Gifts—an immediate way to increase your annual fund revenue is to ask one of the school's closest friends and donors to issue a challenge to his or her classmates. The ratio can be a $1-per-$1 basis with a limit, or require that for every $1 there would be a $2 match from donors.
- Gift Clubs—and honor rolls are lists that group names according to categories of support, such as the Dean's Club or President's Society, or that could be named for a founder or outstanding alumnus. These lists are published and provide an incentive for classmates to be included in similar clubs or societies for peer recognition.
- Special Occasions—be certain to be opportunistic in using any special event or anniversary to pitch a special gift to the Annual Fund that might be a larger gift than usual, what is referred to as a "stretch gift."

Volumes have been written about conducting successful Annual Fund campaigns and the pros and cons of various appeals and methodology. The role of the Annual Fund is a critical first stage for development.

MAJOR GIFTS

The definition of a major gift depends upon the organization. For some, the largest gifts are in the $5,000 to $10,000 range; for others, the threshold is $25,000 or even $100,000. Regardless of the range, the secrets to a major gift are relationships and follow-up. Major gifts involve 95% cultivation and 5% solicitation. Look first to those closest to the school or organization such as trustees, chairs of committees, current or emeriti faculty, or active alumni/ae: "the insiders." These individuals will often have suggestions for major gift prospects, how much the prospect might be willing to give, the most effective approach, or which project(s) would interest the prospect. Like the Annual Fund, prospects for major gifts should be segmented.

Additionally, the group of donors who have made larger or regular contributions to the Annual Fund, a building fund or a special project should be asked to join "the insiders" by taking a leadership role in fundraising. After they have made a commitment, they can be asked to identify others: alumni/ae, colleagues or friends who might be interested in the campaign or project.

A third tier of prospects, those who have given smaller gifts or whose giving has been sporadic, should be contacted. Expanding contacts increases the prospect base and potential support. Consider any legacies of the school; generations of family involvement can lead to a megagift. Tour facilities and research names on existing plaques, consulting archival donor lists for recognition. Tributes are valuable resources.

Major gifts require a customized, individual approach. Not all contacts will result in a gift, but at the very least they will lay the fundraising foundation. Additionally, you are gathering important data about how the school or organization is perceived. This, too, can be helpful in developing prospective contacts related to initiatives and may even provide valuable insights about enhancing current programs and developing new projects. With continued contact and cultivation, future development is facilitated.

ENDOWMENT

It is important to maintain a balance between outright (unrestricted) and endowment gifts. Endowment is a legacy for the school as well as the donor. Wise investment of the principal and allocation of a percentage of the interest annually to be spent for the donor's intention guarantee its permanence. The percentage varies among institutions but often is around 5%. The remaining interest is returned to the principal to ensure its future growth and perpetuity. There is a broad range of endowment gift opportunities, including student support, faculty support or recognition, capital projects (buildings or renovations), programs, research, lectures, library funds and special awards. There is usually a minimum cost to establish an endowment fund; often, however, there is some allowance for individuals to make a pledge with payments over time, typically 3 to 5 years. Many donors find endowment giving very appealing, especially attaching the family name for perpetuity as an honor or memorial.

The named endowment fund provides an excellent opportunity to communicate with donors. Appropriate acknowledgment of all gifts is important, but especially for endowment giving, as recognition was probably a motivator for the gift. Some tangible remembrance, such as a plaque with the family name prominently displayed, a description of the fund's purpose and the date of its establishment, is always welcomed. Also, include endowment donors in publications, honor rolls, or lists of supporters.

RESEARCH

Research is the basis for determining the who, what, and when for fundraising—the resources. While a research department is extremely valuable, much can be accomplished with the proper focus on priority prospects. Information that can provide important clues to a donor's capacity or propensity to contribute includes personal information, such as date of birth, marital status, number of children, home and business addresses, education, career or any financial information on the prospect's company, including compensation and stock options. All of this information is very valuable in determining a feasible gift range. With public companies, information is easy to ascertain from annual reports and income tax returns. Private companies require more thorough research. Additional areas that assist with insights are other relationships with the school, especially legacies, student offices, associations, and sports activities. Information on community activities is helpful particularly if the individual or spouse is a trustee or significant donor. Any information about the prospect's philanthropy will be helpful in targeting how much to request.

If the potential of the prospect is great enough, no source should be left unexplored in preparing for the solicitation. Friends, colleagues and faculty, including emeriti faculty, should be consulted as they often have personal information about the prospect. Gathering background information can make the critical difference in the outcome of your solicitation.

SECURING THE APPOINTMENT

As simple as it sounds, this sometimes proves to be the most difficult. Without a face-to-face meeting, cultivation and solicitation cannot occur. As with other fundraising initiatives, there are many methods and styles used to schedule appointments. Some prefer to make the call themselves; others like to have an assistant make the contact. Development personnel should apply the method that is optimal for the staff and school. Sometimes it is effective to prepare the prospect for the call by first sending an introductory letter. If there is an "insider" who is close to the individual, it might be desirable for that person to secure the appointment. A disadvantage of employing this method is the timeliness and availability of the volunteer caller.

With a busy executive, an assistant who is a "gatekeeper" can be a formidable obstacle. Engage the assistant and enlist him or her to help schedule the appointment. An alternative method is to assume a familiarity with the executive by using his/her first name. Timing can facilitate access, e.g., calling early in the morning, at lunchtime, or after regular hours can sometimes provide direct contact to the prospect. If this fails, a call to the executive's home might be considered.

As a last resort, leave a compelling message on an answering machine, send a fax, or use e-mail. If the message on the machine is informal, be informal in your approach. Try a teaser to get a response: "*I am calling from the president's or dean's office*" or "*Your friend, George, suggested we talk.*" Always maintain control by stating when you will be calling back to schedule the appointment.

Another question that arises is how much information to provide the prospect. Ideally, give only enough information to secure the appointment. Providing too much information or too many details can lead the individual to restrict the conversation to only phone contact or conclude that the information provided was sufficient and there is no need for a personal meeting.

Like so much of development, securing the appointment requires a sensitivity to the prospect. Does the individual sound busy? If so, do not proceed with the appointment request as it will probably not be successful. The most effective callers are those individuals who can immediately engage the prospect. Instead, ask when would be a good time to call back. Positive expectations can elicit positive responses. After the appointment is arranged, confirm it in writing to make certain that all parties have the correct information.

CULTIVATION

The initial step in cultivation is to select the most appropriate individual(s) to meet with the prospect. Past history and relationships are key factors. In some cases, it will be the dean, organization CEO, department chair or faculty member. Additionally, a team comprising a development professional, volunteer, dean or faculty member, or some combination of these individuals, could make the approach. Each situation requires a unique approach and there is no "right" formula.

Cultivation entails establishing or strengthening the individual's interest or involvement in the school or project. It normally involves several meetings with the individual and/or spouse, including special activities designed to increase their affiliation with the school. Each meeting should have a specific goal. The number of meetings should be determined by the response and feedback of the individual prospect.

The first visit with a new prospect is a discovery mission. It is essential to find out how the school is perceived and its value to the prospect's career or personal life. Information the prospect volunteers about relationships, morals, attitudes, and activities can provide important clues in formulating the next step in the cultivation. If the meeting is in the prospect's home or office, take careful note of the surroundings and furnishing styles. These appointments reveal personality; look for items of commonality such as photographs of children or a hobby. These serve as great ice breakers for conversation. Body language and posture, beginning with the handshake, help define personality traits, style, and chemistry with the development team. Specifically, you are trying to discover what will motivate the prospect to make a gift. Why give and why now? What benefits can giving to the school or project present for the donor? People give for a variety of reasons, for example, recognition, immortality, to perpetuate their own beliefs or values, to belong, out of a sense of responsibility, or to ameliorate guilt.

The most effective contacts are usually those in which the prospect does most of the talking, and the development team, the listening. A few well-placed, open-ended questions, attentive listening, and keen observations can accelerate cultivation.

SOLICITATION

With sufficient research and cultivation, the solicitation can proceed. Strategies should be set for the solicitation and the lead solicitor selected in advance. It is usually advisable not to solicit solo; two heads and ears are better than one. Sometimes, rehearsing possible scenarios provides a level of comfort and can help prepare the team to address objections. A positive mind set should be maintained throughout the call. The setting should be comfortable for the prospect, e.g., breakfast, lunch or meetings in the home or office. A predetermined time limit should be followed. As with earlier contacts, the individual's temperament affects the solicitation climate. Engage the prospect in conversation related to an item from earlier discussions or the latest shared experience, either business or personal.

When appropriate, the conversation should segue into the solicitation. Again, there is no "right" way to ask. The request must be clear and unequivocal. Ask for the order. Whatever the style or format, the request must be tied to the purpose, cost and, if applicable, a time limit. It can be straightforward, *"As one of our closest friends, we would like you to consider a gift to ___ of $ ___ to support ___ ."* Another approach could be, *"We know you (e.g., Joan) are committed to the School— how do you want to be identified in this campaign?"* or *"It seems like this project is something you care about, you can help us with a gift of $ ___ to help initiate this program."* If a lighter approach is called for, *"Joan, we appreciate your generous annual fund gift and wondered if you would con-*

sider adding a couple more zeros for this important project." If a volunteer is present, it can be effective for the volunteer to suggest, "*Joan, please join me in supporting this project with a gift of $ ____.*" Sometimes, the volunteer can be a little uncomfortable soliciting a friend. Proper coaching of the volunteer, with a lead-in from the development professional, can often achieve the desired results.

Successful solicitations are not dependent upon the most articulate request; rather, they depend on the rationale for the gift, matching of gift needs, and sincerity of the solicitor. After the proposal, the solicitation team should remain silent and allow the prospect to respond. Too often, the temptation is to keep talking, but silence on the part of those making the request is important. Based on the response, the follow-up, either in the form of a proposal or additional information, should be discussed. If a commitment is made, details, such as pledge forms, should be completed. Affirm the importance of the donor's support.

If the decision is delayed, the solicitor should call in a few weeks to a month to see if the timing is better. A "no" is *not* always a "no" in fundraising and "no" does *not* mean "never." The old sales adage, "a sale begins with the first refusal," often holds true. Timing is a key ingredient; also, there may be another need of the school that is more closely aligned to the prospect's priorities. Above all, persistence does pay. Meetings should always end on a positive note. At the very least, it was a public relations call for the school or organization. A successful solicitation team warrants congratulations and commences the stewardship process.

STEWARDSHIP

An important caveat to remember in fundraising is that a donor can never be thanked too often or by too many people. The solicitation team should send a note; the dean, lead faculty or volunteer should send another note. If appropriate, the president should add an acknowledgment, too. The donor's name should be included on recognition lists (if not anonymous) and the donor and family should be invited to all significant activities. By being as inclusive as possible, the relationship will be strengthened.

If the donor lives out of town, the development staff or primary contact should maintain the relationship and visit when possible.

Visits by faculty or volunteers will keep ties strong. Sending information related to the donor's area of interest and news items also maintains contact. Donors should feel like "insiders" and be treated accordingly. Regular reports should be sent to the donors detailing the use of their funds. Reports should include information on the growth of their fund and market value, the use of their fund, and the program or project that the fund benefits. If the fund is a scholarship fund, it is helpful to send information about the student award recipients, such as their grades, accomplishments, major, and hometown. When possible, a meeting should be arranged so the donor's philanthropy is tangible. Students can be the best salespeople for additional gifts. Often, lifelong relationships are developed through these meetings. If a meeting is not possible, student recipients should be asked to send the donor a thank-you note and tell the donor a little about themselves and their educational experiences, future professional goals, and what the support means to them. Special annual events to recognize significant donors with the board, president, dean and key faculty present, also serve to enhance stewardship and reinforce that the donor and other attendees are truly the school's best friends.

Cultivation, solicitation and stewardship are all a continuum, that is, critical to prospecting for the annual fund, major gifts, and endowments. Today's donors are tomorrow's legacies and can benefit the school in countless ways. It is a win-win situation; the donor feels proud to be part of a quality institution and the school gains support to accomplish its mission.

CHAPTER 12

Strategies for Successful Research Project Management

Elizabeth R. Lenz

Increasingly nurses in clinical facilities, particularly those in leadership positions as administrators, managers, and advanced practice and senior staff nurses, are being expected to participate in research. The most frequently described roles include advocate or supporter, data collector, utilizer of research findings, and investigator. New mandates have heightened nurses' accountability for outcomes management, for variance tracking, and for generating data upon which to base practice innovations and continuous quality improvement. They have resulted in the need for increased involvement by nurses, not just as passive participants in others' research projects, but as designers and implementers of their own studies. Nurses in clinical settings are making important contributions to their institutions and to nursing by designing and carrying out studies addressing highly relevant clinical problems, interventions, and outcomes.

The role of investigator is a relatively new, underdeveloped, and underprioritized one for nursing leaders in clinical environments. Even very experienced clinicians and administrators with extensive experience in managing personnel and the delivery of complex care may have little or no experience in managing research projects. Although many of the strategies that are useful for managing other kinds of projects are also useful for managing research studies, there are also differences. Successful research project management is an

Note: Originally published in *Nursing Leadership Forum*, Vol. 4, No. 1, 1999. New York: Springer Publishing Company.

important leadership skill. It contributes directly to the quality of the research and to the validity and utility of the findings.

Regardless of the scope and complexity of the research itself, successfully managing a funded project is a multifaceted undertaking that requires careful planning, conscientious follow-through, and continuous monitoring. This chapter is designed to provide guidance to the beginning researcher. It was stimulated by the realization that an increasing number of nurses in clinical settings have been successful in securing funding for small-scale studies, but may lack both the expertise and peer support to implement them efficiently and effectively. Although aimed at funded research projects because of the accountability required, the strategies and recommendations are also applicable to research for which no external funding is available. Emphasis is on concrete strategies, particularly those that represent proactive approaches for preventing problems. The observations and recommendations are based primarily on the experiences of the author as a principal investigator of several externally funded large- and small-scale studies, and as a research mentor and facilitator in both academic and clinical settings.

THE PROPOSAL

Any research study is a multistage process. Stages include the preparation of the proposal, notification that the proposal has been funded, the initial start-up period, the implementation of the project, and the wrap-up and write-up stage. The importance of the proposal cannot be overemphasized, because it is the blueprint for the project. Proposals differ in their degree of specificity and completeness. At the very minimum, they specify the purpose and aims of the project, what will be done and how it will be done, the roles of project personnel, the general time frame for the project, and the budget categories and anticipated costs. An approved proposal or protocol constitutes a contract with the funder or sponsor and other significant entities, such as the facility's Institutional Review Board; thus, it is to be viewed as an obligation. Any major departures from the approved proposal must be communicated in advance and be given approval by the appropriate agencies and/or groups before being implemented.

START-UP PERIOD

Generally, the start-up period of a research project begins as soon as notification has been received that it will be funded. In some instances, start-up activities may begin even before formal notification is received. The start-up phase lays the groundwork, so it is absolutely critical to the subsequent smooth operation of the study. During this phase, which precedes any data collection, a variety of important planning activities are carried out: the goals of and vision for the project are reaffirmed, plans are finalized, final approvals for data collection are obtained from sites, human subjects protection procedures are finalized and final approvals secured, personnel are recruited and trained, equipment and supplies are purchased, and the study protocol and instruments are pilot-tested one or more times.

The first step during start-up is to review the proposal to be sure that what was proposed is well understood and remains a viable plan. A work plan then needs to be developed, not only to accomplish the start-up tasks themselves, but also to plan and organize the work of the project. The work plan includes specific activities, the persons responsible for them, and a realistic time line for completing them. One of the most common mistakes made at this point is to anticipate too short a time for accomplishing tasks. The rule of thumb is to anticipate the time needed, then double it in order to provide for unanticipated events that may slow down the study. The most common impediment, particularly in organizations that do not have research as the top priority, is that many other demands compete for the time and effort of project personnel.

An important focus of start-up activity is to finalize and secure the resources that are needed to conduct the study. This includes purchasing equipment and supplies and securing final approvals from the Institutional Review Board and the sites to be used for data collection. Even if formal approval was secured at the time the proposal was developed, it is important to visit each data collection site to be sure that no significant changes have taken place, to reacquaint personnel at the site with the nature of the project, and to reaffirm and/or finalize approval. Meetings with research committees and key administrative personnel at the data collection sites may be required. This visit provides an excellent opportunity to review the study procedures with "grassroots" personnel and to secure their help in troubleshooting problems that may arise in implementing the study.

The start-up period is also the time for recruiting and training study personnel. Staff size varies markedly, ranging from one or two to dozens of persons. Regardless of staff size, the personnel category is the most costly category in most nursing research projects. Therefore, it is crucial that the very best fit possible be achieved between the needs of the project and the capabilities and skills of the recruits. Whether paid or unpaid, study personnel should be screened in terms of their interest in the project and willingness to commit the kind of effort that will be required. Before the study gets underway, it is important to clarify reporting and collaborating relationships among the members of the team and to develop written a priori agreements about aspects of the study, such as coverage during weekends, holidays and vacations, ownership of data, publication expectations, ground rules for authorship, and order of authorship. Such matters are among the most problematic in collaborative research (Wilcox, 1998).

Because staff are key to the success of the project, thorough training during the start-up period is a good investment of time. Among the objectives to be achieved by the end of the training period are that the staff agree with and "buy in" to project goals, understand the study and their individual roles, can answer questions about the study that might be posed by subjects, use data collection instruments correctly, execute the protocol accurately and consistently, recognize and handle or report any problems in the execution of the protocol, and anticipate and avoid any pitfalls or errors that may occur as the protocol is executed.

The final phase of the start-up period is one of putting the finishing touches on the protocol. That means pilot-testing instruments, treatments, and procedures individually; making any needed modifications; then retesting the entire protocol. Pilot testing is a crucial activity, because it points out unanticipated problems that can then be prevented during the study. When finalized, all materials for data collection are secured, duplicated if necessary, and prepared for use.

PROJECT PERSONNEL

The project team is viewed as a collaborative unit. Roles and responsibilities of project personnel are determined at the time the study is designed. Before the project begins, the plan for personnel should be reviewed and responsibilities finalized; however, the division of labor for the project and the roles of specific personnel are reviewed periodically and in the event of any personnel changes.

All studies have a designated principal investigator (PI), the individual who is ultimately responsible for all administrative, operational, and scientific aspects of the study. Specific responsibilities include assuring the successful conduct of the study and the quality of the data and results; monitoring scientific progress and adherence to the protocol; making decisions about any departures from the protocol (with approval from the IRB and funding agency); planning and managing the budget; hiring and supervising personnel; communicating with others about the project; preparing reports; and taking the lead in deciding which publications and presentations will be produced to disseminate study findings. In some instances the PI does not have a staff and is solely responsible for all aspects of the study, but much nursing research involves collaboration with others and the support of a study team.

The co-PI shares responsibility for the total project with the PI and is able to stand in for the PI in his or her absence. Generally, a co-investigator (co-I) or assistant investigator has a more limited scope of responsibility than either the PI or co-PI. A co-I may have scientific responsibility for particular substantive or procedural aspects of the study, such as developing and overseeing a particular aspect of the protocol, developing and testing instruments, or investigating a particular research question. Both co-PIs and co-Is are expected to attend all project meetings and to participate in publication, usually serving as first author on publications that report aspects of the study for which they were primarily responsible.

The project director (PD) is responsible for the day-to-day operation of the project, including recruiting and retaining subjects, supervising personnel, coordinating and scheduling data collection, monitoring progress of the study and adherence to the protocol, assuring accurate record keeping and documentation of all project activities, and monitoring budget expenditures. The PD often participates in publishing and presenting results and attends all project meetings. In randomized clinical trials of drugs and devices, the individual assuming the role analogous to that of the PD is usually called the clinical research coordinator (Raybuck, 1997).

Other roles that may be included in nursing research projects are the following: (1) research assistants, who help with recruiting subjects and collecting and analyzing data and who communicate regularly with the PI and/or PD and participate in project meetings; (2) a data manager or analyst, who develops and maintains the study data base, conducts data analyses, and summarizes results; (3) a statistician or biostatistician who provides advice about data analysis strategies, and may actually analyze the data; (4) a project secretary, who is generally responsible for preparing correspondence, filing, maintaining records, ordering supplies, and possibly data entry; and (5) consultants or an advisory board, usually external to the institution, who provide expert advice, may preview reports and publications, and may attend one or two meetings a year. These and other roles that are involved in clinical trials are described by Spilker (1996, pp. 954–957).

PROJECT IMPLEMENTATION AND OVERSIGHT

The procedures to be followed in a study and the projected timeline for implementation are specified in the proposal, and detailed logistical and operational planning takes place prior to implementation. The progress of the research project, however, must be monitored continually and "mid-course" corrections made when necessary to assure its integrity. It cannot be assumed that the study will run smoothly just because the plan was well conceived. It is essential to be alert to events and biasing factors that may have an impact on the timing, and, therefore the expense of the project, as well as the findings themselves.

Generally, the first-line responsibility for overseeing the progress of a study is in the hands of the project director, with ultimate responsibility being the PIs. Oversight of progress includes monitoring the following elements: (1) whether subjects are being recruited at the anticipated rate (and if not, to determine why not); (2) whether subjects are being retained in longitudinal studies; (3) whether any difficulty is encountered or breakdown occurs in executing the protocol; (4) whether data are being gathered and stored appropriately; (5) the extent of missing data and rate of subject refusals and withdrawals; (6) whether the results of the preliminary analyses of data indicate unanticipated problems; and (7) whether records are being kept appropriately.

Subject recruitment and retention are particularly important aspects of research project management. Subject recruitment may be carried out by the project staff or may be delegated to individuals who are in regular contact with potential subjects (e.g., staff nurses in clinics or inpatient units). The recruitment process is planned in accord with Institutional Review Board (IRB) guidelines and is often a multistep process. It involves screening potential subjects using predetermined inclusion and exclusion criteria and obtaining informed consent. A roster containing the names of all persons approached to participate and the disposition of each (i.e., enrolled, ineligible, refused) must be maintained. A critical question in any research study is whether those who agree to participate differ systematically from those who refuse to do so (Spilker & Cramer, 1992).

As more studies address long-term outcomes of nursing interventions, the retention of subjects over time has emerged as a critically important aspect of project implementation. Strategies include the following: (1) securing valid information at the outset about how the subject can be reached, including the addresses and phone numbers of two or three contact persons; (2) regularly letting subjects know that their participation is appreciated and contributions valued; (3) providing incentives for participating as a subject; and (4) making participation in the study as easy and enjoyable as possible. Should a subject choose to withdraw, the date and reason for withdrawal should be clearly noted and recorded.

The best way to maintain oversight of a project is to hold regular staff meetings. Open discussion facilitates the detection of any problems while implementing the study and encourages the staff to participate in finding workable solutions. Regular staff meetings also help assure that scientific integrity is being maintained, because the data are discussed on a regular basis. Team meetings should be held regularly, with frequency usually ranging from weekly to monthly. Written minutes of the meetings, which are considered official records of the study, should be distributed so that all staff members are informed of progress and decisions, and they should be stored in a safe place.

Several of the management tools that are available for use with other types of projects are equally relevant to research project management (Findley, Daum, & Macedo, 1991; Hayes, 1989; Perce, 1998; Thomasett, 1990). For example, project plans with an associated time line and flow diagrams of the process to be carried out are particularly helpful (for example, see Berry, 1994). Project management and budget management software are also available. For example, Turbo-project® Express™ is a project planning and scheduling tool that can be used to help organize activities for projects of any kind. A number of resources are also available to help researchers who are managing randomized clinical trials to meet the requirements for Good Clinical Practice, the processes required to assure high quality in these closely controlled studies (e.g., Hutchinson, 1997). They provide valuable guidance to all researchers.

RECORD KEEPING

With the current emphasis on the importance of scientific integrity, thorough, accurate, and complete record keeping is essential. Record keeping is expected by the funders, by the institutions in which the study is being carried out, and by the scientific community. Records can be considered to fall into two categories: those concerning individual subjects and those about the conduct of the study as a whole.

In addition to all data collected from and about each study subject, records regarding individual subjects include signed consent forms, descriptions of each telephone or in-person contact, copies of all correspondence, description and documentation of all interventions carried out, and documentation of any adverse event or complication experienced. Raw data, as well as the case report forms in drug and device trials, are stored in locked files. They are usually identified with code numbers, but without identifying names (which are stored separately in locked files). Research data are subject to the same guidelines for confidentiality as medical records; that is, they must be handled, transported, and stored carefully only by authorized personnel, and cannot be left lying around. The consent forms and the raw data have to be stored for varying periods ranging to 15 years, depending on the rules of the funding agency, the employing institution, and the IRB.

Records regarding the project as a whole include: (1) minutes of all meetings; (2) documentation of all decisions (with supporting rationale); (3) correspondence with the funding agency, regulatory agencies and boards, IRBs, institutions, project staff, subjects and consultants; (4) rosters of prospective subjects approached and recruited; (5) personnel files; and (6) copies of any reports or scientific publications resulting from the study. All project personnel are expected to participate in accurate record keeping and documentation, and all records must be stored carefully, with access limited to those requiring them.

Reports of study progress are accountability mechanisms, and they are the responsibility of the PI. The funder, the IRB, the employer, and the institutions in which data collection is taking place may require progress reports at varying intervals (usually yearly). The amount and type of information to be included in an interim progress report is specified by the entity requiring the report, and it varies. The guidelines and deadlines should be followed carefully, because an interim report may be a crucial determinant of continued funding and continued ability to enroll subjects and collect data. Inevitably, a final report about the entire project and its results is required. Failure to provide the final report in a timely manner can jeopardize future funding from the same organization.

BUDGET MANAGEMENT

Budget management actually begins during proposal development, and decisions made at that time can have a negative or positive impact throughout the life of the project. An estimated budget and budget justification are part of virtually all research proposals. Because this projected budget (which may be amended by the funding agency before funding the study) defines how much will be spent on what, it must be prepared thoughtfully. Cost estimates for multiyear projects, for example, should take into account projected inflation and cost-of-living increases.

Once approved, budgets are difficult to change. Changes may, however, be necessitated by such unanticipated occurrences as increases for equipment, postage, utilities, fringe benefits, and so forth; unavailability of equipment and the consequent need to substitute other brands, models, or vendors; or changes in the protocol requiring increased or decreased expenditures. Increases in the "bottom line" are very difficult to secure; however, reallocation of funds within and among budget categories is possible, but may require prior approval of the funding agency. It is advisable to review carefully all policies of the funding agency regarding budget, as they may vary considerably in their specificity. For example, some funding agencies require that prior approval be secured for any departure from the approved budget, while others are more lenient and require approval for departures only over a given percentage or within specific budget categories. Requests to carry over unexpended funds to the next project year, to extend the term of the project (with or without additional funding), or to amend the approved budget should be made in writing, and copies kept of all correspondence.

Budget management is the responsibility of the PI, even though assistance may be obtained from others, such as the PD, secretary, and institutional budget office. Careful record keeping about all project expenditures and income is essential, even when the institution has centralized departments for budget, payroll, and purchasing. It is wise to maintain an independent accounting of income and expenditures by setting up and continually updating a spreadsheet that lists and tallies all expenditures and income. A number of spreadsheet software packages such as Lotus 1, 2, 3® and Excel® are relatively easy to use, and can greatly simplify the process of budget tracking. The status of actual and projected expenditures should be assessed regularly (at least monthly) to avoid shortfalls or surplus at the end of the budget year. With the exception of the start-up period, during which a disproportionate percentage of the expenditures often occurs (primarily because of one-time equipment purchases), it is wise to allocate operating expenditures relatively evenly across the entire budget period.

The PI is responsible for knowing and following the financial and administrative policies and operating procedures of the institution. There are inevitably rules about how grant funds can and cannot be spent. They are generally categorized as restricted funds, because they must be spent on the project and for the purposes for which they were obtained.

WRAP-UP

The final stage of a funded study is often termed the "wrap-up and write-up" stage. Although summary, closeout and dissemination activities constitute the focus of activity at the end of a study, it is important to point out that they also occur at other points along the way. Periodically it is essential to take stock of the progress that has been made and to think ahead to identify the objectives and deliverable outcomes that will be produced during the next phase of the project. For most grants funded by governmental agencies and large foundations, the PI is expected to file a progress report annually; however, more frequent stocktaking may be required and certainly is advisable. Progress reports reflect not only retrospective reporting, but also prospective thinking about what is yet to be accomplished, and what is being planned for the future. Ideally research projects by a given investigator or group—even small-scale projects by clinical scholars—are not isolated undertakings. Rather, they are parts of a more extensive program of research in which several related studies build on and extend one another. Prospective planning should be done in the context of the overall program of research.

Although reports of the major findings of a study may not be publishable before data collection and analysis are complete, it is often possible to publish or present some interim or preliminary findings during the course of the study. For example, it may be possible to publish findings about short-term post-intervention outcomes while data about longer-term outcomes are still being collected. It may also be possible to write theoretical or methodological articles that do not report study findings but communicate activities and thinking that are part of the proposal preparation or research process.

Activities that are undertaken as the study comes to a close following the end of data collection and analysis include: (1) communicating with the study sites and the IRB that data collection is complete; (2) checking data files for completeness; (3) securing locked storage for archiving data and other study materials; (4) providing a summary of study findings to study sites, either in oral or written format, to the IRB, and, if promised, to the subjects; (5) preparing the final report to be submitted to the funding organization; and 6) continuing to plan and prepare publications and presentations to disseminate the results of the study to relevant audiences.

Dissemination of the results is an inherent part of conducting research and is a key responsibility of the PI and other investigators. As noted above, some aspects of the study or preliminary findings may be presented or published while the study is underway; however, the majority of dissemination activity occurs at the final stage of the research. Even though many of the ground rules about publishing study results are agreed upon at the outset of the study, it is well to revisit these issues when the study is complete.

The study team as a whole participates in decisions about the number and focus of publications and presentations to be developed and the role of each team member on each publication. Generally more than one publication can be generated from any given study. This may include several different types of articles (e.g., methodological, data-based, clinical, and theoretical), which would be submitted to those journals that commonly publish articles of that type or are directed toward specific audiences such as researchers, clinicians, clinical specialists, administrators, educators, case managers, and evaluators. Because of copyright considerations, given results should appear in only one journal. Where there is a question of possible duplication or overlap, it is advisable to submit, along with the manuscript, a copy of any other publications about the same study that have appeared in print or have been accepted for publication.

Authorship order is determined based on previously agreed upon criteria and standards held within disciplines. Ideally, consensus is reached about these matters before these scholarly products are generated. For example, individual members of the research team have particular interests and strengths, and would be the logical first authors of publications reporting those aspects of the study. Agreement also needs to be reached about which members of the team will be able to access the data in the future, and how much access will be permitted for others, such as students or colleagues who may wish to access the data set for secondary analyses. Ideally, the decision making about these matters should include investigators who may have left the institution, but who played major roles in some aspects of the study, as well as the team members who are present at the termination of the project. See Duncan (1999) for helpful guidelines regarding publication of research findings.

CONCLUSION

Beginning researchers may not appreciate the complexity of implementing a study, or the degree or rigor and precision involved. Some of the factors that may introduce error into, confound, or invalidate results are beyond the investigator's control; however, many can be prevented or ameliorated through conscientious research project management. Both effective project management and mismanagement can have profound implications for the outcomes and ultimate contributions of the research. A conscientious approach to managing research projects yields more accurate, reliable, and valid results, and thus more meaningful nursing science.

REFERENCES

Berry, R. (1994). Project management for nurses: Guidelines for success. *Journal of Intravenous Nursing, 17*(1), 28–34.

Duncan, A. M. (1999). Authorship, dissemination of research findings, and related matters. *Applied Nursing Research, 12*(2), 101–106.

Findley, T. W., Daum, M. C., & Macedo, J. A. (1991). Research in physical medicine and rehabilitation: Research project management. *American Journal of Physical Medicine & Rehabilitation, 70*(1 Suppl.), S49–S60.

Hayes, M. E. (1989). Project management: A guide. *Info-line, 4,* 1–18

Hutchinson, D. (1997). The trial investigator's GCP handbook: A practical guide to ICH requirements. Richmond, Surrey, UK: Brookwood Medical Publications.

Perce, K. H. (1998). Project management skills. *AAOHN Journal, 46*(8), 391–405.

Raybuck, J. A. (1997). The CNS as research coordinator in drug trials. *Clinical Nurse Specialist, 11*(1), 15–18.

Spilker, B. (1996). *Guide to clinical trials.* Philadelphia: Lippincott-Raven.

Spilker, B., & Cramer, J. A. (1992). *Patient recruitment in clinical trials.* New York: Raven.

Thomasett, M. C. (1990). *The little black book of project management.* New York: AMACOM.

Wilcox, L. J. (1998). Authorship: The coin of the realm, the source of complaints. *Journal of the American Medical Association, 280*(3), 216–217.

An earlier version of this chapter was presented as part of a symposium titled, "I have the funding, now what?", at the Sigma Theta Tau International Annual Scientific Sessions, Indianapolis, Indiana, December, 1997.

CHAPTER 13

Twelve Principles of Successful Fundraising

Joyce J. Fitzpatrick

Health profession schools traditionally have been dependent upon public support and tuition support for academic programs. This article is focused on generating private support from a range of sources. Attention will be paid to the structures and the processes to generate new avenues of private support for academic programs. Successful examples that have been used at Case Western Reserve University are given to highlight the principles addressed.

The goal of philanthropy is to improve the human condition. Two of our noblest institutions, hospitals and universities, have been built upon philanthropy and have evolved through numerous kinds of gift-giving programs. It is of interest to note that philanthropy increases as the economy declines. It is an important foundation of philanthropy to note that people give to people. Thus, the personal approach can make the difference in any effort to generate support for academic programs. The art of asking involves the *right* program, the *right* purpose, and the *right* amount.

Individuals may give for a variety of reasons: They want to maintain their own immortality; they want to live in perpetuity; they want to perpetuate their own beliefs; they want to belong to something; they want recognition; or they want to alleviate ills. For many people, giving is based on a sense of duty, a belief that one should support the future generations. On a related note, as educators it is important for us to instill in our students the sense of responsibility

Note: Originally published in *Nursing Leadership Forum*, Vol. 2, No. 1, 1996. New York: Springer Publishing Company.

and duty that they must give to the students who come after them.
The following 12 principles are presented as a basis for fundraising activities.

PRINCIPLE 1:
VOLUNTEERS ARE AN IMPORTANT RESOURCE IN
GENERATING PRIVATE SUPPORT

Structures that we have put in place to increase the activities of volunteers include a formal advisory committee and campaign/development committee structures with subcommittees. For example, we have volunteers assisting with our recruitment activity for students for the School of Nursing. We have volunteers participating on various campaign committees. We have a very structured volunteer organization among our alumni. We have many different committees participating, but the important point is that the volunteers have a lot of the responsibility for generating support for our programs. In the last decade, alumni giving has increased by approximately 70%; we could not have done that without our volunteer structure. Peer solicitation is what makes the difference. If you are asked to support the alumni association by a classmate who graduated in the same year, then you are more likely to participate in that activity. We use our volunteer structure for all of our fundraising activities. Each of our six endowed chairs that we have generated in the last 10 years can be traced to a volunteer who had been actively involved in the solicitation.

PRINCIPLE 2:
PUBLIC AND PRIVATE SUPPORT ARE
OFTEN INTERTWINED

In a private institution you find most clearly the relationship between public and private support. A few examples are relevant here. One is the specific activity of Congresswoman Frances Payne Bolton, who as a private citizen endowed our School of Nursing, then became a Representative of Congress and was very active in the public funding not just of nursing at Case Western Reserve University but of nursing nationally. It is very important to find ways to link private funding with public funding. We have discovered that there most often are links that can be developed. We have recently created a new primary health care center as a part of our faculty practice in the School of Nursing. Because of the private support that we were able to generate for this particular project, we also were able to secure a federal grant to support activities of the center.

PRINCIPLE 3:
MAINTAIN AND NURTURE THE RELATIONSHIPS
THAT YOU DEVELOP

Every week we talk about our activities in fundraising and friend-raising. Once you develop a circle of friends, it is important to support every link in the circle. Keep everybody involved in the development activities at all times. One example of continued involvement is as follows. In 1988, we completed a $5 million campaign. There were key volunteers involved in the committee structure; we asked them to stay on for the next campaign committee, and gave them responsibility as consultants to the new committee. Thus, we try to nurture the relationships that we develop and keep volunteers involved over time.

PRINCIPLE 4:
IT IS IMPORTANT TO BE SUCCESSFUL IN YOUR GOAL

In the campaign that we completed in June 1994, we struggled with identifying a campaign goal. Our 1988 campaign goal for the School of Nursing was $5 million and was the most we had ever raised in a campaign for the school. So we needed to be cautious. At the same time, we had uncovered a great deal of potential, so we knew that we had to be somewhere beyond $5 million, but realistic in setting a goal. Most important, we needed to set a goal that we could achieve. We set a goal of $15 million, knowing that we could achieve $15 million. The struggle was to set the goal at $15 million and not at $25 million. Over the five-year campaign, we raised $26 million. We were able to boast that we went $11 million over our goal, whereas, if we had set it at $25 million, we would only be $1 million over goal. It is more impressive to be $11 million over goal than to be $1 million over. The most important point is to set a goal that you know you can achieve; everyone wants to support a winner. Create the system so you can win.

During the campaign that closed in 1994, we raised $7 million from corporations. Prior to this campaign, that is, prior to 1989, we had not raised more than $100,000 from any corporation in any single year. We focused on generating foundation support and were able to raise close to $9 million from foundations. Previous to 1989, we had not had a very strong showing in foundation funding. Prior to this 1989–1994 campaign, most of our support had been from individuals.

PRINCIPLE 5:
DEVELOPMENT REQUIRES A LONG-TERM PERSPECTIVE

It is important to plant the seeds for one's successors. It takes time to identify the relationships that fit with the particular development goals. Of course, for academic institutions and for many other private institutions, endowment is the foundation for all of the other development activities. Endowment funding is an investment in the future.

In academic institutions, an endowed chair represents the ultimate form of an institutional legitimization of disciplines. Endowed chairs were noted as early as 1449. An endowed chair provides funding support for scholarly pursuits at the highest academic level. It is interesting to note that in 1928 the first endowed chair in nursing was committed by nurses themselves. Many of the individuals who contributed were alumni of the University of Virginia, and many of them were not. They were all members of the Virginia Nurses' Association. It was several years before any others were endowed. Endowed chairs provide an opportunity for high visibility for both the professor and the school.

What follows is a description of some general aspects of philanthropy in the United States. These figures can be traced each year. If increases in contributions over the last 5 years are traced, there is an approximately 5.5% or 6% increase annually in the contributions. If you think about approximately $124.3 billion being given privately to support programs, it seems that many schools are not getting a fair share of that $124.3 billion. Individual giving accounts for 89% of every dollar given. This is important because, in terms of long-term development activity, it really makes sense to focus on individuals. Although it may be easier to write foundation proposals or corporate proposals, the greater payoff is in individual support. In 1992, $7.78 billion were given in individual bequests alone. Foundation grants were only $8 billion in 1992. Corporate giving was only $6 billion. Individual giving accounts for most of the private support, close to 9 cents out of 10. Yet it requires a lot more activity and more of a long-term perspective, particularly with new alumni, because it takes them a while to accumulate resources. In 1992, gifts to education were $14 billion and gifts to human services were $111 billion.

The following is an example used in our previous two campaigns. Individuals were offered the opportunity to name scholars in the academic programs. The students know who their sponsor is, and the donors know who their students are. Interactions between donor and students are encouraged. Our expectation is that this relationship will continue over the years. We hope we are building in the responsibility to the students so that they know that they have been supported by an individual in their academic career and they will feel some responsibility to support future students.

PRINCIPLE 6:
IT MATTERS WHOM YOU KNOW

It is important to nurture relationships and to try to know everybody that you possibly can. For example, we found that we often had physicians telling us that nurses were not like they used to be and if we prepared them better, everything would be like it used to be. So we said, "OK, you can help, folks. Here is how you can do it, you can help us, you can give us some money, we will prepare them differently and you can be involved." We set up a physicians' advisory committee, but we also set up a scholarship fund. We did get all of our friends to participate and were able to raise close to $250,000 from physicians who wanted to support nursing education, and most important, who wanted to be involved in some way. The way they were involved is through an advisory committee that recommended students to us. We have a number of students who were recommended by physicians in the community because they knew more about our program. We sent our physician friends a lot of literature about our programs. By way of involvement, we did set up a separate physicians' scholarship fund and we monitor that yearly; we report to them yearly about whom they are supporting and what kind of support they are providing. That circle of friends we knew in the physician community was extremely important to us in raising the money. We did presentations at medical staff meetings in community hospitals and we made house calls to physicians' offices to tell them about the program. We approached banks and businesses where we knew that somebody happened to know a nurse. We involved corporate executives who had a particular interest in health care. We have started involving people in public policy discussions with the expectation that we will extend our network.

PRINCIPLE 7:
COLLABORATION WITH OTHER ACADEMIC
PROGRAMS PROVIDES A FOUNDATION

In our community and in our university, there is no way we could have initiated the programs and generated the support we have without the collaboration of academic programs. We have a strong collaborative activity around certain academic programs, but it is very clear that that collaboration was a key to our success both in terms of program planning and in terms of product support. An example of our collaboration is our previously mentioned Nursing Health Center, which is a primary health care and birthing service developed in an underserved area. Here we have been able to generate approximately $1 million in private foundation support. Important, collaboration with the School of Medicine was required to launch this project because every time we came up against some regulatory barriers to advanced nursing practice, the phone calls about what was happening did not come to the School of Nursing, they came to the School of Medicine. So we require that we be involved in communication with colleagues, particularly in the School of Medicine.

PRINCIPLE 8:
TAKE RISKS

Almost all the programs that we have launched in the last 8 years have been launched through outside funding. Almost all of them have involved some degree of risk. For example, we began an acute care pediatric nurse practitioner program in collaboration with two hospitals in the community. We have discovered that there are questions about certification of graduates from this program. We have to be involved in setting standards at the national level to clarify the "gray area" of certification.

PRINCIPLE 9:
INVOLVE FACULTY AT ALL LEVELS

I almost never can speak as well about the academic programs as the faculty. It is very typical to have the key faculty members present the case for funding because, although it is important for me to be there as the academic administrator, it is more important to have someone there who can answer the questions. We have found that it is most important to have the expertise of the faculty in all of our efforts to generate academic program support.

PRINCIPLE 10:
ALUMNI ARE FOREVER

We treat our alumni as if they are forever because we know they are key to our outreach efforts, as well as to our annual fund efforts which serve as the base for our overall development. We have many programs orchestrated to keep our alumni active at all levels.

PRINCIPLE 11:
YOU HAVE TO SPEND MONEY TO MAKE MONEY

Sometimes this is particularly difficult if you do not already have a lot of money to spend. When I received the first commitment for the $5 million campaign that we launched in 1983, we turned a few faculty positions into staff positions for development. It was important to invest in that campaign in order to be successful. Also, in development it is expected that expenses will be justified. In the campaign completed in 1994, the School of Nursing had the lowest investment in our development costs; fewer than 10 cents on the dollar raised was tied to development expenses. We are constantly weighing all of our expenditures for generating funds and have to look at the long-term perspective. For example, some of the investment in our alumni will not pay off until 20 years hence.

PRINCIPLE 12:
VISIBILITY IS THE KEY TO SUCCESS

Visibility is important for students, faculty, and the administrative staff. We must participate in all of the community activities that involve health care and human services. Only when we are visible in the community will people want to invest in our academic programs.

Frequently asked questions and answers about fundraising are as follows:

Q. What drives your fundraising?

A. Strong academic programs, new programs and flexibility are important keys to our development success. In our strategic planning in the 5-year period prior to the campaign, a motto for our school—"a tradition of innovation"—characterized our programs. It has served us well in launching new programs and in supporting all programs.

Q. What drives your collaborative relationships?

A. Strong academic programs, new programs, and flexibility in developing programs drive collaboration.

Q. What is the key to your development system?

A. Communication. We constantly communicate with everybody, whether they are previous donors from a foundation or a corporation, or whether they are current students who will be future alumni.

Q. What is the relationship between the School of Nursing's development effort and the university's development efforts?

A. Efforts are coordinated, requiring a great deal of communication. The coordination is necessary with the university because there are a number of professional schools interested in the same foundations and the same donors. Before we approach a donor, we must request clearance from the university's development office which acts as a clearinghouse.

Two principles are used in making the decision for clearance: which is the largest gift and the closest relationship or the closest potential relationship.

Q. Do you employ your own staff?

A. Yes, we are a decentralized university so that each management center stands on its own. Therefore, we are totally responsible for generating our own funds for all of our programs. Whatever resources we generate, we can spend.

Q. How big is the development team in the School of Nursing?

A. While finishing a campaign, we are staffed at our campaign level of four professional development staff and two support staff. In 1982, we had one half-time staff member assigned to development in the School of Nursing.

Q. Can you identify some potential audiences that could be targeted for a development campaign?

A. The immediate potential is for foundation support and individual support, knowing that individual support takes longer to generate. There are a number of foundations—local, regional, and national—committed to health care or new programs that address health care issues. There is much more potential for generating foundation support in health science schools. Piggyback on the successes of other institutions. Find out everything about what potential there is in the area. Find a good mentor. Relate to your local community. If the locals do not view you as a star, then you will have a hard time getting national support.

Q. Of the monies that you talked about, what share was for endowment and what share was for operating revenue?

A. About a third of our campaign commitment was endowment support. We would have liked that to be 50%. Since 1982, our endowment has increased from $8 million to $27 million. Over the years we have purposely focused on generating endowment support because we believe that will put us in the best long-term position. Given a choice, we would always like to have endowment. It is often a struggle because you do have programs that you want to support, so it is a judgment call. Many foundations only give to operating and current program support. With the individual gift it is a hard judgment call, and I always lean on the side of endowment. If you have a situation where there is a current operating deficit, obviously it is important to get out of that deficit position before you can start building an endowment.

Q. What percent of your budget is from tuition?

A. Approximately 50%. In the last 12 years we have not varied much in our tuition as a percentage of our overall revenues.

Q. In your relationship with the rest of the university with coordination, when you want to approach a major corporation, do you need to clear it within the university system so that everybody cannot approach at the same time?

A. Yes, and we have not always won, but we keep trying. In fact, it is a challenge to always be there when the decision is made. If you are not there, if you don't have a current relationship with somebody you think has the potential of supporting your programs, then it is a hard sell. You have to build the potential relationship. I can give you a good example of that. We have a program that we have started in home care. I have to say that we invested in the program before it was clear that that was the direction in which the world was going.

I have summarized what I believe to be the common themes in all of the principles that I have noted. These values are collaboration, communication, and cooperation.

PART III

Enhancing Patient and Employee Satisfaction

CHAPTER 14

Reflections on Empowerment: A Developing Concept or an Outdated One?

Barbara A. Backer, C. Alicia Georges, and Diana J. Mason

For a number of years, we have grappled theoretically and experientially with nursing's use of empowerment and how nursing empowerment relates to leadership and, ultimately, to patient empowerment. In 1991, the publication of the article "Toward a Feminist Model for the Political Empowerment of Nurses" (Mason, Backer, & Georges, 1991) was the result of creative thinking based upon the leadership and empowerment literature and our lived experiences with nursing, feminism, and political action. Subsequently, we applied the described model of empowerment in practice, academic, and organizational settings.

The nursing literature suggests that nurses continue to struggle with developing empowerment (Backer, Costello-Nickitas, & Mason-Adler, 1994; Carlson-Catalano, 1992; Chandler, 1992; Kramer & Schalenberg, 1993). Empowerment assumes new significance as nurses individually and collectively cope with today's realities of downsizing, mergers, redesign, retrenchment, and layoffs. Styles (1994) writes that in the decade leading to the 21st century, nurses are "being challenged to reach beyond independence toward interdependence, to join our growing powers to a full partnership with citizens, govern-

Note: Originally published in *Nursing Leadership Forum,* Vol. 2, No. 2, 1996. New York: Springer Publishing Company.

ment, and all health care providers to transform the health care system in the face of new realities" (p. 78).

This chapter presents further delineation of the 1991 model based on experiences with implementing it, research, continued review of the empowerment literature, and ongoing dialogue with each other and colleagues. We speak and write from our particular perspectives and with developing awareness of how our own races and classes as much as gender influence these perspectives. We recognize how our own work with empowerment as a concept and empowerment as an action has influenced our thinking, careers, and relationships. These ideas and actions of empowerment move in a continuing spiral from abstract to personal to political to discouragement to critique. As we write this paper, there is much to say, yet there are no definitive answers to our own questions.

There is also recognition that the term empowerment may no longer be in vogue, having been overused and abused to the extent that it has become a cliche. "Empowerment . . . has grown satiated by its own success" (Burghart, 1995, p. 1), albeit often as mere rhetoric. It was the buzzword of the late 1980s and early 1990s that perhaps explained what many people were feeling and were trying to do in terms of self-actualization. Burghardt (1995) suggests that people have moved beyond empowerment, recognizing that individual development and freedom cannot produce results without collectivity. While the rhetoric of empowerment may be passé or misused, the 1991 model continues to be relevant for nursing's present and future. It needs to be more fully developed and expanded rather than abandoned, however, because it did not rest solely on development of the individual, but was grounded in the connection of empowerment to the collective.

POLITICAL EMPOWERMENT MODEL 1991

Empowerment as originally discussed in 1991 was defined as "the enabling of individuals and groups to participate in actions and decision-making within a context that supports an equitable distribution of power. Empowerment requires a commitment to connection between self and others, enabling individuals or groups to recognize their own strengths, resources, and abilities to make changes in their personal and public lives. It is a process of confirming one's self and/or one's group" (Mason, Backer, & Georges, 1991, pp. 72–73). The proposed political empowerment model suggested the development of three dimensions: (a) raising consciousness of the sociopolitical realities of a nurse's world; (b) strong and positive self-esteem; and (c) the political skills needed to negotiate and change the health care system (Beck, 1983; Mason, Costello-Nickitas, Scalan & Magnuson, 1991). These dimensions were viewed as interdependent and overlapping, suggesting an interactive rather than linear development.

We maintain our original formulation that a politically empowered nursing profession can change a health care delivery system that is dysfunctional to patients and people working in it. We recognize, more so than in the earlier paper, the degree of empowerment, dignity, and self-esteem that many nurses have when they complete a daily patient assignment safely and with care, then leave. In keeping with the 1991 definition of empowerment, these nurses are empowered to the extent of having weighed the pros and cons of situations, the benefits and the risks, and made the choice to provide care (or teaching, supervision, administration). Such actions support nursing's commitment of caring for patients and the significance of the connection between self and others. Therefore, we expand the use of the concept "political empowerment" to encompass all of nurses' empowerment as political.

We acknowledged the difficulties of participating and promoting collaborative and collective action in systems that are based on a competitive, cost-driven product orientation. Health care systems continue to maintain this orientation as seen in the recent quote of a CEO who was describing his hospital's patient population: "People look at our neighborhood and go 'yuck' . . . But frankly, 500,000 people live here who have nowhere else to go and if we can capture their business we can succeed" (Speck, cited in Rosenthal, 1995, p. 22). Further, we offered encouragement to nurses to seek "safe havens" with others of like mind to continue their efforts in transforming health care and maintaining nursing's commitment to caring.

Was this an "ivory tower" conceptualization of political empowerment? We think not. Empirically and conceptually, we recognize now that contextual factors influence the development and enactment of each of the model's three dimensions more extensively than the initial proposal. The remaining part of this paper revisits these contextual factors.

RAISING CONSCIOUSNESS

In the original paper, we stressed the significance of nurses becoming aware of the sociopolitical reality of their unequal status in the health care system. Additional contexual factors that nurses need to understand include how this unequal status reflects trends in the society at large, how these trends influence nurses' relationships with each other and their profession, and how they influence the care that patients receive. Consciousness-raising about these factors can stimulate nurses to 'think out of the box'; i.e., to think about alternative and perhaps innovative ways of relating and thinking about the health care system, themselves, their profession, and their patients.

Nurses' unequal status in the health care system remains unchanged, and indeed it now may be more regressive, as health care organizations determine that nursing departments are passé, that unit managers need not be nurses, and that nursing care need not be provided by nurses. In New York State, the legislature has even discontinued its Nurse of Distinction Program that recognized and honored the achievements and work of nurses in the state. Begun during the height of the nursing shortage, the program's demise was announced in 1995. Faludi (1991) notes that a backlash has been occurring against women's increasing power. It would seem that the power that nurses gained during the end of the last shortage has led to efforts by others to undermine that power. This is consistent with other societal movements to try to reinforce traditional power structures. For example, the current efforts to dismantle affirmative action policies speak to the power and extent of the backlash, and to the need for nurses to understand the connection between their own personal or professional issues and the broader health and social issues of the times.

The sociopolitical reality of nursing itself also indicates that the profession continues to perpetuate unequal status among its members:

> A glass ceiling does not exist in the nursing hierarchy, a human ceiling does. It forms an encrusted barricade of nurse after nurse perched on the stooped shoulders of former colleagues. It is perpetuated by self-serving isolation, containment of power, and retention of privilege. (Renz, 1993, p. 88)

The competitive context of capitalism, health care, and academic systems is pervasive in many of our nursing deliberations. In one discussion of nurses' oppression, a leadership group became involved in an argument as to which ethnic group of nurses experienced more discrimination than the others. The group divided into ethnic subgroups and was unable to move beyond their own interests. There was no acceptance of the commonalities in different realities.

The idea of being able to "empower" someone implies a hierarchical order in which one person (power-full) allocates some power to another person (less power-full) while still maintaining a power-over position. The nursing literature supports this assumption to some extent (Clifford, 1992; Havens & Mills, 1992; Johnson, 1992). The organizational structures of most health care and academic institutions, as well as of that most basic of social structures, the family, employ a hierarchical order based on power allocation. Interestingly, the Cumulative Index of Nursing and Allied Health Literature (CINAHL) up until 1991 indexed empowerment under authority and power. Since 1991, empowerment has been defined as a "process by which people gain mastery over their affairs" (CINAHL, 1993, p. 382).

Although we try to live our premise that to empower means to facilitate person/group self-development, and to utilize the feminist approach of power-sharing (Miller, 1976, 1982), we and our colleagues continue to put each other in the power-over position. Students will say to faculty, "tell us what you want in this paper"; staff nurses and supervisors say to directors of services, "you make the goals for this department." We fall easily into the mode of giving the answers and making decisions as the demand for numbers, time, and outcomes continues to rise. We rationalize to each other: "but 'they' won't assume any responsibility for making the decision!"

Culture, race, ethnicity, and comfort with the status quo may influence responses to power-sharing and empowerment. One of us worked with a group of master's-prepared nurses who felt more comfortable framing their group work in the business language of "a self-directed work team" rather than discussing their structure in feminist terms of nonhierarchical, consensus-building, and equal relationships. Perhaps feminist terms are too loaded and misunderstood. And yet, the ground rules this group established for their team reflected these feminist concepts. Another of us worked with a seminar group of culturally diverse registered nurses studying for their BSN degrees. The nurses in this group viewed feminism and its concepts of power-sharing more in the context of a White middle-class movement in which White women are seen as part of an overall oppression that minority women and minority men experience. People in positions of organizational power in relation to patients, staff, and students may use the comfort of those positions to espouse power-sharing, perhaps on some level knowing that institutional power will support us if power-sharing "gets tough."

Nursing may also have contributed to maintaining its level of unequal status through collective bargaining. In some parts of the country, staff nurses are earning substantial salaries, often based on contracts negotiated by bargaining units of state nurses' associations or labor unions. Salaries have increased, but how has the collective of nursing moved forward educationally and professionally? Certainly, collective bargaining agents have enabled nurses to feel some measure of protection in speaking out about the "re-engineering" of health care into "product lines." Nurses represented by the New York State Nurses Association, for example, have participated in a highly publicized "Every Patient Deserves an RN" campaign by wearing buttons at work, testifying before the legislature and pointing out to people through ads on subways and bus kiosks that effectively raise the issue of who will be providing nursing care to you or your family member when you need it. Nevertheless, too often the issues articulated by unions and state nurses associations are self-interests. While these have been important to nurses' empowerment, more balance is needed to address the impact of changes in health care and nurses on the patients. The withdrawal of the California Nurses Association from the American Nurses Association (ANA) threatens the viability of the national association at a time when cohesion within the nursing community and a focus on the external environment are paramount. Although the withdrawal was purportedly a response to ANA's failure to address staff nurse issues sufficiently, the very action of withdrawal undermines the power of staff nurses everywhere by diverting efforts to internal dissension.

Part of nurses' consciousness-raising must be in relation to what happens to the health and health care of people during this time of "reform." Currently there is much emphasis on caring for patients in the community and nurses' roles in this area. But many of these patients in the community include people who need long term care or are elderly, have AIDS, or are substance abusers. These are groups of people for whom health care practitioners have not traditionally rushed to provide care. Does this movement of nurses and patients out of the hospital and into the "community" signify improvement of quality patient care? Or is it perhaps another movement to maintain/ignore the status of oppressed groups (nurses and patients) in the power hierarchy?

Remember what happened when we "de-institutionalized" mental patients? The programs and systems that were deemed necessary for this community care model to be successful were never fully developed or supported. In a thought-provoking article several years ago, Anderson (1990) pointed out that the self-care movement was ostensibly supported by policy makers but without the necessary financial backing. In fact, the money saved was used to further fuel the development and use of high technology in acute care, rather than supporting families providing care to chronically ill children. One must likewise ask, 'Who is benefiting from the movement of patient care from the hospital to home?' While we fully support community-based care, we *must* question how all but the wealthy will be able to afford the supportive care that one needs for recovery from illness. This would be particularly oppressive to women since they are the primary caregivers for family members. Actual and proposed cuts in respite care and adult day care (Freudenheim, 1995) suggest that Anderson's perspective continues today.

The question remains as to whether nurses will see and articulate the connections between their own jobs and self-interests and the interests of patients and the public. In our attempts to implement the model, we have found that nurses give varying degrees of recognition and acknowledgment to their unequal status within nursing and the health care system. Some have not thought much about it and are excited about putting into words the feelings of oppression they have experienced in this role and their own individual empowerment. Others are understandably somewhat leery about "being empowered" through efforts of nursing leadership, since these efforts are often attempts to get staff to do what management wants them to do rather than true empowerment. For example, in a qualitative study of nurse empowerment, some nurses identified the idea of shared-governance as another oppressive strategy of administration

(Backer, Costello-Nickitas, & Mason-Adler, 1994). In 1987, Allen noted that shared governance programs generally address only "relations within the department and leave nursing's position relative to administration and medicine essentially unchanged" (p. 17). One might still question whether shared governance models currently perpetuate nursing's unequal status in hospital governance or move it into mainstream decision-making.

Nurse leaders have many opportunities to bring nurses together to explore the sociopolitical context of nurses' lives. This can be through informal discussions, support groups, professional meetings, or regular business meetings that include time for discussing trends in health and society. Concomitantly, nurse leaders need to examine their own use of power, and how their behaviors do or do not foster empowerment. The development of positive self-esteem, the second dimension in the political empowerment model, interacts with the raising of consciousness of sociopolitical realities and suggests further understanding of the model's components.

DEVELOPING POSITIVE SELF-ESTEEM

The literature on oppressed groups was reviewed in the 1991 article (Mason, Backer, & Georges, 1991, p. 74) and noted that members of such groups have difficulty in achieving the degree of self-esteem and sense of competence necessary for political action and empowerment. If nursing is an oppressed group, as suggested by Roberts (1983), then we might expect nurses to have difficulties in these areas. Indeed such conditions do exist, but not for all nurses. There are many nurses who are politically active, who themselves hold elected public office. It is true that nurses and students in other aspects of their lives outside the health care system and nursing are far from oppressed. Some have leadership positions in churches, school boards, PTAs, and community agencies. Others own independent businesses, are heads of three generational families, manage property in this country and outside the US, and speak and write in several languages.

Current developments in the health care system threaten nurses' self-esteem in overt ways and sometimes in insidious ways. In nursing practice and administration, enormous efforts and time have been committed to move hospital-wide initiatives forward as health care adopts a business orientation. This orientation includes doing more with less, streamlining, downsizing, rightsizing, redesigning, reorganizing, restructuring, etc . Nurses we know report feeling reduced to incompetency after meeting with consultants of health care delivery redesign who have "suggested" that their work needs creativity and 'thinking out of the box,' even though thinking out of the consultants' box is not acceptable. Some are coping with watching their work defined in terms of a series of discrete tasks that are taught to technicians in 6 weeks to 6 months. Staff nurses consistently are on the front line of fielding complaints and criticisms from physicians, patients, families, and other nurses while attempting to provide care to a patient caseload that is escalating in number and complexity, requiring the highest levels of critical thinking, interpersonal and technical judgement and skill, and stamina. Often there is little or no acknowledgement of these daily heroic accomplishments. To the extent that self-esteem is dependent upon meeting professional standards for safe, ethical, competent nursing practice, nurses' empowerment in today's health care environment is threatened. That nurses continue to stay in these harsh systems may be in and of itself an act of courage and empowerment. Granted they stay for many reasons, economics being a major one; people responsible for families do not go lightly into unemployment.

Nurses may leave systems that are personally and professionally demeaning to themselves if those systems cannot be changed. This does not necessarily mean giving up; it can instead indicate a positive regard for self-integrity. Nurses have a reputation for altruism, heroics, and courage. Certainly, Florence Nightingale set the example for these characteristics, which are associated with high, not low, self-esteem. On the other hand, there are nurses who treat patients disrespectfully and uncaringly. We believe these nurses suffer from a lack of caring, perhaps because they have been too long in uncaring environments, and that this behavior can be associated with a low self-esteem (Ameigh & Billet, 1992; Quinn, 1992). On the other hand, the authors have all witnessed the empowerment that occurs from role modeling with other health care colleagues, patients, and their families.

We have also been impressed with the extent to which mentoring of nurses is mutually empowering. For example, one of the authors was involved with implementing the first one-month sabbatical leave developed for nurses with 25 years of experience in a particular acute care facility. The first nurse to apply for the sabbatical had asked for one week for each of four years to attend a national conference in her specialty. Realizing that sabbaticals are foreign to most staff nurses, the author denied the nurse's proposal and requested that they meet to design an appropriate leave. The nurse arrived in the author's office with anger about the denial. When the author suggested that they begin fresh with the nurse identifying her interests, the nurse was taken aback. After reporting on her interest in history and photography, the author asked the nurse, "If you could do anything you wanted with this leave, what would you do?" The nurse responded, "Do you really want to know? I would lay on a beach!" When the author wrote this on the list of interests, the nurse was amazed and began to open up to the possibilities for a renewing and creative sabbatical. The nurse designed one that involved journeying to her ancestors' country of Greece and studying health and health care there from current and historical perspectives. She gave a presentation on her trip to the medical center using slides that ended with a picture of her swimming in the Aegean Sea. Subsequently, she encouraged her eligible colleagues to meet with the author to develop a sabbatical that was renewing and challenging. Risk-taking with this nurse confirmed the importance of mentoring staff.

Lack of recognition of nurses' (and women's) contributions to society's health and welfare is problematic in systems other than health care. In the academy, we have experienced the adage that one must leave one's own campus for acknowledgement of professional accomplishments. In looking at the social and political structure of academia, one writer wondered ". . . what on earth could motivate people to participate in a hierarchy of constant competition and showing off?" (Malterud, 1993, p. 367). In fact, we believe that many faculty in schools of nursing have stronger egos than self-esteem and are threatened by the full participation in the collective. The profession's and academy's emphasis on solitary scholarship, until recently, and on issues such as 'first authorship' for tenure, work against collective identities and strategies. How then will faculty teach nursing students about collective empowerment? Does the process of nursing education enable students to learn about empowerment— ". . .to recognize their own strengths, resources, and abilities to make changes in their personal and public lives?" (Mason, Backer, &

Georges, 1991, p. 73). It is important for nurses to value themselves and each other in order to form a nursing collective that can use political skills to initiate system change.

DEVELOPING POLITICAL SKILLS

Our original paper discussed empowerment of nurses as requiring the development of political action skills that enable change and influence decision-making. These skills were oriented toward the feminist model of power involving a collective approach emphasizing consensus-building and group process (Wheeler & Chinn, 1991). We have used this approach as part of our daily work situations which by and large involve working with nurses who perceive themselves as nursing leaders. We see changes in that some of the nurses have grown personally and professionally as evidenced by their own and organizational recognition, and have been instrumental in improving patient care. These are empirical observations, but this area of model implementation has been one of struggle for us.

An important side effect of empowerment to consider is the polarization that can occur when oppressed groups gain and advantaged groups lose (or think they lose) advantage (Schwartz, 1994, p. 10). Again, this occurs when the definition of empowerment focuses on power-over rather than on power-sharing and the release of personal power within individuals and groups. The current health care institutional movement toward continuous quality improvement or total quality management (TQM) may be a feminist blessing in disguise:

> The overt message, at least as institutions approach TQM, is to abandon the traditional model of paternalistic or hierarchical management in favor of one that empowers the employee and makes decisions by consensus. Top managers become leaders and coaches rather than authoritarian heads of bureaucratic institutions. (Lanza, 1994, pp. 8–9)

How likely is it that there will be changed relationships and ways of working together? Without the education of staff on group process and TQM tools (e.g., problem-solving processes and methods of analyzing data), staff will continue to need managers to lead the process. And even with this education, if management controls when the TQM process will be applied, it limits collaborative problem-solving and opportunities for true empowerment. In addition, we have found that, consistent with women's ways of knowing (Belenky, Clinchy, Goldberger, & Tarule, 1986), nurses often define issues and problems through their stories rather than data. While we believe that health care organizations need to value these stories as legitimate ways of understanding problems and potential solutions, until this happens nurses must be able to use the tools that are viewed as legitimate.

While writing this part of the paper in revisiting political action skills, we have become more aware of the exclusion of women's experiences in the conceptual models and methodologies used to analyze organizational structures. One reason for this may be a fear of marginalization (being situated on the border, not central to the main focus), that because women write about values that are associated with women such as consensus-building and nurturing they will be trivialized (Bensimon, 1989). Nurse leaders live this marginalization risk daily as many of their colleagues both in other disciplines and nursing tell them their ideas of empowerment cannot be done because of time and cost considerations. In addition, the covert message here often is "get with the program or get out."

We live with the reality of co-optation, often visiting this within ourselves or advising or criticizing our nursing colleagues in leadership positions as to what they "should" do/have done, as we have done in this paper. The importance of a collective of politically empowered nurses increasingly becomes important, as at any given time one nurse or group of nurses may need/choose to be less active, and others will need to take up the slack. We have learned to live more openly, although not necessarily more comfortably with the contradictions, the ambiguities, and the fluidity of political empowerment.

CONCLUSION

We have learned from implementation of this model that empowerment takes many forms in nurses' lives. It interfaces with life stages of personal as well as professional development. With this developmental perception, we no longer assume that all nurses want to become empowered at any one time to transform health care delivery. We acknowledge that our own life stages have brought us to this point of participating in system changes. Political empowerment for nurses means moving nursing forward, not losing the legacy of nursing that has been inherited, and leaving something for the next generation. It also means true reform of health care and society's approaches to health and social issues. We are firmly grounded in the belief that ultimately the collective is responsible for such empowerment.

REFERENCES

Allen, D. G. (1987). Professionalism, occupational segregation, gender and control of nursing. *Women and Politics, 6*(3), 1–24.

Ameigh, A. Y., & Billet, H. (1992). Caring: A key to empowerment. *Nursing Administration Quarterly, 16*(3), 43–46.

Anderson, J. M. (1990). Home care management in chronic illness and the self-care movement: An analysis of ideologies and economic processes influencing policy decisions. *Advances in Nursing Science, 12*(2), 71–83.

Backer, B. A., Costello-Nickitas, D., & Mason-Adler, M. (1994). Nurses' experiences of empowerment in the workplace: A qualitative study. *Journal of the New York State Nurses Association, 25*(2), 4–7.

Beck, B. (1983). Empowerment: A future goal for social work. *Working Papers in Social Policy.* New York: Community Service Society of New York.

Belenky, M. E., Clinchy, B. M., Goldberger, N. R., & Tarule, J. N. (1986). *Women's ways of knowing: The development of self, voice and mind.* New York: Basic Books.

Bensimon, E. M. (1989). A feminist reinterpretation of presidents' definitions of leadership. *Peabody Journal of Education, 66,* 143–156.

Burghardt, S. (1995). Community-building. *Update: School of Social Work, Hunter College of the City University of New York,* Spring, 1, 3.

Carlson-Catalano, J. M. (1992). Empowering nurses for professional practice. *Nursing Outlook, 40,* 139–142.

Chandler, G. (1992). The source and process of empowerment. *Nursing Administration Quarterly, 16*(3), 65–71.

Cumulative Index of Nurses and Allied Health Literature (CINAHL). (1993). Glendale, CA: CINAHL Information Systems.

Clifford, P. G. (1992). The myth of empowerment. *Nursing Administration Quarterly, 16*(3), 1–5.

Denmark, F. L. (1993). Women, leadership, and empowerment. *Psychology of Women Quarterly, 17*, 343–356.

Faludi, S. (1991). *Backlash: The undeclared war against American women.* New York: Crown.

Freudenheim, M. (1995, September 15). An exam for home health care: A way to cut hospital costs, or a system out of control? *The New York Times*, D1–D2.

Havens, D. S., & Mills, M. E. (1992). Staff nurse empowerment: Current status and future projections. *Nursing Administration Quarterly, 16*(3), 58–64.

Johnson, L. (1992). Interactive planning: A model for staff empowerment. *Nursing Administration Quarterly, 16*(3), 47–57.

Koerner, J. G. (1994). Encouragement versus empowerment: A nurse executive responds. *Journal of Nursing Administration, 24*(4), 12, 16–17.

Kramer, M., & Schalenberg, C. (1993). Learning from success: Autonomy and empowerment. *Nursing Management, 24*(5), 58–59, 62, 64.

Lanza, M. L. (1994). Total quality management: A feminist perspective. *Journal of Nursing Administration, 24*(4), 8–9, 15.

Malterud, K. (1993). Voices in the medical culture. *Health Care for Women International, 14*, 365–373.

Mason, D. J., Backer, B. A., & Georges, C. A. (1991). Toward a feminist model for the political empowerment of nurses. *Image: Journal of Nursing Scholarship, 23*(1), 72–77.

Mason, D. J., Costello-Nickitas, D., Scanlan, J. M., & Magnuson, B. A. (1991). Empowering nurses for politically astute change in the workplace. *Journal of Continuing Education in Nursing, 22*(1), 5–10.

Miller, J. B. (1976). *Towards a new psychology for women.* Boston: Beacon.

Miller, J. B. (1982). *Colloquium: Women and power.* Stone Center for Developmental Services and Studies, Wellesley College.

Quinn, J. (1992). Holding sacred space: The nurse as healing environment. *Holistic Nursing Practice, 6*(4), 26–36.

Renz, M. C. (1993). Nursing's noblesse oblige. *Revolution: The Journal of Nurse Empowerment, 3*(4), 42–43, 88.

Roberts, S. J. (1983). Oppressed group behavior: Implications for nursing. *Advances in Nursing Science, 5*(7), 21–30.

Rosenthal, E. (1995, July 8). Leading academic hospital squeaking by, seeks merger. *The New York Times*, pp. 1, 22.

Schwartz, R. H. (1994). Encouragement versus empowerment. *Journal of Nursing Administration, 24*(4), 10, 13–14.

Styles, M. M. (1994). Empowerment: A vision for nursing. *International Nursing Review, 41*(3), 77–80.

Wheeler, C. E., & Chinn, P. L. (1991). *Peace and power: A handbook of feminist process* (3rd ed.). New York: National League of Nursing.

The authors acknowledge and thank Harriet R. Feldman, RN, PhD, FAAN, for her thoughtful review of this manuscript.

CHAPTER *15*

The Impact of Organizational Climate on Nurse Satisfaction: Management Implications

Linda D. Urden

INTRODUCTION

The stresses and demands on nurses currently in practice and those who manage nursing environments are far greater than they were just a few years ago and will only escalate in the future. The purpose of the study described in this chapter was to examine the relationship of organizational climate dimensions on registered nurse job satisfaction. The sample consisted of 232 pediatric registered nurses who worked in all pediatric specialties. There was a statistically significant relationship between five climate dimensions and job satisfaction (p < .01–.001). Emphasis is placed on implications for nurse administrators and managers who can greatly impact the climate of the nursing unit and department. It is essential for nurse administrators and managers to plan and implement approaches that will meet the unique needs of their staff and institution in these particularly challenging times.

Redesign, restructure, downsizing, rightsizing, merger, cross-train, delegation, efficiency, productivity, quality, outcomes, collaboration, and systems thinking—these are common initiatives today as dramatic changes force a new reality in health care and nursing envi-

Note: Originally published in *Nursing Leadership Forum*, Vol. 4, No. 2, 1999. New York: Springer Publishing Company.

ronments (Pierce, Hazel, & Mion, 1996; Relf, 1995). Due to decreased lengths of stay, hospitalized patients have higher acuities and greater teaching needs and discharge plans to initiate (Relf, 1995). Additionally, more demands are placed on nurses regarding nondirect care requirements, that is, documentation and maintenance of technologic devices (Patterson, Blehm, Foster, Fuglee, & Moore, 1995; Pierpont & Thilgen, 1995). Many nurses perceive the bureaucratic hospital environment as not allowing for professional practice and as being only interested in meeting fiscal goals. This has led to frustration and disillusionment with the job, hospital, and profession.

Turnover is frequently associated with frustration with the organizational work climate and job dissatisfaction. It has been assumed that a majority of nurses leave for reasons that managers and administrators can control. Hence, organizations that design strategies that lead to employee satisfaction should be able to decrease turnover. Changes in nursing operational and governance structures have been shown to increase satisfaction (Fullam, Lando, Johansen, Reyes, & Szaloczy, 1998). Quality of work life and environment for registered nurses have also been shown to impact satisfaction with the work environment (Irvine & Evans, 1995; Kovner, Hendrickson, Knickman, & Finkler, 1994; Tumulty, Jernigan, & Kohut, 1994).

FRAMEWORK

Many social and psychological factors impact behaviors and interactions in hospitals. There are unique lines of authority, sources of power, and complex communication networks that differentiate hospitals from other organizations. In addition, the hospital structure has been traditionally based on a bureaucratic model with administrative authority interfacing with professional attitudes and actions. There are frequently conflicts between organizational mission and goals of the professionals who work there (Ellefsen, 1995). Thus, organizational climate may greatly influence the attitudes, commitment, and performance of the various professional staff members. Organizational climate consists of measurable attributes of the work environment that are directly or indirectly perceived by the persons working in the environment. Interpersonal relationships among coworkers and between managers and staff are indicators of climate in organizations (Duxbury, Henley, & Armstrong, 1982; Halpin & Croft, 1962). These climate perceptions are thought to influence motivation, satisfaction, and behavior of the workers (Gillies, Franklin, & Child, 1990). Assessment of climate provides a basis for organizational change and improvement, motivation and commitment of employees, improved communication, and redirection of goals. Organizational climate as defined by Duxbury and associates (1982) forms the conceptual framework for this study. Organizational climate is described in terms of six behaviors: disengagement, hin-

FIGURE 15.1 Definition of organizational climate.

Organizational climate consists of organizational characteristics that are relatively stable, differentiate organizations, and influence behaviors of members in the organization. Climate is perceived by individuals in terms of subordinate behaviors (disengagement, hindrance, esprit, intimacy) and leader behaviors (aloofness, thrust).

Disengagement describes a group that is going through the motion and not in gear with respect to the goal at hand.

Hindrance refers to feelings that one is burdened with routine duties, committee demands, and other apparently necessary requirements which, however, are construed as unnecessary busy-work.

Esprit refers to subordinate morale or to the feeling that social needs are being satisfied, and that at the same time there is a sense of accomplishment in the job.

Intimacy refers to the subordinates' enjoyment of friendly social relations with each other and describes a social-needs satisfaction not necessarily associated with task accomplishment.

Aloofness refers to behavior by the leader that is characterized as formal and impersonal. The leader goes by the book, and is guided by rules and policies rather than dealing with subordinates in an informal, face-to-face situation.

Thrust is behavior by the leader that is characterized by an evident effort to move the organization and by the leader's attempts to motivate subordinates through the example he or she personally sets.

drance, esprit, intimacy, aloofness, and thrust. Figure 15.1 defines these behaviors.

Job satisfaction, the degree to which employees like the various components of their work and their position in the organization (Stamps & Piedmonte, 1986), consists of six components: pay and benefits, autonomy, status, organizational requirements, task requirements, and interactions. Job satisfaction in nurses has been studied in multiple settings and has been shown to impact absenteeism, morale, productivity, quality of care, and turnover (Agho, 1993; Goodell & Coeling, 1994; Klinefelter, 1993; and Tumulty et al., 1994). McNeese-Smith (1997) found that nurses were dissastified when their managers did not provide recognition or support, criticized them in a crisis, and did not follow through on issues. Nurses who felt comfortable with their ability to delegate to nonprofessional staff demonstrated greater job satisfaction (Parsons, 1998). Transformational leadership style has been shown to positively affect job satisfaction because of its influence on one's feeling of empowerment (Morrison, Jones, & Fuller, 1997).

Early studies reported from the fields of psychology, management, and organizational behavior established relationships between climate attributes and satisfaction (Downey, Sheridan, & Slocum, 1975; Friedlander & Margulies, 1969; Halpin & Croft, 1962; Pritchard & Karasick, 1973). In health care, organizational climate variables have been demonstrated to affect job satisfaction among staff (LaFollette & Sims, 1975) and to differ among staff and managers (Ivancevich, Matteson, & McMahon, 1980). Duxbury, Henley, and Armstrong (1982) formulated an instrument to measure organizational climate in nursing (Nursing Organizational Climate Description Questionnaire) which had been adapted from a tool used in elementary education (Halpin & Croft, 1962). Their study of neonatal intensive care nurses from 18 different settings revealed that nurses are most satisfied with their jobs when there is teamwork and concern for peers, high morale, and a leader who is a good, progressive, role model. Another early study examining organizational climate and satisfaction among nurses reported that climate variables influence work stress and job satisfaction of nurses (Gray-Toft & Anderson, 1985). Weisman, Alexander, and Chase (1981) conducted a longitudinal study and determined that organizational attributes were consistently predictive of job satisfaction. Gillies, Franklin, and Child (1990) reported a pilot study in which there were significant correlations between satisfaction and climate variables of warmth, support, identity, and responsibility.

Blegen (1993) reported a meta-analysis in which 48 studies were examined describing relationships between job satisfaction and variables most frequently influencing satisfaction. There were high correlations between satisfaction and the following variables: communication with supervisor, autonomy, recognition, routinization, communication with peers, fairness, locus of control, stress, and organizational commitment. A more recent meta-analysis (Irvine & Evans, 1995) showed that work content and work environment had strong relationships with job satisfaction.

Dissatisfaction with job and organizational climate are often only two components of larger problems within an organization. Each institution must be analyzed for problems that are amenable to tailor-made solutions for that particular institution. It is crucial in today's fast-paced and everchanging health care environment that these issues be addressed and appropriate and timely strategies implemented. This study examined the relationship between organizational climate variables and pediatric nurse job satisfaction.

METHODS

The study consisted of a convenience sample of 232 subjects, determined by power analysis based on the procedures described by Cohen (1977). Respondents were female and male registered nurses who worked per diem, part-time or full-time on all shifts. They held direct care positions and had been employed for a minimum of 6 months in one of three southern California children's hospitals.

The mean age was reported as 32 years, with an average of 5.3 years of employment in the institution and 8.2 years as a registered nurse. Just over half of the nurses were prepared at the baccalaureate level; 30% held associate degrees; 14% had obtained diplomas; and 1% had master's degrees. The majority of participants worked the day shift (60%), with 6% on the evening shift and 34% on the night shift. Participants worked an average of 65.9 hours per 2-week schedule. Major nursing specialties represented were neonatal intensive care unit (NICU) (33%), general medical-surgical (31%), and pediatric intensive care unit (PICU) (14%); the remaining 20% were accounted for by work in the emergency room, outpatient department, oncology, operating room, and intermediate care departments.

The *Nurse Organizational Climate Descriptive Survey* (NODCQ) is a 26-item, Likert-type scale which measures six dimensions of organizational climate (refer to Figure 15.1). Scale items are scored using a 4-point range from 1 = "rarely occurs" to 4 = "very often occurs" (Duxbury et al., 1982). One item is reverse-scored, and all items are summed for a total score. Individual subscale reliabilities have been established; no overall reliability is reported. The survey has been used repeatedly in studies and has established strong reliability of the subscales. The Cronbach alpha coefficient for the subscales ranged from .74 to .84 for the current study.

The Index of Work Satisfaction (IWS) Part B is a 44-item, Likert-type scale which measures the current level of satisfaction for each of six work components: pay and benefits, autonomy, status, organizational requirements, task requirements, and interactions. Scale items are scored using a 7-point scale, ranging from 1 = "completely disagree" to 7 = "completely agree" (Stamps & Piedmonte, 1986). Half of the items are reverse-scored and results are summed to derive an indicator of individual satisfaction. This instrument has been used extensively in nursing satisfaction studies and has strong reliability. The Cronbach alpha coefficient for the current study was .88 for the overall scale.

An initial meeting was scheduled at each site with the chief nurse executive and nurse managers to discuss the study purpose, procedure, and timing of the proposed research. After human subject approvals were obtained from all study sites, 600 subjects were randomly selected from the work schedule rosters at each study site. Research packets containing the cover letter, informed consent form, instruments, and self-addressed stamped envelope to the investigator were distributed to subjects by the nurse managers of the unit or department. A total of 232 completed packets were returned to the investigator within 1 month, indicating a 39% return rate.

FINDINGS

The relationship of each organizational climate dimension with job satisfaction was examined using the Pearson Product Moment

Correlation Coefficient. Correlations are listed in Table 15.1. Each of the organizational climate variables correlated with job satisfaction except for the "intimacy" dimension. Strong positive correlations were demonstrated between job satisfaction and thrust ($p < .001$), and esprit ($p < .001$). Negative relationships were revealed between job satisfaction and aloofness ($p < .01$), disengagement ($p < .001$), and hindrance ($p < .001$). Thus, there was less satisfaction in nurses who perceived that their supervisors were aloof, placed obstacles in their way, and who felt disengaged from the group goals.

DISCUSSION

The importance of organizational climate and job satisfaction was demonstrated in the current study by strong correlations among the variables. The findings were not surprising since they validated previous research and are consistent with what many organizations know and strive to implement. Although the generalizability of this study is limited to pediatric nurses in a given geographical area, this research is consistent with earlier studies that established relationships between climate and various indicators of nurse satisfaction. It includes communication, management practices, and autonomy (Agho, 1993); communication with peers and supervisor, autonomy, and management practices (Blegen, 1993); thrust, esprit, and disengagement with satisfaction (Duxbury et al., 1982); support, warmth, and respon-

TABLE 15.1 Pearson Correlations for Organizational Climate Dimensions and Job Satisfaction

Dimension	Pearson Correlation
Thrust	.4037***
Esprit	.5875***
Intimacy	.0190
Aloofness	−.1885**
Disengagement	−.3956***
Hindrance	−.4370***

$**p < .01.$ $***p < .001.$

sibility (Gillies et al., 1990); supervisory relationship, leadership, autonomy, and participation (Irvine & Evans, 1995); autonomy and interactions (Kovner et al., 1994); and autonomy, work relationships, and management characteristics (Tumulty et al., 1994).

IMPLICATIONS FOR MANAGERS AND ADMINISTRATORS

There is no panacea or simple answer to managing the organizational climate. Rather, a combination of approaches is necessary to address these complex issues. In today's unstable health care environment, the recommendations may be difficult to implement. Although what should be done is known, in reality the current managed care environment may not make this feasible. Managements of health care organizations today face a particularly challenging task in having to design and implement approaches to meet staff needs, while at the same time meeting the goals and demands of an often financially challenged and changing organization. Strategies addressing the climate variables of thrust, aloofness, hindrance, esprit, and disengagement will directly impact nurse job satisfaction.

Proactive management that enables individual autonomy and flexibility while maintaining a known set of values can greatly influence staff commitment and quality work performance. Open communication between nurse administrators and nurses, involving staff in the change process, and providing opportunities for input may decrease aloofness and disengagement and allow staff participation in decisions that affect their practice and work lives. Leaders who are able to demonstrate genuine respect and caring for all staff create a satisfying work environment.

Aloofness and hindrance can be diminished in a work climate that fosters and encourages risk-taking and entrepreneurship. Such an environment allows for growth and development of both individuals and groups, and results in commitment, ownership, and pride. Research, committee work, special projects and development, temporary job reassignments, and participation in new programs support the entrepreneurial nurse. Although these types of activities may appear to be beyond budgetary means, staff members who are interested and committed to such activities will participate and develop new skills. It is through these activities that cost reduction, increased productivity, and innovation in care modalities often occur. Team-building programs and activities that will increase and maintain group motivation and cohesiveness will positively impact the esprit and disengagement components of the staff nurse work environment.

Esprit and disengagement can also be influenced through recognition for a job well done, resulting in improved morale and self-esteem, professional and organizational commitment, pride in the profession, and overall satisfaction. Recognition activities can play an important role in an overall, ongoing, and comprehensive retention program. For example, an annual nurse recognition day or week provides an opportunity to acknowledge the unique contributions that nurses make. Promotions and acknowledgment of outstanding performance and special accomplishments can take place both on the unit and institution-wide throughout the year. Such recognition activities can also decrease disengagement, increase esprit, and serve as group and individual motivators.

Internal promotion and career advancement opportunities acknowledge individual growth and reward expertise, and may also serve to increase esprit and decrease disengagement. Career ladder programs allow staff to specialize in an area of practice, for example, clinical, administrative, or education, and enhance job status, self-concept, and commitment. Temporary or interim assignments of staff nurses into expanded role or special project positions provide more global insights and serve to open new opportunities for future personal direction. Credentialing of nurses through professional organizations recognizes competence and excellence in clinical practice, leadership, and education. Acknowledgment of such accomplishments by management will reinforce the importance of these activities and encourage others to strive for the needed certification or credential.

Traditional bureaucratic organizational structures in nursing departments have limited decision-making powers at the staff level regarding professional practice. Alternate nursing care delivery models, such as case management, partners-in-practice, or specialized nursing care centers promote autonomy, decision-making authority, and empowerment of the staff nurse. Current staff nurse responsibilities need to be assessed for workflow, appropriateness, and necessary skill level to diminish hindrance. Obstacles for nurses that prevent fulfilling professional role components, such as clerical tasks, housekeeping duties, transport of patients, and various kinds of paperwork that are not directly related to patient care, need to be removed and reassigned. New technologies, such as computerization of the medical record and other hospital information systems, can serve to increase efficiency with the non-direct care components of the staff nurse role.

Input into scheduling and flexibility in hours and staffing patterns are other areas for staff nurse involvement that may promote esprit. Efficient and effective scheduling benefits both the staff nurse and the institution. No one method is universally successful and the needs of the individual units or client populations must be considered. Job share can also be an option for staff who are committed to the positions and team, and who are attempting to meet family or personal goals.

Peer review is another strategy by which nurses have input into personal and peer practice. Shared governance models allow for varying degrees of management/staff control over practice. Joint practice committees demonstrate collaboration between medicine and nursing and mutually acknowledge each other's areas of expertise. All of these activities are indicative of leader thrust and may decrease aloofness, hindrance, and disengagement.

SUMMARY

These research findings establish a strong relationship between organizational climate and nurse job satisfaction, and corroborate findings of past research. Several strategies to enhance nurse satisfaction were delineated. Since this study utilized a total pediatric sample in one geographic region, additional research is necessary in other populations in other geographic locations. Intervention studies based on these findings could be designed that examine the impact of strategies addressing climate components. It is essential for nurse administrators and managers to plan and implement approaches that will meet the unique needs of their staff and institution in these particularly challenging times facing all of health care.

REFERENCES

Agho, A. (1993). The moderating effects of dispositional affectivity on relationships between job characteristics and nurses' job satisfaction. *Research Nursing & Health, 16*, 451–458.

Blegen, M. (1993). Nurses' job satisfaction: A meta-analysis of related variables. *Nursing Research, 42*(1), 36–41.

Cohen, J. (1977). *Statistical power analysis for the behavioral sciences.* New York: Academic Press.

Downey, H., Sheridan, J., & Slocum, J. (1975). Analysis of relationships among leader behavior, subordinate job performance and satisfaction: A path-goal approach. *Academy of Management Journal, 18*(2), 253–262.

Duxbury, M., Henley, G., & Armstrong, G. (1982). Measurement of the nurse organizational climate in neonatal intensive care units. *Nursing Research, 31*(2), 83–88.

Ellefsen, B. (1995). Bureaucratization of professionals. *Nursing Leadership Forum, 1*(3), 100–106.

Friedlander, F., & Margulies, N. (1969). Multiple impacts of organizational climate and individual value systems upon job satisfaction. *Personnel Psychology, 22,* 171–183.

Fullam, C., Lando, A., Johansen, M., Reyes, A., & Szaloczy, D. (1998). The triad of empowerment: Leadership, environment, and professional traits. *Nursing Economics, 16*(5), 254–257, 253.

Goodell, T., & Coeling, H. (1994). Outcomes of nurses' job satisfaction. *Journal of Nursing Administration, 24*(11), 36–41.

Gillies, D., Franklin, M., & Child, D. (1990). Relationship between organizational climate and job satisfaction of nursing personnel. *Nursing Administration Quarterly, 14*(4), 15–22.

Gray-Toft, P., & Anderson, J. (1985). Organizational stress in the hospital: Development of a model for diagnosis and prediction. *Health Services Research, 19*(6), 753–774.

Halpin, A., & Croft, D. (1962). *The organizational climate of schools.* Chicago: Midwest Administration Center, University of Chicago.

Hayes, E. (1993). Managing job satisfaction for the long run. *Nursing Management, 24*(1), 65–67.

Irvine, D., & Evans, M. (1995). Job satisfaction and turnover among nurses: Integrating research findings across studies. *Nursing Research, 44*(4), 246–253.

Ivancevich, J., Matteson, M., & McMahon, J. (1980). Understanding professional job attitudes. *Hospitals and Health Services Administration, Winter,* 53–58.

Klinefelter, G. (1993). Role efficacy and job satisfaction of hospital nurses. *Journal of Nursing Staff Development, 9*(4), 179–183.

Kovner, C., Hendrickson, G., Knickman, J., & Finkler, S. (1994). Nursing care delivery models and nurse satisfaction. *Nursing Administration Quarterly, 19*(1), 74–85.

LaFollette, W., & Sims, H. (1975). Is satisfaction redundant with organizational climate? *Organizational Behavior and Human Performance, 13*, 257–278.

McNeese-Smith, D. (1997). The influence of manager behavior on nurses' job satisfaction, productivity, and commitment. *Journal of Nursing Administration, 27*(9), 47–55.

Moos, R. (1981). *Work environment scale manual.* Palo Alto, CA: Consulting Psychologists Press.

Morrison, R., Jones, L., & Fuller, B. (1997). The relation between leadership style and empowerment on job satisfaction of nurses. *Journal of Nursing Administration, 27*(5), 27–34.

Parsons, L. (1998). Delegation skills and nurse job satisfaction. *Nursing Economics, 16*(1), 18–26.

Patterson, P., Blehm, R., Foster, J., Fuglee, K., & Moore, J. (1995). Nurse information needs for efficient care continuity across patient units. *Nursing Management, 25*(10), 28–36.

Pierce, L., Hazel, C., & Mion, L. (1996). Effect of professional practice model on autonomy, job satisfaction and turnover. *Nursing Management, 27*(2), 48M–48T.

Pierpont, G., & Thilgen, D. (1995). Effect of computerized charting on nursing activity in intensive care. *Critical Care Medicine, 23*(6), 1067–1073.

Pritchard, R., & Karasick, B. (1973). The effect of organizational climate on managerial job performance and job satisfaction. *Organizational Behavior and Human Performance, 9*, 126–146.

Relf, M. (1995). Increasing job satisfaction and motivation while reducing nursing turnover through the implementation of shared governance. *Critical Care Nursing Quarterly, 18*(3), 7–13.

Stamps, P., & Piedmonte, E. (1986). *Nurses and work satisfaction.* Ann Arbor: Health Administration Press.

Tumulty, G., Jernigan, I. E., & Kohut, G. (1994). The impact of perceived work environment on job satisfaction of hospital staff nurses. *Applied Nursing Research, 7*(2), 84–90.

Weisman, C., Alexander, C., & Chase, G. (1981). Job satisfaction among hospital nurses: A longitudinal study. *Health Services Research, 15*, 341–362.

CHAPTER 16

Improving Patient Satisfaction Through Focus Group Interviews

Kathleen Leask Capitulo

Long used by the social science community, focus groups have been increasingly used by nursing leaders to obtain information and feedback. Use of the focus group interview (FGI), a qualitative research method, allows the nurse executive the opportunity to obtain data on a variety of topics. In order for the findings to be meaningful, however, the researcher must adhere to basic FGI design and data analysis. Like other research methodologies, the focus group offers advantages and disadvantages that must be evaluated for appropriateness and feasibility. This chapter illustrates the use of the FGI to spark the creation of patient-focused care and significant increases in patient satisfaction in an academic medical center.

Challenged to change the philosophy of a large Maternal-Child Health service from a traditional, provider-focused academic model to that of patient-focused care, the Clinical and Operational Directors of the service utilized patient focus group interviews. Data from the focus groups spawned 18 process redesign teams which led to dramatic changes in the service, resulting in statistically significant ($p = .05$) increases in patient satisfaction. When nursing and health care leaders are in need of data and feedback to create and evaluate programs, traditional quantitative methods, such as written surveys, may be difficult to adapt to a variety of practice areas and issues. Focus

Note: Originally published in *Nursing Leadership Forum*, Vol. 3, No. 4, 1998. New York: Springer Publishing Company.

groups offer the flexibility to investigate numerous topics using a standardized, user-friendly design.

A focus group is "a carefully planned discussion designed to obtain perceptions on a defined area of interest in a permissive, non-threatening environment" (Krueger, 1994, p. 6). Focus group interviews (FGI), a form of qualitative research study (Kingry, Tiedje, & Friedman, 1990), are conducted by a facilitator or moderator, often with an assistant facilitator. Focus groups were first used by Bogardus (1926), a sociologist, to study race relations, leisure activities, and boys' work experiences. At the time, however, focus groups were not embraced by the social science community. In fact, the literature remained markedly devoid of focus group reports until the second part of this century.

World War II brought new uses to focus groups. Merton initially published his work in 1956 and is credited with vitalizing the use of the FGI (Merton, Fiske, & Kendall, 1990). The FGI was used to elicit marketing information about the war as well as evaluating army training and morale (Smith, 1995). By the 1960s, advertising and marketing professionals began utilizing the FGI to do market and consumer buying surveys. By the late 1970s this familiar marketing technique was rediscovered by social and health scientists (DiIorio, Hockenberry-Eaton, Maibach, & Rivero, 1994). The business community found FGIs very helpful in anticipating consumer needs as well as in cost-avoidance, preventing losses that would be incurred by the creation of products not wanted by consumers (Stevens, 1996).

In the 1990s, nursing and health researchers embraced this qualitative research technique to investigate many health care issues. Stevens (1996) pointed out that a focus group "provides a means of reality reconstruction in which the basic source of data consists of stories members of a subculture tell about their lives, their health and environments in which they live" (p. 171). The FGI technique has been used to identify social service concerns of HIV positive women (Seals et al., 1995), communities' health care needs in Chicago (Stevens, 1996), health and wellness education needs in rural areas (Watts, Brockschmidt, Sisk, Baldwin, & McCubbin, 1997), and, in the author's practice, registered nurses' evaluation of educational programs and patient satisfaction in hospitals.

Currently, focus groups in health care research are used to obtain feedback and suggestions from user groups, both professionals and patients, to plan and evaluate systems, develop programs, and design change. They are also used for reliability and validity testing on research instruments, such as surveys. In contrast, the use of focus groups for market research is primarily to obtain consumer feedback and to identify ideas for an advertising campaign (Carey, 1995). Focus groups can also be used to explore the meaning of behavior, "to develop hypotheses for subsequent quantitative study . . . [and] for obtaining information that can serve as a basis for the development of research instruments" (DiIorio et al., 1994, p. 176).

As in other research, the first step in focus group design is to identify an objective. For example, the Watts and colleagues (1997) focus group study was designed to assess the beliefs and attitudes on health promotion and wellness in five small rural communities outside of Chicago. Based upon the objective of a study, a review of the literature should be done and an interview guide created. The guide that is used to conduct the focus group includes a brief introduction of the concept to be discussed, followed by 6 to 12 open-ended questions, and a summarizing conclusion. The facilitator should begin with broad, simple questions and progress to more specific, sensitive questions (DiIorio et al., 1994). Carey (1995), however, suggests that questions be limited to four or five.

FACILITATOR/LEADER

The facilitator/leader of the FGI, who may or may not be part of the research team that is responsible for the project, should receive special training to conduct a focus group. Watts and associates (1997) note that "failure to be prepared properly for this unique information gathering experience can lead to diminishing returns on the investment of the time and energy of many people" (p. 250). The role of the facilitator is to introduce the topic to the group, ask the open-ended questions, facilitate the discussion, and provide feedback to the research group. Depending on the size of the group, many researchers suggest the use of an assistant moderator, who can take "comprehensive notes, being attentive to time and environmental conditions, summarize key ideas and issues . . . and debrief with the moderator and other investigators" (Watts et al., 1997, p. 250). The facilitator also may utilize an observer, a nonparticipant who "will not be involved in directing discussion, sits away from the group or behind a one-way mirror . . . to monitor the nonverbal behavior of group members" (p. 250). Observers can also assist with tape recorders and refreshments, and maintain a nondistracting environment (DiIorio et al., 1994).

RECRUITMENT

Recruitment may pose the greatest challenge, since participation in the study is optional and out of the control of the researcher. Depending on the topic, individuals can be recruited by utilizing written and electronic communication as well as personal contact. If participants are needed from outside the organization, advertisements can be put in newspapers or journals that they are likely to read. Paid advertising, however, can be costly, with little return on the investment. Newer recruitment approaches include posting notices on the Internet. Bulletin boards and professional lists offer outstanding, no-cost access to large groups of individuals interested in a particular subject. For example, the *Perinatal Nursing List Serv*, e-mail address, PNATALRN@LISTSERV.ACSU.BUFFALO.EDU, has over 1,000 perinatal nurse members, a source of recruitment for perinatal studies.

In my work coordinating focus groups of previously hospitalized patients, phone invitations were extended to 15 to 20 people who had been discharged from a particular area of the hospital in the past 4 to 8 weeks. Written letters of confirmation were sent to all those invited asking them for a response. Few responded spontaneously. All those invited were again contacted by phone to obtain their response. Reminder calls were made within 24 hours before the meetings were to be held.

The "no-show" rate of participants can be very high, reaching as high as 50% to 90%. It is essential, therefore, to invite more participants than needed (DiIorio et al., 1994). Incentives, such as cash, prizes, gift certificates, or holding the group meeting in an attractive location, may enhance recruitment. For example, I was recently invited to an FGI conducted by a publishing house at a famous restaurant, where dinner and $100 were offered for participation. In this case, recruitment was easy but required a substantial financial investment.

PARTICIPANTS

Focus groups should contain 4 to 12 participants. It is helpful if groups are homogenous (Kingry, Tiedje, & Friedman, 1990, p. 124). DiIorio, Hockenberry-Eaton, Maibach, and Rivero (1994, p. 176–178) recommend, however, that "a balance between homogeneity and diversity" is desirable. This approach enables individual opinions to be heard in the context of a common theme. In addition, they state that the ideal focus group has eight participants. Fewer participants limit the breadth of the discussion, while larger numbers do not permit adequate discussion.

In the discharged patient surveys mentioned previously, participants were grouped by the clinical area in which they had been hospitalized, e.g., new mothers for maternity focus groups, separate interviews for parents and patients from general pediatric units, and parents of children in two critical care units, Neonatal Intensive Care and Pediatric Intensive Care. Combining the NICU and PICU parents worked well, as many had children who had been in both units. Groups should represent diversity reflected in the studied population. For example, in the case of the maternity and pediatric patient/family groups, members came from diverse racial, ethnic, and socioeconomic backgrounds. Some had been cared for by private physicians and others by the hospital's clinics. At the same time, homogeneity was maintained in that all had personal experience as inpatients on particular services in the last two months.

CONDUCTING THE GROUP

The location of the focus group is important. It should be held in a comfortable, nonthreatening, easily accessible setting. Participants should be arranged in a circle to promote discussion. A table poses a barrier to discussion but can be helpful for placement of refreshments during the meeting. Distractions, such as noise or an uncomfortable room temperature, should be minimized (DiIorio et al., 1994, p. 178–179).

At the time of the focus group, the facilitator utilizes the interview guide previously described. Data are collected using a tape recorder. (DiIorio et al., 1994, p. 176). The facilitator and, if present, assistant or observer, take notes (Kingry et al., 1990, p. 125). During the introduction, the facilitator emphasizes confidentiality, that "there are no right or wrong answers," and that the audiotape will be transcribed without reference to anyone's name. Participants and leaders should be on a first name basis, with identifying name tags in front of each individual (Watts et al., 1997, p. 251). A demographic tool may be used to collect data from each participant.

Generally, a group meets once for a period of 1 to 3 hours. Groups which are utilized to create change, however, may be reconvened to comment on progress of the project. Nursing and interdisciplinary redesign groups in the author's practice were reconvened to evaluate progress toward patient-focused care. The extent of expected participation should be explained at recruitment.

During the group meeting, the facilitator should keep the discussion focused and allow participation from all individuals, using group facilitation techniques. As in other groups, care should be taken to prevent domination of the FGI by an individual (Watts et al., 1997, p. 251). At the conclusion of the meeting, the facilitator should thank participants.

Following the FGI, the facilitator and assistant/observer should be debriefed immediately by the research team. The audio tapes should be transcribed and analyzed separately by each investigator. "Analysis should be done by someone who observed the session, although not necessarily the leader. [A] description of group interaction and nonverbal behavior will be useful in helping to interpret the transcripts or tape recordings" (Carey, 1995, p. 493).

A summary of advantages and disadvantages of the FGI appears in Table 1. The cost/benefit of conducting an FGI needs to be viewed within this context and in light of the kind of information desired.

ANALYSIS OF DATA

Krueger (1994, p. 143–144) suggests four methods of data analysis: transcript-based analysis, tape analysis, note analysis, and memory analysis. Analysis of the tape transcripts is the most tedious, necessitating 10 to 16 hours. Tape analysis involves the researcher listening to the audio tapes and creating a summary. This can take 4 to 6 hours. For note analysis, the facilitator and observers summarize the con-

TABLE 16.1 Advantages and Disadvantages of Focus Group Interviews

Advantages	Disadvantages
• Data collection from several participants simultaneously	• Facilitator with expertise in group work is needed
• Synergy of the group	• Recruitment can be difficult
• In-depth discussion	• High "no show" rates (50%–90%)
• No need to have preconceived ideas of responses to craft interview	• Group-think phenomena
	• Participants' disclosure of sensitive information may pose ethical dilemmas
• Participants may be more open in a group setting than a one-to-one interview	• Negative opinions are magnified
	• Data analysis is time consuming
• Costs can be kept low	• Costs
	• Facilitator may have a bias

Taken from the works of: DiIorio, Hockenberry-Eaton, Maibach, & Rivero, 1994; Carey, 1995; Smith, 1995; and Kingry, Tiedje, & Friedman, 1990.

tent of the FGI, a process of 2 to 4 hours. Memory analysis involves the facilitator and observer debriefing the research team immediately following the FGI, which takes about an hour.

Data should be analyzed and summarized, creating clusters or groupings of ideas to identify key themes (Kingry et al., 1990, p. 125). Participants' statements should be listed under appropriate themes. In addition, "verbal communication, nonverbal communication, and observations of behavior" should be analyzed. "Verbatim transcripts, notes, and debriefing summaries provide the decision trail, which is the basis for auditability, confirmability, and credibility." Putting the analysis away for some time and reanalyzing it later may help with data reduction and the identification of "big ideas" for the final analysis (McDaniel & Bach, 1996, p. 57–58).

In my own practice, I have held focus groups in hospitals to obtain consumers' opinions on what should be changed and what should be kept in systems, processes, policies, and facilities in the Maternal-Child Health Care Center. One obstetrics group consisted of seven new mothers who brought their babies. The research group consisted of the clinical director, operational director, and members of the care center's patient satisfaction committee. The research group created the questions, recruited participants, and planned the meeting. An experienced facilitator from the Human Resources Department was selected as the neutral facilitator. The directors attended the FGI as nonparticipant observers, with a noncaregiver member of the research team as a recorder. No caregivers were invited to attend in order to facilitate open discussion in the group. Participants were not asked to sign consents. Since their attendance was voluntary and required returning to the institution, attendance of the participants implied consent.

Initial FGIs were designed to elicit suggestions and directions for process redesign for the patient-focused care initiative. At the beginning of the FGI, participants were told that we were about to redesign the maternity and pediatric services and wanted their input. Two questions were posed: "What do we do that we should change" and "What do we do well that we should keep?" Major themes which were identified included participants' recommendations for an enhanced breastfeeding program, dramatic changes in visiting hours, creation of mother-baby processes, and major facility redesign.

Feedback from the FGI was shared with the interdisciplinary re-engineering team. Utilizing these data, as well as results of telephone patient satisfaction surveys, and patient complaints, major changes were made in the philosophy, policies, processes, programs, and design of the obstetric service. A hospital Breastfeeding Committee, comprising nurses, physicians, lactation consultants, and clinical nurse managers, and a Breastfeeding Mothers Support Group for patients were established, which followed the principles of the Baby Friendly Program. To obtain designation from the World Health Organization as a Baby Friendly Hospital, the gold standard of institutional breastfeeding support, a hospital must meet rigorous standards. Mother-baby primary nursing was introduced to provide continuity of nursing care. Mothers and their newborns were transferred together from Labor and Delivery to the Post-Partum units which were renamed the Mother-Baby units.

Policies surrounding visiting were dramatically changed to create open, family-centered visiting. Previous policies had limited grandparent and sibling visiting to only two hours in the afternoon. Other family and friends were only welcome in the evening for two hours. Husbands were welcome at any time during the day. New policies were predicated on a new definition of family: anyone who is designated by the patient to have a significant role in her/his life. Family visiting was open all day. Primary visitors (spouse, significant others, partners, or anyone designated by each mother) were banded, as was the mother, with the newborn's band and were welcomed at any time, including 24-hour visiting in single rooms. Recommendations were made to families to keep visits short to promote the mother's rest and to limit the number of people in the room at any time for safety.

In Pediatrics, parents focused on the need for amenities, such as a washer and dryer on the unit to wash their clothes, as most never left their child during the period of hospitalization. Some focused on the desire for enhanced colors to decorate the units. All children and parents complained about the lack of child-friendly food. As a result, the pediatric menus were revamped. Children now can order pizza, hot dogs, hamburgers, and sandwiches. Peanut butter is kept as a stock item on all pediatric units. Through foundation support, colorful bedside curtains were added, treatment rooms were decorated by artists creating the illusion of an undersea environment and a fairy land, and washers and dryers were ordered for pediatric floors.

Because these changes were very significant to staff, educational programs, group meetings, and teambuilding workshops were provided to all staff. Following the implementation of these changes, results of the telephone patient satisfaction surveys demonstrated statistically significant increases in patient satisfaction scores. The hospital's Survey Center research staff conducted 125 phone surveys of patients, discharged in the last 4 weeks, per Care Center in a 3-month period. Surveys consisted of 71 questions, 62 on patient care and 9 on patients' health status, in the following domains: nursing care, health status, medical care accommodations, team care, information, food, general evaluation of care, and communication. Validity of the survey was established by a factor analysis and alpha coefficients for internal consistency. Cronbach coefficient alphas ranged from .7 to .8. Items in the nursing care factor domain relate to timely response to requests for assistance, patient education, discharge preparation, and pain management. Reports are sent quarterly to the Care Center's Patient Satisfaction Committee which analyzes the data for trends and patterns and identifies the need for specific interventions.

Prior to changing to a model of patient-focused care, the Maternal-Child Health Care Center had the lowest patient satisfaction scores of the eight Care Centers. Following the implementation of the redesign initiatives, the Maternal-Child Health Care Center consistently rated among the two highest scores. In addition to the reports, evidence of the effectiveness of the changes was seen in the 50% decline in patient complaints. Inversely, letters of compliment, now published in the Care Center's quarterly newsletter, number 40 or more per quarter.

I also have used focus groups in my work with professional nurses in terms of patient/family education. To meet the standards for patient/family education documentation established by the Joint Commission, the committee I chair created a Patient/Family Education form to be incorporated into the patient's medical record. To obtain feedback from the actual users of the form prior to and after its implementation, we utilized focus groups. Staff were able to articulate what they liked about the form as well as what should be revised. Based upon their recommendations, changes were made in the tool that has increased compliance in its use.

Focus groups also were used to evaluate the beta testing of an on-line patient/family education product. Krames, a proprietary company known for printed patient education literature, provided the software for the hospital's intranet site. After a trial period, groups of professionals were asked key questions about the system which they had been able to test. Groups were questioned about the content, format, readability, utility, and ease of use. Recommendations were made to the vendor for incorporation into the final product.

CHALLENGES

A major challenge in the use of the focus group in my work with patient satisfaction was recruitment of participants. A subcommittee retrieved demographic data of recent patients and made numerous phone calls, followed by written invitations and reminder calls 24 hours prior to the meeting. Despite these extensive recruitment efforts, the no-show rate averaged 50%. One focus group, held on a winter evening, had only one participant. The only incentives given to participants were transportation costs and lunch or dinner. Due to the high no-show rate, invitations were extended to 17 participants, hoping to secure eight in the FGI.

Recruitment of participants for staff focus groups posed less of a challenge. Staff were invited by their superiors and were able to participate during work hours. The key was to instill in the managers who would assign staff the need to participate. Most participants were eager to share their feedback on the clinical issues being discussed: patient/family education, on-line services, and documentation. Philosophical support for the use of FGI was strong. The emphasis on shared governance for staff and patient satisfaction made the use of the FGI a natural. The facilitator from the Human Resource Department for the patient-focused group participated as part of the organization's commitment to patient-focused care, without cost to the department. Administrative support, however, was more challenging. The FGI leaders had to rely on their own departmental staff and secretary to support the process. In addition, data analysis, when running several groups, was very time consuming.

Barriers were encountered during the implementation of these major changes. Resistance, particularly from physician staff, was challenging. Obstetricians voiced opposition to the concept of family-centered care and visiting. Approaches to changing the resistance were the creation of a family-centered philosophy and mission, a literature review on family-centered care, a survey of family-centered processes and visiting hours at comparably sized institutions, and a consistent reminder of the feedback of the consumers from the FGI.

RELIABILITY AND VALIDITY

Measuring reliability and validity of an FGI differs, greatly, from other types of qualitative research. The researcher may choose to interview different groups about the same topic; however, each group remains an entity. Carey (1995, p. 489–490) states that each group's "information can be considered as an accurate representation of the perceptions of reality for the group members and, therefore, valid." Groups can take on a life of their own, creating a "synergistic, bandwagon effect similar to 'groupthink.'" Participants will be influenced by the opinions of others. This influence may be decreased by asking participants to come to the FGI with written responses or ideas about the topic, which can be used to guide them with the discussion during the interview. Participants are, thus, more likely to recall and verbalize their own opinions.

In the case of the maternity FGI, participants were told on the phone that they would be asked for feedback about the maternity services, including what should be changed and what should be kept. They were asked to bring written comments, including those of their partners, to refer to during the interview, in an attempt to minimize the groupthink phenomena.

McDaniel and Bach (1996, p. 54) suggest that establishing reliability of an FGI can be done by standardizing for all groups the FGI process, including recruitment, questions, and data analysis. In the case of the patient satisfaction and staff FGIs, identical recruitment procedures, questions, and data analyses were used for all groups within the individual projects.

Validity cannot be measured by traditional methods. Instead, McDaniel and Bach (1996, p. 55) suggest that the FGI process be evaluated based upon "trustworthiness, which is composed of credibility, dependability, confirmability, and transferability." Credibility can be established by asking participants for feedback to confirm the investigator's interpretation of the FGI. Peer debriefing can also be used. In this method "the researcher asks a disinterested peer to question or examine the researcher's interpretations and to probe for possible researcher biases that could influence the interpretation of the data." Dependability can be established by having two investigators review that the FGI process was followed consistently. Confirmability is the ability to audit the process of the FGI. Transferability relates to the ability to generalize results and create implications and conclusions.

For patient satisfaction FGIs, subjects were invited from a convenience sample that reflected a diverse mix of providers and patient residences. To minimize any effect from facilitator bias, a neutral, expert facilitator from the Human Resources Department, was utilized. Staff that interacted directly with or cared for the patients during their hospital stay were not permitted to attend. The Clinical Director and the Operational Directors of the Maternal-Child Health areas were nonparticipant members of the group. At the beginning of the interview they were introduced as observers. They sat at the table, took notes, and did not voice any comments during the FGI. At the conclusion of the interview, they were available to group members who wished to speak to them. This opportunity was utilized to clarify issues.

Focus groups are increasingly used in nursing practice and in health care for data collection in qualitative research, for feedback, to obtain opinions with which to create measurement surveys and change, and for market research. Useful data, however, can only be obtained when the researchers and participants follow the methodology and guidelines for planning and holding the FGI as well as analyzing its data.

As health care systems respond to enormous economic and consumer demands, leaders are challenged to implement more than "black bottom line" change. The visionary leader must design cost-effective changes that improve patient care and outcomes and decrease costs. Nurse executives should utilize the opportunity to plan and participate in focus groups to elicit feedback from their colleagues, their staff, and their clients.

REFERENCES

Bogardus, E. (1926). The group interview. *Journal of Applied Sociology, 10*, 372–382.

Carey, M. (1995). Comment: Concerns in the analysis of focus group data. *Qualitative Health Research, 5*, 487–495.

DiIorio, C., Hockenberry-Eaton, M., Maibach, E., & Rivero, T. (1994). Focus groups: An interview method for nursing research. *Journal of Neuroscience Nursing, 26*(3), 175–180.

Kingry, M., Tiedje, L., & Friedman, L. (1990). Focus groups: A research technique for nursing. *Nursing Research, 39*(2), 124–125.

Krueger, R. (1994). *Focus groups: A practical guide for applied research* (2nd ed.). Newbury Park, CA: Sage Publications.

Merton, R., Fiske, M., & Kendall, P. (1990). *The focused interview: Manual of problems and procedures.* New York: Free Press.

McDaniel, R., & Bach, C. (1996). Focus group research: The question of scientific rigor. *Rehabilitation Nursing Research, 5*(2), 53–59.

Seals, B., Sowell, R., Demi, A., Moneyham, L., Cohen, L., & Guillory, J. (1995). Falling through the cracks: Social service concerns of women infected with HIV. *Qualitative Health Research, 5*, 496–515.

Smith, M. (1995). Ethics in focus groups: A few concerns. *Qualitative Health Research, 5*, 478–486.

Stevens, P. (1996). Focus groups: Collecting aggregate-level data to understand community health phenomena. *Public Health Nursing,* *13*(3), 170–176.

Watts, P., Brockschmidt, B., Sisk, R., Baldwin, K., & McCubbin, J. (1997). Use of focus groups to determine the need for health promotion and wellness education services in rural communities. *Journal of Health Education, 28,* 249–252.

CHAPTER 17

A Self-Efficacy Approach to Nursing Leadership for Shared Governance

Louise S. Jenkins and Nora E. Ladewig

Drawing from social-cognitive theory, Bandura (1977) articulated self-efficacy theory in the mid-1970s from an interactive model of human behavior in which individuals selectively attend to various sources and types of information about their own capabilities (efficacy) with regard to specific behaviors. In self-efficacy theory, the cognitive appraisal that the individual makes of this information creates *efficacy expectation.* This key component of self-efficacy theory is defined as the confidence an individual has in his/her ability to carry out a specific behavior at the current time. In literally hundreds of research reports dealing with diverse behavioral domains ranging from snake phobias to recovery from cardiac events, from career choices to diving board performance, efficacy expectation has consistently been a key, though not sole, predictor of behavior performance. In summary, the higher one's level of confidence in his or her ability to carry out a specific behavior, the more likely the individual is to: (a) choose to perform the behavior; (b) expend effort on the behavior; and (c) persist in performance of the behavior (Allen, 1988; Bandura, 1986; Jenkins, 1988). In this study, self-efficacy theory was used as the theoretical framework to consider aspects of nursing leadership for shared governance in the hospital setting.

Note: Originally published in *Nursing Leadership Forum,* Vol. 2, No. 1, 1996. New York: Springer Publishing Company.

BACKGROUND

The introduction of shared governance as a model for decision making for nursing care issues has placed large numbers of practicing nurses in pivotal leadership roles in their organizations. A shared governance model provides the nursing staff with the opportunity to accept ownership of their work and accountability to make decisions about practice, quality, and education (McMahon, 1992). Because most models of shared governance are implemented with a representative body of nursing staff placed in decision-making groups for a defined period of time (Bernreuter, 1993), leadership skills are a requirement rather than an option. Further, successful application of the staff leadership role is essential for the quality of the process and outcomes of decisions made in the governance groups (Porter-O'Grady, 1992).

Staff members are often reluctant to undertake leadership roles because the degree of risk and the uncertainty of the role sometimes argue against assuming these roles (Bernreuter, 1993; Porter-O'Grady, 1992). In some cases, the environment for nursing practice has not always been supportive of the decision-making authority of the staff nurse. Havens' (1994) data from hospitals across the country reflect that despite a great deal of emphasis in the literature, perceived staff nurse involvement in decision-making is minimal and very unequally shared with administration management. To counteract such ideas, the clinical and organizational leadership must converge if nurses are to establish their roles as critical, influential providers of care (Clifford, 1991).

There is increasing recognition that those furnishing direct patient care hold significant potential for providing leadership (Clifford, 1991; McMahon, 1992). It is also becoming evident that new leadership in nursing, designed to manage uncertainty and diversity, while involving many individuals dispersed throughout systems, must look different from leadership of the past (Dickenson-Hazard, 1994; Porter-O'Grady, 1992; Wilson, 1994).

Preparing staff nurses to step forward and exhibit leadership and decision-making skills has provided a challenge to the implementation of shared governance (Bernreuter, 1993). This is complicated by the difficulties experienced by management personnel when relinquishing control for decision making (McMahon, 1992). Successful strategies to help both groups with managing change and learning new roles are seen as beneficial for the successful implementation of the shared governance model (Jones, 1994).

Kouzes and Posner (1993) point out the key role of self-perceptions in the level of challenge individuals choose to pursue. It follows that those staff nurses feeling confident of their abilities to take on a leadership role in shared governance would be the ones seeking nomination and then election to such roles. Once a nurse is elected, organizations may facilitate the transition of staff nurses into their roles in the decision-making process. Orientation to the expectation of the role as a member of the governance group or as leader is often needed. The ability to apply skills for problem solving and creating new and different solutions requires practice for successful performance (Wilson, 1994). A training program providing the essentials of the leadership role, covering such topics as group process, group dynamics, problem-solving, priority setting, consensus seeking, and agenda writing, is an appropriate way to indicate solid support for the effectiveness of the leader. Lack of preparation for the role and lack of the requisite supports are often the greatest barriers to the success of the staff leadership role (Porter-O'Grady, 1992).

Study Aims

The purpose of this project is to study aspects of leadership in newly elected and continuing leaders in shared governance at a 700-bed community hospital in a midwestern city. Specific research questions identify leadership skills that participants bring to their roles in shared governance and address aspects of leadership in four selected behavioral domains: communication, conducting meetings, leadership style, and professional development. Further, the impact of a structured leadership development session and time on these selected aspects of leadership is examined within the context of a theoretical framework derived from self-efficacy theory.

Theoretical Framework

Implicit in the aims of this project is a focus on identifying, explaining, and predicting behavior in selected domains of leadership behavior. The appropriate theoretical approach guiding this study must be supportive of this focus. Self-efficacy theory provides such support.

Sources of efficacy information can be broadly categorized as: (a) behavior performance—that is, actually carrying out the behavior; (b) vicarious experience (modeling)—seeing someone like the individual carry out a behavior; (c) verbal persuasion—providing cues (whether spoken or written) to the individual about his or her capability to carry out a behavior; and (d) physiologic state—internal cues experienced by the individual, such as fast heart rate (Bandura, 1977, 1986).

In relation to this study, more specific examples of efficacy information can be offered. Behavior performance of a leadership behavior such as developing an agenda for a meeting (behavioral domain of conducting meetings) could be provided either in prior experience that the individual brings, such as doing so for a church group, or in role-playing in which the individual would be guided through the experience; this source involves actually carrying out the behavior personally. Vicarious experience (modeling) could be provided if the individual actually "saw" either personally (e.g., role-playing) or in an audiovisual aid such as a video, a peer (i.e., another elected leader in shared governance) carry out an activity such as interacting with staff having diverse levels of investment in shared governance (an activity in the communications behavioral domain). An example of verbal persuasion would be someone "telling" (either personally or in written or audio form) the individual information about his or her capability to carry out an activity such as bringing a group to consensus (behavioral domain of leadership style). Information from the physiologic arousal source could be in a "flush" or fast heart rate, or other physical cues the individual experiences in relation to carrying out an activity such as accepting criticism with grace (behavioral domain of professional development).

Participants in this study were offered the opportunity to participate in a structured leadership development session. This session forms the quasi-experimental "intervention" for this study. It was anticipated that multiple and diverse sources of efficacy information would be provided in that experience. Although the physiologic state source may have provided efficacy information during this session, it is composed of experiences that are not observable and unique to the individual. Thus, efficacy information from this source could not be documented in this project.

It is important to note two additional points. First, efficacy information can range in impact from positive to negative. Second, previous studies have demonstrated that perceptions of self-efficacy expectation are highly dynamic because the content and sources of efficacy information, as well as cognitive appraisals of efficacy information at different times, vary. Likewise, the impact of various sources of efficacy information varies over behavior as well as over time. What may be a potent source of efficacy information at one point in time may not be at another point; also, sources of efficacy information impact differentially for different behaviors. These findings have implications for measurement in that efficacy assessments must be done at more than one point in time and carefully analyzed by each behavior (Jenkins, 1988).

Research Questions

Research questions posed in this study are as follows. In elected leaders of a shared governance organization:

1. What is the level of efficacy expectation for selected behaviors (communication, conducting meetings, leadership, and professional development) and self-reported behavior performance before, immediately after, and 6 months after, a scheduled voluntary structured leadership development session?
2. To what extent do efficacy expectation and behavior vary over time for each of the selected behaviors?
3. What is the relationship between self-efficacy expectation and behavior performance for each of the selected behaviors at each of the data collection points?
4. What is the impact of a voluntary structured leadership preparation session on self-efficacy expectations and behavior performance of selected behaviors?

To adequately capture the intervention session, an additional question was included regarding the extent to which the sources of behavior performance, modeling, and verbal persuasion were used as sources of efficacy expectation in the voluntary structured leadership development session.

Assumptions and Limitations

Implicit in self-efficacy theory is the assumption that the individual has the capability to carry out behaviors being considered. A further assumption is that study participants will accurately self-report responses to questions posed.

The quasi-experimental design selected to answer the research questions posed does not allow for random assignment of subjects to participation in the structured leadership development session; thus, participants versus nonparticipants were compared on all key variables. Likewise, because random selection of subjects was not feasible, generalizability of findings is limited.

METHODS

Design

A quasi-experimental, repeated measures design was used. The comparison groups for the quasi-experimental portion of the design were formed on the basis of participation in the structured leadership development session.

Instrumentation

Three types of instruments were used in this study: self-efficacy expectation assessments, activity self-reports of behavior performance, and demographic information.

Efficacy Expectation Assessments

For each of the four behaviors considered in this study, a separate scale listing a series of various activities ("items") was developed. The number of items on each scale varies to adequately tap the behavioral domain being considered: communication (17), conducting meetings (16), leadership style (15), and professional development (9). Respondents are asked how confident they are of their ability to perform each of the activities now (presently). The response format is that of a numerical confidence scale anchored by 0 = "not at all" and 10 = "totally". Respondents are instructed to mark the number for each activity that best reflects their confidence in their ability to carry out that activity. For each of the four behaviors, responses for all the activities on the respective scale are summed and then divided by the number of activities on that scale to produce a self-efficacy expectation score for that behavior that reflects the mean level (strength) of confidence in ability to carry out the behavior. These scores, called efficacy expectation scores for each respective behavior, can thus range from 0 to 10.

Activity Self-Reports of Behavior Performance

These four measures list the same activities for each behavior as found on the efficacy expectation assessments; however, the question posed is, to what extent are respondents actually carrying out each activity? The response format is again a numerical confidence scale anchored by 0 = never and 10 = always. If the respondent has not had the opportunity to carry out the behavior (e.g., a council member may rarely, if ever, make out a meeting agenda), there is a column that can be checked to so indicate. These measures are scored in exactly the same manner as the efficacy expectation scales. The resulting scores, called behavior scores, can vary from 0 to 10 and reflect the extent to which respondents report behavior performance in each of the four areas.

Demographic Information

At Time 1, respondents were asked to indicate their role, highest level of education, how long they have been a registered nurse (RN), and whether they have had previous experience in an elected position in any organization(s) other than shared governance. Also, they were asked whether they were newly elected or continuing in their role in shared governance. At Time 2, respondents were asked to indicate whether they attended the structured leadership development session.

Sampling and Data Collection

All newly elected and continuing shared governance leaders ($N =$ 40) received a letter describing the project, the nature of participation, and study materials via interdepartmental mail. Each was assigned an arbitrary subject identification number with the corresponding name known only to the secretary preparing the materials. This number was used for tracking data over time. All 40 potential participants received materials at baseline and at the 1-month period. Only those who returned a completed packet at either of the first two data collection points were sent the packet at the 6-month point. Data were collected from a total of 34 voluntary participants for an 85% participation rate: at baseline ($n = 26$); at 1 month ($n = 24$); and at 6 months ($n = 23$).

Intervention

The intervention used in this study was a voluntary, all-day structured leadership development session. This session was already developed and there was no attempt to influence content or presentation style. Objectives for the session included preparing participants to: (a) describe key elements of the shared governance structure; (b) articulate roles and responsibilities; (c) demonstrate skills of effective meeting facilitation, group process, and decision-making; (d) describe strategies for success in shared governance; (e) discuss the inherent gains of shared governance; and (f) explain communication pathway purpose, function, and accountability. Attendance at all or part of the session formed the comparison groups in this study.

To ascertain the extent to which this intervention provided sources of efficacy information for behaviors of interest in this study, an investigator attended the session and used a checklist to record both the frequency and the type of efficacy information presented for each activity listed on the measures of self-efficacy expectation and behavior.

RESULTS

Subjects

Answers to questions about basic demographic information revealed that the respondent group was composed of RNs who were as follows: 58% were staff RNs; 44% had bachelor's degrees; 44% had been RNs for 5 to 15 years; and 62% reported having previously held an elected position in some type of organization. Half were newly elected and 50% attended all or part of the leadership development session offered just before the 1-month data collection point.

Instrument Reliability and Validity

Internal consistency reliability was estimated using Cronbach's alpha. The values obtained for the self-efficacy expectation scales ranged from .83 to .98. The alpha values obtained for the behavior scales ranged from .90 to .97. Indices of content validity ranged from .75 to 1.00 for the activities (items) included in the scales.

Self-Efficacy Expectation

Mean self-efficacy expectation scores by behavior and time are displayed in Figure 17.1. Repeated measures analyses of variance revealed that although the trend in self-efficacy expectation scores for all behaviors was to increase over time, significant ($p < .01$) increases were found between Time 1 and Time 3 for all four behaviors. Between Times 1 and 2, there were only increases for meetings ($p < .05$) and professional development ($p < .01$). Between Times 2 and 3, there were also significant increases ($p < .01$) for all behaviors except professional development, where the increase was less significant ($p < .05$).

Behavior Performance

A similar trend, though less pronounced, was seen in behavior performance scores for each behavior as in Figure 17.2. The increases between Times 1 and 3 were significant at $p < .01$ for all behaviors. Between Times 1 and 2, significant ($p < .05$) increases were noted

FIGURE 17.1 Self-efficacy expectation.

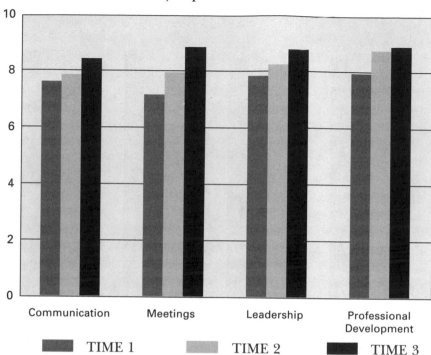

only for leadership style and professional development; between Times 2 and 3, significant increases were noted only for leadership style ($p < .05$) and communication ($p < .01$).

Correlations

With self-efficacy theory, the ability of self-efficacy expectation to explain and predict behavior is always an interesting aspect. As seen in Figure 17.3, at each data collection point, for each behavior, the correlations obtained were *all* significant at $p < .01$. These findings support the tenets of self-efficacy theory and offer evidence for criterion and construct validity of the measures.

Impact of Intervention

There were no significant differences in self-efficacy expectation or behavior performance scores for any behavior at any point in time by whether participants had attended all or part of the intervention.

FIGURE 17.2 Behavior performance.

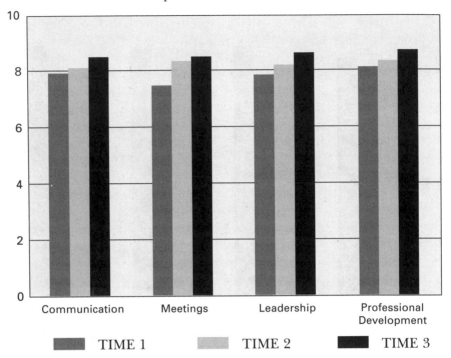

FIGURE 17.3 Self-efficacy expectation and behavior correlations.*

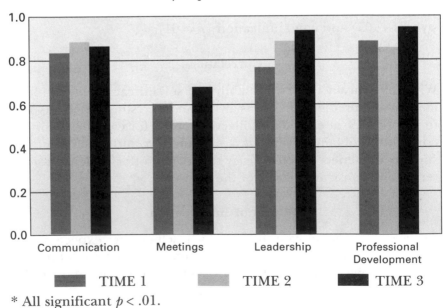

* All significant $p < .01$.

In fact, the only variable by which there were some statistically significant differences was previous leadership experience. At Time 1, those subjects had significantly higher self-efficacy expectation for communication ($t = -2.59$, $p = .016$), and professional development ($t = -2.69$, $p = .13$). No other significant difference in either self-efficacy expectation scores or behavioral performance scores was revealed at this or subsequent data collection points.

Frequency of Use of Scores of Efficacy Information

The frequencies with which various scores of efficacy information were provided by behavior at the intervention session are seen in Figure 17.4. The most frequently used source, in all cases, was verbal persuasion; modeling was used the least. The behaviors for which the most sources of efficacy information was documented were leadership style ($n = 30$), then conducting meetings ($n = 29$), communication ($n = 24$), and professional development ($n = 18$). Of the 100 instances of use of a source of self-efficacy information, 72% were in the form of verbal persuasion.

FIGURE 17.4 Leadership self-efficacy sources.

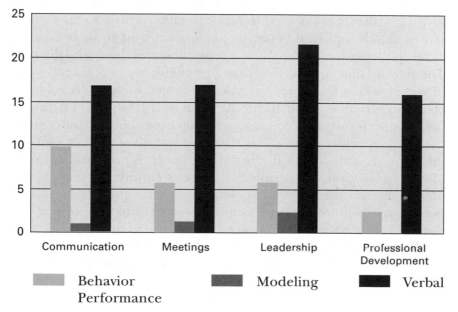

DISCUSSION

In discussing the results of this project, it is critical to keep in mind that the leadership development session used as the intervention was traditional in teaching style and the content was predetermined. Because we did not influence content or teaching method, a self-efficacy approach was not used. Rather, the shared governance leaders included what they thought would be most helpful to participants. Indeed, we were told that evaluations of the offering and its helpfulness were quite positive.

In applying self-efficacy theory to this intervention, we learned that, not surprisingly, the "traditional" methods used provided few sources of efficacy information to the participants. Using verbal persuasion (the most frequently observed source) employs what we know from study of other behaviors to be typically the least potent source of efficacy information. The use of behavior performance, typically the most potent source of efficacy information, was limited for all behaviors (24% of sources of efficacy information documented), especially professional development. The rare use of modeling is striking (only 4% of sources of efficacy information documented) and overlooks teaching strategies, such as role-playing, that could be employed even more easily than the enactive mastery of behavior performance.

Given the absence of self-efficacy basis in the intervention, it is not surprising that there is no difference in either efficacy expectation scores or self-reported behavior performance of study behaviors between those who attended the intervention and those who did not. The finding that some differences in self-efficacy expectation were observed at baseline based on whether subjects had previous leadership experience points to the strength of the impact of previous behavior performance. Previous leadership experience provides enactive mastery, which typically is the most potent source of efficacy information. Indeed, this finding also supports Kouzes and Posner's (1993) contention that people with greater confidence seek particular challenges. Previous leadership experience provided enactive mastery as a source of efficacy information; if this experience was positive, it may have even reinforced confidence in the ability to carry out leadership behaviors.

Self-efficacy expectation and behavior performance scores increased over time, with the greatest increases noted from the beginning to the end of the study. This finding is expected because, over time, these shared governance leaders had the opportunity to perform, indeed "practice," study behaviors. Wilson (1994) points to the need for allowing this opportunity as well as encouraging such activities in the hospital setting.

When comparing the trajectories of self-efficacy expectation and behavior performance, there is a surprising finding in that these trajectories are highly similar with nearly comparable scores at each of the data collection points. In self-efficacy research, increases in self-efficacy expectation are usually sharper over time and precede increases in behavior performance (Foster et al., 1995). One reason for the different pattern found in this study may be that subjects did not have a great deal of choice as to whether they were going to carry out the leadership behaviors. The need was there, so the decision was made to carry out the various behaviors; although we did not quantify the amount of effort put into the behavior performance, this element could have been influenced.

The statistically significant correlations between self-efficacy expectation and self-reported behavior performance at all three data collection points provide dramatic evidence of the predictive ability of self-efficacy expectation. It is interesting to note that this ability held even in behaviors having the fewest sources of efficacy information provided during the intervention. One explanation for this could be that even though some sources of efficacy intervention were used during the intervention, they were delivered at one time point in a study spanning a 7-month period from Time 1 to Time 3. Individuals experience many sources of efficacy information; it is those they choose to pay attention to and how they organize the information provided that count (Bandura, 1977, 1986).

The results of this study have led to several changes in the shared governance operations at the hospital where it was conducted. When nurses are expected to perform in new or different roles than those that they previously held, opportunities to learn their new roles are provided in different settings and practice is encouraged.

For example, as preparations were underway for educating staff nurses to assume leadership positions on peer review panels for clinical advancement, the use of modeling via videotape was instituted to assist these nurses with learning to communicate difficult panel decisions to peer applicants. This process uses the vicarious experience source of efficacy information as nurses see nurse colleagues carry out the behaviors involved in communicating difficult decisions as well as the immediate consequences of doing so. In another example the shared governance organization bylaws were changed to provide incoming council chairs with a 6-month training period before they assumed the leadership role of chair of a council; this provided much needed "practice" opportunities. In addition, the nominations committee of the shared governance organization now actively seeks candidates from among those nurses who have served in unit leadership positions or in leadership positions for other organizations or groups. Both of these strategies draw on the potent information source of the individual actually carrying out the behavior (enactive mastery). The value of role preparation through practice of relevant leadership behaviors has made an impact on learning leadership skills for shared governance organizational positions.

In this study, the basic tenets of self-efficacy theory were supported; the ability of self-efficacy expectations to predict behavior was clearly demonstrated for all four of the leadership behaviors studied. The findings suggest the potency of previous enactive mastery and vicarious experience in modeling by others as "practice" for leadership behaviors. We recommend drawing on these sources of efficacy information in developing strategies supportive of leadership development of RNs for shared governance in hospital settings.

REFERENCES

Allen, J. K. (1988). Self-efficacy in health behavior research and practice. *Cardiovascular Nursing, 24*(6), 37–38.

Bandura, A. (1977). *Social learning theory.* Englewood Cliffs, NJ: Prentice-Hall.

Bandura, A. (1986). *Social foundations of thought and action.* Englewood Cliffs, NJ: Prentice-Hall.

Bernreuter, M. (1993). The other side of shared governance. *Journal of Nursing Administration, 23*(10), 12–14.

Clifford, J. J. (1991). The practicing nurse as leader. *MCN, 16*(1), 8–20.

Dickenson-Hazard, N. (1994). On beginnings and leadership. *Reflections, 20*(1), 2.

Foster, C., Oldridge, N. B., Dion, W., Forsyth, G., Grevenow, P., Hansen, M., Laughlin, J., Plichta, C., Rabas, S., Sharkey, R. E., & Schmidt, D. H. (1995). Time course of recovery during cardiac rehabilitation. *Journal of Cardiopulmonary Rehabilitation, 15,* 209–215.

Havens, D. S. (1994). Is governance being shared? *Journal of Nursing Administration, 24*(6), 59–64.

Jenkins, L. S. (1988). Self-efficacy theory: Overview and measurement of key components. *Cardiovascular Nursing, 24*(6), 36.

Jones, P. K. (1994). Developing a collaborative professional role for the staff nurse in a shared governance model. *Holistic Nursing Practice, 8*(3), 32–37.

Kouzes, J. M., & Posner, B. Z. (1993). *Credibility: How leaders gain and lose it, why people demand it.* San Francisco: Jossey-Bass.

McMahon, J. M. (1992). Shared governance: The leadership challenge. *Nursing Administration Quarterly, 17*(1), 55–59.

Porter-O'Grady, T. (1992). *Implementing shared governance.* St. Louis, MO: Mosby Year Book.

Wilson, C. K. (1994). The new business paradigm: Demands for nursing leadership. *Aspen's Advisor for Nurse Executives, 9*(8), 3–6.

We acknowledge, with appreciation, the contributions of the volunteer participants J. Fleege and C. Lageson for assistance with data management/analysis, the support of the Nursing Research Center and St. Luke's Medical Center, and J. Gaynor for assistance in manuscript preparation.

CHAPTER 18

Nursing Empowerment Through Computers: A Personal Saga

Karen DuBois

As a new clinical nursing instructor for neurology and psychiatry, I was searching for innovative teaching strategies to replace what seemed to me outdated ones. My teaching peers, who had participated in creating self-learning modules with Dorothy Del Bueno at a time when this concept was new, were still applying these strategies. I suspected, however, that there had been many new developments since that time. These teaching modules were literally kept in sweater boxes and consisted of videotapes and paper pre- and post-tests for use during staff orientation and for continuing education. As a computer literate person, I realized the underutilization of computer technology in the nursing department at this large medical center.

When you do not have your own computer you learn to use whatever system is available to you and so it was with me. I was in a department of nurse clinicians surrounded by computer terminals networked into a user-unfriendly word processing system. I learned to use the system for convenience sake and found its limitations could be overcome by people who had prior computer knowledge. My own experience with Macintosh and IBM word processing systems had given me the necessary foundation. Other members of the department were unfamiliar with computer technology and easily frustrated by

Note: Originally published in *Nursing Leadership Forum*, Vol. 1, No. 2, 1995. New York: Springer Publishing Company.

the system. They needed to be exposed to computer technology another way if they were to view it favorably.

The in-house system, used primarily for administrative functions, was rapidly losing favor, even with its few advocates, because a bigger and better network existed in the hospital clinical areas. That network was an Integrated Academic Information Management System (IAIMS). It was not connected to the network used by nursing administration, which puzzled me. Nurses used it to access lab data and MEDLINE. I knew MEDLINE was connected to the medical center campus library and this led me to the media center in the medical center library. Previously I had always used the microcomputer lab in the media center for word processing on Macintosh and IBM.

The media center can be an exciting place for someone searching for innovative teaching techniques. That is where I met the CAI (computer assisted instruction) guru of our institution who exposed me to CAI programs. CAI programs allow the learner to absorb information, then respond to questions or scenarios generated by the computer program. He showed me a laser disc with a fluorescent brain that twirled, peeled, sliced, moved forward and back in sequence or freeze frame. The laser disc is similar to a videotape and is played in a laser disc player similar to a videotape player. Using digital technology the laser disc could be moved instantly to any point on the disc. I was amazed and full of ideas for how this technology might replace slide lectures. Then we viewed an interactive videodisc program. The computer terminal functioned as a television screen with short film clips of a patient in a medical setting. Text and questions for a self-study program flashed across the screen, and I could access a glossary at any time to clarify terms. My mind was spinning with ideas of how I could update the sweater boxes developed by my colleagues.

Bursting to share this news with my peers, I ran back to the director of my department. She supported me and agreed to use our 2-hour staff meeting time to demonstrate CAI technology to the clinical instructor group. I felt certain everyone would be as excited as I was with this new discovery. I coordinated a demonstration in the computer classroom of the media center. Chills ran down my spine as we sat in this room full of computers watching a demonstration of all the multimedia teaching tools available in health care education. I envisioned computer simulations of clinical experiences enabling our nurses to acquire and demonstrate knowledge in a realistic and sophisticated manner.

To my surprise the reaction of the nursing education group was mixed. Those who had graduated recently or were actively in school had some knowledge of computer technology. Their responses were enthusiastic. Other clinical instructors were guarded, hesitant, or negative concerning what they had just seen. My knowledge of computers helped me maintain objectivity regarding their reactions.

The technology was changing so quickly that many people fell behind. I felt obligated to bring these instructors up to date. To start, I backed up, and coordinated a second more basic class so that the instructors could learn how to use the library and its computers to find the very information they needed to stay current in their nursing specialty areas. This had to be done in a nonthreatening manner that recognized the faculty as a group of accomplished individuals with valuable clinical skills.

As the "new kid on the block" it was obvious that I was not the proper teacher. The personnel in the library, however, were pleased to conduct this class. Nevertheless, it was not long before instructors and others began to come to me and share their experiences and feelings about computer use. They realized that I knew more than they did and that computers could make their work easier even if they were not sure how. My role developed into that of a role model, leader, and facilitator with computers even though I was only a few steps ahead of them. I continued to educate myself by using the CAI programs myself and trying them out with the nursing staff and orientees. In addition I attended classes to further refine my existing knowledge base.

On Nurse Recognition Day 1992, my career in computers received official recognition. I was acknowledged as a computer expert by the Vice President of Nursing at the medical center and was asked to meet with her that week. I was overcome with anxiety and fear. Anyone who had ever met with the Vice President of Nursing had returned with assignments that kept them working for months. In addition I could not believe that out of over 1,000 nurses in this institution I could possibly be the most computer-literate. What would become of me? What about my work with the staff nurses and my orientees? When would I have time to continue learning about these wonderful CAI programs and the equipment used with them?

I wore my best suit to the meeting with the Vice President. I went to the top floor of the administrative building. I still felt inadequate. I had begged the director of my department to find someone else, but there was no turning back. I saw my daily life flash before my eyes and then I met the Vice President of Nursing. I couldn't believe it. She was nice. She gave me no assignment except to attend and support her in meetings that were related to nurses' use of computers. I do not remember exactly what was said because my anxiety blotted out details, but her suggestions sounded exciting!

The first relevant meeting was with the Director of Clinical Information Systems of the medical center. I listened very carefully to everything said and watched my nursing leader for cues when to interject. While she personally did not know a lot about the technology, she understood that it was the future for nursing. She wanted her staff to be a part of it, she had a vision. This conceptual thinking was new to me in a practice setting, but I could see it working. Frontline, firsthand organizational politics and I was in a supporting role . . . WOW!

Networking became a vital part of my existence. It was my duty to keep the Vice President of Nursing aware of all information I could find beginning with the IAIMS that already existed in this medical center. Why didn't nursing have full access to this system I asked the Vice President? Why didn't they have an access code like the physicians had? Why didn't they have access to other applications like electronic mail? Information of this sort gave the Vice President of Nursing an advantage in the computer power game, which she played successfully to empower the entire Division of Nursing.

My assignments grew and I worked hard, caught up in the vision of the Vice President. Because I was focused on the quest for computer access to the IAIMS, my original intention of teaching the Vice President to use the computer was lost. Then I realized that this was not her role. She did not need to be the computer expert; she had given me that assignment. She was depending on me to provide her with the right information so that she could strategically make decisions about computer technology to guide her staff into the future.

I was learning how power could be gained from information management. After reading everything the Director of Clinical Information Systems would give me, I started to get the concept. This man had received a grant to build one of the biggest computer networks in use in a teaching hospital setting.

Remember my role as a clinical instructor? Don't think I was excused from those duties to pursue this new interest, even though it took up most of my time. Like any good nurse, I exercised creative use of time. Among other things I kept educating the instructor group about CAI, ordering programs for preview and assigning individual instructors to view them in the media center. They then gave me feedback about how they could use such programs to replace those instructional programs in sweater boxes. Meanwhile, I used the new CAI programs to teach the orientees and staff as part of my own experimentation with this new technology.

My career took the next major turn when a leader in nursing informatics came to visit our medical center as a consultant. When she mentioned CAI, I managed to give her an account of my progress. In the subsequent conversation, it became clear that we needed to expand our use of the technology in the hospital setting as well as to communicate with more people within and outside our institution concerning its use.

The Vice President decided it was time to educate all nurses to the present IAIMS. This was a seemingly impossible task because we had an informatics department of two people, a nurse and a programmer. Once again I turned to the media center for support. One of the two people in our informatics department learned to use a liquid display panel (that projects computer screens up on the wall for display purposes). Within 2 months all staff nurses had an access code for the IAIMS that was connected with the Clinical Information System. Of course the leadership group had to be taught in a nonthreatening manner before their staff could be educated, nor could they be made to feel embarrassed about their lack of knowledge. As with the instructors earlier, this group received special classes in the media center computer lab, taught by the library personnel.

Then one day, as I was walking into the library, my beeper sounded. It was the Vice President's secretary asking from which airport I would be flying. WHAT? I was to accompany the Vice President and the Director of Clinical Information Systems to the National Institutes of Health (NIH) for a demonstration of the NIH bedside system. This had gone so far so fast! What about the nursing staff and my orientees? What did I know about bedside computer systems? WHY ME?

Preparing for my trip to Washington, D.C., I decided to optimize the opportunity presented by the travel. I made an appointment to meet with the Director of Nursing Information Systems at a Veterans Administration (VA) hospital in Maryland before the NIH meeting. I was going on a fact-finding mission, still slightly fearful that I was playing out of my league. Rain was pouring down as the car, about to overheat, conveyed me to the VA hospital. I tried to maintain a cool and confident professional attitude. Yet as I walked into the hospital it was with the same feeling I'd had when I first met the Vice President of Nursing. The VA representative, I thought, would think she was wasting her time with me. Not so. She was a perfect hostess and pleased to demonstrate her system.

After 4 hours of intense one-to-one education about Clinical Information Systems and how they interface with IAIMS, I had the concepts. Everything I had learned earlier fell into place. In addition to the technology, the VA representative shared with me her vision of nursing and the role technology played in it. She told me about her own experiences and let me get some hands-on time with a bedside charting system she had reprogrammed to suit her institution's needs. I was spellbound by her intelligence and modesty. To this day I try to emulate the attitude she has about computers and nursing—that computerization is not in competition with nursing but comprises the discipline's movement into a future where all knowledge can and should be shared.

When I arrived at the NIH, I felt an inner peace about my role in the computer knowledge quest. I was able to view the NIH systems critically and ask questions that I could not have imagined 24 hours earlier. Yet my new level of understanding regarding computer systems made this fact-finding adventure frustrating. My mind raced with questions about how data were transferred and accessed technologically. How should nurses utilize the power of this technology? I was reassured by the Director of Clinical Information Systems that understanding the concept was a critical first step.

My primary interest was still CAI. While we were at the NIH, I also visited the Lister Hill Computer Learning Center where I saw the latest advances in CAI technology. Having gone to school in Washington, I was familiar with the National Library of Medicine but had not been there in years. I quickly lost my nostalgia when I walked into this new part of the library and saw an oasis of CAI hardware and software. It was like being turned loose in a room of toys. I stayed there playing until they closed that evening and politely kicked me out with an armful of reading materials.

The Vice President of Nursing was well on her way to grasping the potential of computer use in health care. Once we were back in our own institution, she took immediate action and hired a Director of Nursing Research/Director of Nursing Information Systems. The Vice President recognized the magnitude of the computer network in this medical center and that it could be a pilot for all futuristic health care settings.

I continued to share my interest in CAI with the Vice President of Nursing, who supported my attendance at an interactive video conference in Washington, D.C., that following week. I listened intently to every word said at the conference and on the last day met with my soon-to-be mentor is this area of educational technology. By now I had my own vision of networking CAI programs on the IAIMS network already at my disposal. It was at this conference that I negotiated my first site license to pilot CAI materials on the network.

At this point it was clear to me that health care would be continuously adapting to the technological changes in information systems. To be an influential part of this change process, I would need a leadership position from which to continuously educate peers about the ongoing technological growth. Coincidentally a leadership opportunity availed itself to me at a state facility next door to the medical center. Knowing that this state facility would soon be connected to the IAIMS network at my present place of employment, I decided to take a chance and accept the position of Director of Nursing Education.

I did not want to stop my work with the Vice President of Nursing because it would have been a job half finished. I explained my plight to the Vice President, who took a chance and retained my services with grant money. When I met the other people employed by the grant I was astonished. They were nursing leaders whom I had only read about and there they were advising me about the direction of technology and my role with it. They too had visions of nursing for the future.

I have now developed my own CAI programs. In addition, with the help of the CAI expert at the media center, I developed a teaching strategy for use with clinical instructors and faculty professors to encourage use of CAI in their teachings. Finally I revisited the Lister

Hill Computer Learning Center at the National Library of Medicine as a facilitator for an invitational workshop offered to nursing leaders in hospital and college education in the United States. The purpose of this series of workshops is to disseminate knowledge throughout the nursing profession about the use of computers in education and health care.

My enthusiasm and self-education about computers and CAI technology have enhanced my nursing career. With the recognition and support of nursing leaders, some strategic planning, and a lot of hard work, I believe I have become a change agent for nursing in education technology. This experience has given me influence in my profession and a talent usable wherever my career takes me.

CHAPTER 19

Funding for Nursing Excellence: The Endowment for Nursing . . . A Capital Idea

Gertrude Rodgers, Barbara Callaghan, and Susan Brusilow

While many hospitals encourage learning through tuition reimbursement for continuing education, they may suffer from a major void in providing opportunities for advanced learning and practice. The Fund for Nursing Excellence at Fairfax Hospital in northern Virginia was gestated and born of rising aspirations and inspirations for excellence in practice, research, and patient care among the hospital's nurses. The focus on excellence is in keeping with the hospital's ambience. Fairfax Hospital, barely 30 years old, has achieved continuous commendation for medical care and community service. High on the list of America's 100 best medical centers, it enjoys a "magnet hospital" designation, attracting the best and the brightest care deliverers and health practitioners. Essential to the hospital's qualifications is the renown of its nursing practice.

The increasing acuity of patient illness and the critical demands of clinical technologies notwithstanding, nurses today crave and covet continuing education to perfect skills and practice. Fairfax Hospital, a "learning" organization, offers an established Clinical Ladder

Note: Originally published in *Nursing Leadership Forum*, Vol. 2, No. 3, 1996. New York: Springer Publishing Company.

Program[1] and is guided by a unique Nursing Practice Congress.[2] Nursing excellence is a key phrase heard throughout the hospital.

The Fund for Nursing Excellence at Fairfax Hospital is a permanent endowment uniquely conceived and supported by Fairfax Hospital nurses. It is a tax-exempt entity, organized by nurses from all clinical services and is directed in its operations by a 19-member steering committee. The goal of the Fund is to achieve a one-million-dollar endowment. While other existing charitable endowments and permanent funds support critical hospital needs, none touches the entire health and science community as does The Fund for Nursing Excellence.

The Fund for Nursing Excellence was created by nurses, for nurses, and is supported by nurses. The initial idea was conceived by the Chief Nurse Executive for External Affairs, Gertrude Rodgers, in 1993.

Gertrude Rodgers and Susan Brusilow, the Assistant Administrator of Development at Fairfax Hospital, composed and proposed the formal endowment agreement now in existence between the Fund and the Hospital's Foundation. Once the official step was completed, it was time to gather other key nursing leaders for their endorsement. In this endowment agreement the basic agreements include what the Fund was to support and how the decisions would be made to distribute monies. This formal endowment agreement was signed in March of 1993, signaling that the Fund for Nursing Excellence was now a fund-raising priority for the institution.

THE INSTITUTIONAL BACKGROUND

Inova Health System (formerly Fairfax Hospital Association) became involved in its first capital campaign in its history in 1992.

As Inova began its first capital campaign (an intensive 3- to 5-year fund-raising drive), it recognized the benefits of soliciting all constituencies for gifts. Included among those many constituencies were physicians, executive staff, and the senior management team. Soliciting these groups became part of the strategic plan to raise specific designated dollar amounts from each group.

Philanthropy was new to the senior managers and required some thought on their part. They learned to think as philanthropists would think. How can this institution best use my gift? What should I support? Will it be well spent by the hospital? What do I expect in return, if anything? These are not easy questions with which to grapple. It requires not only leadership but a vision of how one individual or group can make a remarkable difference within an institution.

Among the group of senior administrators present for Inova's start-up was Gertrude Rodgers. It was from this initial presentation that she was inspired to launch The Fund for Nursing Excellence at Fairfax Hospital.

THE VISION

From this inspiration a concrete vision of the Fund began to take form. The Fund would provide an opportunity to raise needed dollars. It would gather a like group of people together in a cause. It would advance nursing to the next level of achievement. It would provide an endowment that would last in perpetuity. It would serve as a national model for nurses to advance entrepreneurial thought.

HISTORY

The first planning meeting took place in November 1993, and Ms. Rodgers provided an overview of the concept of The Fund for Nursing Excellence. An executive committee of nurse leaders discussed the desired structure and operation of the Fund. By the end of the meeting, the executive committee members were ready with recommendations. First, a steering committee would need to be designed. This committee would eventually replace the executive committee and be responsible for overseeing the fundraising portion of the Fund. To be a member of the steering committee required making a gift to the Fund. An advisory committee would set criteria and have oversight as to the use of the funds. Both committees would need leadership from the staff nurse membership. Other representation would be added later, such as medical staff and community constituents. To educate the executive committee members a literature review was completed on models of nursing fundraising initiatives. Although overall information in the literature was scant, two models assisted us in designing our own Fund for Nursing Excellence: The Center for the Advancement of Nursing Practice at Boston's Beth Israel Hospital and the Center for Nursing Innovation at Houston's St.

Figure 19.1 The Fund for Nursing Excellence at Fairfax Hospital

---

The purpose of the fund is to provide unique opportunities for nurses at Fairfax Hospital. The fund will support initiatives that promote excellence in patient care, professional practice, education, and research.

Goals:
1. Capitalize on a rich clinical learning environment to advance clinical practice.
2. Provide support and consultation to developing clinicians to assist them in patient care delivery issues.
3. Assist staff with professional growth and development.
4. Continue to investigate ways to provide experienced Nurse Clinicians III and above with opportunities for recognition of their contributions.
5. Promote the development of knowledge through both practice and research.
6. Provide support for nurse managers which will also provide support for staff.
7. Provide a mechanism for interdisciplinary forums to support projects and research development.
8. Build stronger consultative and collaborative relationships with our colleagues in nursing academia.

Luke's Episcopal Hospital Friends of Nursing Program.

The purpose and goal of the Fund were established in writing (Figure 19.1). The composition and responsibilities of the executive and steering committee were also defined (Figure 19.2). Gertrude Rodgers and co-chairman Barbara Callaghan, Patient Care Administrator, Oncology, Medicine and Surgery Services, provided additional leadership to move this fund forward. The committee began to identify staff nurses for the steering committee. All understood the importance of a staff-driven initiative. The executive committee would be disbanded once the steering committee was formed and functioning.

In January 1994, the executive committee received its first lesson in fundraising. Characteristics needed in a fundraising committee, the structure of gift-giving levels and the potential funds to be raised based on the structure were reviewed with the group. Much discussion ensued around the gift-giving levels. Of particular interest was the development of a certain "look" for the Fund. A pledge card and letterhead were designed. A formal letter requesting participation on the steering committee was composed and sent to selected staff members. A variety of fundraising strategies were visited.

GOAL-SETTING EXERCISE

Setting a dollar goal was an interesting challenge. During one of the first committee meetings, the group engaged in a goal-setting exercise by outlining the number of nurses at each job classification level. The level of jobs at Fairfax Hospital included Associate Administrator, Patient Care Administrator, Patient Care Director, Assistant Patient Care Director, Staff Nurse, Clinical Educator and Clinical Nurse Specialist. For a comprehensive look at what might be achieved, each of these groups was listed with the number of employees in those positions. A frank discussion took place concerning how much each of these groups might give, projected from an average base salary.

After much debate, the steering committee asked each nurse for 5% over the next five years or 1% of base salary each year. The group felt that this amount could be expected across the board at all levels.

Table 19.1 shows the exercise described above. We hoped to raise a total of $933,000; however, we estimated that realistically only one of four nurses solicited would make a gift, so we divided our total dollars by one quarter, leaving expected returns at $233,520. Keep in mind these gifts were projected to come from the nurses only. There were numerous additional avenues for support that would also be pursued.

TIMETABLE OF ACTIVITIES

In order to establish a goal, the committee needed a timetable and list of activities necessary to build momentum for this effort. The timetable included the following:

1. Kickoff Event

In October of 1994, Fairfax Hospital and Inova Health System officially launched The Fund for Nursing Excellence at an invitation-

FIGURE 19.2 The Fund for Nursing Excellence at Fairfax
Hospital Steering Committee

---

*The Fund for Nursing Excellence at Fairfax Hospital Committee will consist
of two co-chairmen and the steering committee. The responsibilities of this volunteer group are to:*

1. Provide oversight of the project.
2. Help formulate strategies to promote The Fund for Nursing
   Excellence.
3. Establish relationships with potential Fairfax Hospital donors
   and recruit their help and assistance with the goal.
4. Make introductory contacts, either through letters, phone calls,
   or personal meetings.
5. Participate in direct solicitation efforts with potential donors.
6. Assist the co-chairs in the formulation of the advisory committee, whose function will be to determine the appropriate
   use of the funds.
7. Make one's own gift to this project.

*A volunteer organization of broad scope and substantial depth will be essen-
tial to ensure the success of The Fund for Nursing Excellence. The responsibility of these volunteers at every level will be:*

1. To articulate clearly the specific goals and objectives of The
   Fund for Nursing Excellence.
2. To set an example in personal giving.
3. To cultivate prospects and solicit their support for the campaign.

---

only dinner. This event was hosted by the President of Inova Health
System, the Administrator of Fairfax Hospital (a nurse herself), and
the medical staff leadership. It was vital to the momentum of this initiative that the Fund be recognized by the institution as an important part of its future. Its importance was twofold: (1) to provide
monies to promote nursing, and (2) to emphasize the importance
of the nursing community in the future of our health care system.

2. Special Events: Play at the Reston Town Playhouse

Special events can be successful fundraising tools. One of the committee members was involved in a local community playhouse and was

able to have the proceeds of one evening's ticket sales donated. This event increased the visibility of the Fund to the general community.

3. Potential Major Donors Taken on Tour of Hospital

Each committee member was asked to compile a list of potential prospects including former patients who might be grateful for the care they have received at our hospital.

Once identified, these individuals were invited to tour Fairfax Hospital as the first stage in a 12-month cultivation process. Through this cultivation process, the members of the steering committee hoped to receive not only financial support, but involvement from the community. The long-term goal of the Fund was to have an extensive group of lay leaders from the community joining the nurses in raising money for this endowment.

4. Presentation to Fairfax Administration for Gala '95

The largest public event held by Inova Health System is its annual black tie dinner dance known as the Fairfax Hospital and Inova Health System Foundation Gala. Through a rigorous selection process, programs in the hospital may submit a request to become a beneficiary for the gala.

In 1995, The Fund for Nursing Excellence competed with seven other prominent programs at the hospital. Representatives from each program made a 10-minute presentation to the decision-making committee (made up of the Chairman of the Board of the Inova Health System Foundation, The Gala Committee Chairmen, the President of the Medical Staff, the Medical Director of the hospital and the Administrator of Fairfax Hospital). The Fund for Nursing Excellence was selected by vote. In 1995, the Gala raised $300,000 for the Fund.

5. Presentation to Fairfax Hospital Auxiliary

Another source of philanthropic funds is the Fairfax Hospital Auxiliary, comprised of persons who provide essential volunteer support to the hospital, as well as revenue from our gift shops, thrift shops, and aux-

TABLE 19.1 The Fund for Nursing Excellence at Fairfax Hospital Exercise One—Possible Solicitations

# of Employees	Title	Ask Amount	Average Salary	Average Gift	Dollars Raised
3	AA	10%			
9	PCA	5%	$70,000	$3,500	$31,500
40	PCD	2.5%	$62,000	$3,100	$124,000
65	APCD	2.5%	$50,000	$1,250	$81,250
12	Educator	5%	$55,000	$2,750	$33,000
12	Clinical Specialist	5%	$55,000	$2,750	$33,000
11	AD	5%	$55,000	$2,750	$30,250
1200	Staff Nurses	$500		$500	$600,000
			TOTAL DOLLARS POSSIBLE : $933,000		

Historically only 1/4 of these people will give gifts. $933,000 divided by 4 = $233,250

TABLE 19.1 (*continued*) Exercise Two—Possible Solicitation Results

# of Employees	Title	Ask Amount	Average Salary	Average Gift	X 5 Years	Per Pay Period	Dollars Raised
9	PCA	1%	$70,000	$700	$3,500	$26.92	$31,500
40	PCD	1%	$62,000	$620	$3,100	$23.85	$124,000
65	APCD	1%	$50,000	$500	$2,500	$19.23	$81,250
12	Educator	1%	$55,000	$550	$2,750	$21.15	$33,000
12	Clinical Specialist	1%	$55,000	$550	$2,750	$21.15	$33,000
11	AD	1%	$55,000	$550	$2,750	$21.15	$30,250
1200	Staff Nurses	1%	$40,000	$400	$2,000	$15.38	$2,400,000
						TOTAL:	$2,733,000

Historically only 1/4 of these people will give gifts. $2,733,000 divided by 4 = $683,250.

iliary special events. Once a year the Fairfax Hospital auxiliary votes on supporting hospital programs. The Administrator of Fairfax Hospital makes a formal presentation of needs to the Auxiliary Board asking for special dollar amounts that are needed. In 1996 The Fund for Nursing Excellence at Fairfax Hospital received $100,000.

6. Establishment of a Communications Subcommittee

A tremendous amount of work, outreach, and fundraising has occurred since the kickoff event in October of 1994. In order to keep the momentum going the committee decided to establish subcommittees, the first of which was the communications subcommittee. We felt that communications would be key to the continued success of all activities.

FINALIZATION OF GOAL

As a result of these comprehensive activities, The Fund for Nursing Excellence established a two-part goal. Phase 1 launched an initiative to raise $500,000 by December 1995. This goal was achieved. Phase 2, begun in January of 1996, aimed to raise an additional $500,000 bringing the total endowment goal to $1,000,000.

The Fund, established in perpetuity, recognizes that excellence in nursing arises out of daily practice and is quickened by personal achievement. The Fund has a unique premise. Though not eschewing private and corporate donors, it is conceived as an endowment largely relying on efforts and contributions by nurses themselves. Contributions from past, present, and future nurses will be the bedrock platform upon which the Fund will grow. We hope that the Fund will be enlarged by donations from other caregivers and patients and families served by the hospital. The opportunity for research and advanced clinical study by nurses will rebound to the entire community in improved health and prolonged lives.

Why an endowment for nursing excellence? Why not? Why indeed not?

NOTES

1. Clinical professional advancement program for nurses with levels I–V.
2. Staff Nurse clinical decision-making body for Nursing Practice.

CHAPTER 20

Nominating a Colleague for a Recognition Award

Theresa Stephany

Qualities that comprise leadership have long been of interest to nurses, and there is surely no dearth of literature on this topic. In an article, however, when Manfredi (1995) listed ". . . leaders create climates" among the five roles for a leader, I was struck by the simplicity of the statement. I realized that the nurse managers I have most respected did just that: fostered *climates* that promoted excellence. Despite confusing and difficult economic times, these managers made nurses feel supported and valuable, and they were openly proud of their staff.

Unlike actors, accustomed to applause, standing ovations, and curtain calls for their performances, nurses find that their best work usually goes unnoticed. Few patients, if indeed any, say, "Gee Nurse, you did a great job of maintaining sterile technique while accessing that port," or, "Your astute observations prevented my wound infection from escalating into a systemic sepsis." Often, only another nurse knows when a colleague has made a particularly important contribution. Every nurse, regardless of title or formal education, can assume a leadership role: "create a climate" by nominating a colleague for a recognition award. The following guidelines demystify the process:

1. List potential nominees by identifying *local nurses* that you admire. Who is the "angel of mercy" at your workplace? Who

Note: Originally published in *Nursing Leadership Forum,* Vol. 1, No. 4, 1995. New York: Springer Publishing Company.

would you want caring for your loved one? Who did you look up to when you were new on your unit or at your agency?

2. Who are your *professional heroes/heroines*? What author, researcher, or educator has most influenced you? Who wrote that great article that you saved for years and still reread? If you remembered the article after so many years, chances are others did, too, with good reason.

3. Become familiar with existing recognition awards. Calls for nominations usually appear in national nursing journals or local chapter newsletters. If an award sounds right for your colleague, telephone or write for an official nomination packet. Note the deadline for submission, and send the completed package, by certified mail, well before the deadline.

4. Carefully review the written criteria for the award. Awards committees spend a great deal of time articulating exactly which activities/qualities they wish to honor. When composing the narrative or writing a letter of support, be sure to clearly address *each* criterion.

5. Write from the heart. Relate your colleague's accomplishments in your own words, as though you were speaking to members of the awards committee face to face. Clear, simple sentences are best.

6. Show concrete examples of the nominee's work. If she or he has developed a patient education pamphlet, written a memorable article, or delivered a particularly stirring speech, enclose a copy. Let the awards committee see for itself why the nominee is worthy of this honor.

7. Secure letters of support from as broad a geographic area as the award itself. For example, if the award is given by the local chapter of a specialty organization, request letters of support from local sources. If the award is a statewide award, letters of support should come from different regions of the state. If the award is national in scope (American Nurses' Association, National League for Nursing, etc.), request letters from supporters who live across the country (East, South, West, and Midwest).

8. Request letters of support from a broad-based, multidisciplinary population. This is particularly important if the award is at the state or national level. For example, if the nominee worked in government relations, ask for a letter from the legislator with

whom she or he worked, as well as from an agency that bene-
fitted from the nominee's work.

9. Request letters of support *only* from people who know the nominee well and who will write with genuine enthusiasm about his
or her work. Awards committees are not fooled by lukewarm
responses from "big names" who are simply "paying off a debt"
by adding their signature to a letter.

10. Ask the nominee for an updated copy of his or her curriculum
vitae, and say why you need it. Nominators must list basic information correctly on the nomination forms, and even if your
nominee is not selected to receive the award, she or he will be
honored that you remembered his or her work.

11. If your nominee is not selected to receive an award this time,
resubmit his or her name for the same award next year. Do not
give up. Important work deserves to be recognized, and, eventually, justice *will* prevail.

Without a doubt, nominating a colleague for a recognition award
requires extra time and work for the nominator. It may require a
financial outlay for long-distance phone calls and postage; however,
learning that your nominee was chosen to receive the award is almost
as thrilling as receiving an award yourself. Most importantly, whether
or not your nominee was selected, you will be acting as a leader by
creating a climate that supports and rewards nursing excellence, and
you will be encouraging others to do the same.

REFERENCE

Manfredi, C. (1995). The art of legendary leadership: Lessons for
new and aspiring leaders. *Nursing Leadership Forum, 1,* 62–64.

CHAPTER 21

Cost Control Heroism: Strategies to Reduce Operating Expenses

Cynthia Caroselli

Confronted with an estimated $949.4 billion spent on health care in 1994 (Pear, 1996), and with an estimate exceeding $1.616 trillion for the year 2000 ("News notes," 1992), health care administrators search desperately for ways to contain health care costs and expenditures. While hospital-specific price inflation shows some signs of slowing (Pear, 1996), it has risen generally faster than prices in the general economy (Ashby & Lisk, 1992). Given the gravity of this situation, health care organizations exert tremendous effort to move from the "cost unconscious" mindset of the past (Enthoven, 1988) to a fierce struggle for cost containment with increasingly scarce resources (Campbell & Dowd, 1993). Recently, cost containment efforts in business and health care have shifted from downsizing personnel to savings accrued from better managed supplies (Deutsch, 1996). This study details strategies available to nurse managers (NM) to achieve budgetary savings without eliminating positions.

GENERAL STATE OF KNOWLEDGE

Nursing is the largest and most labor intensive component of hospitals (Dison, 1992), representing over 50% of hospitals' operating

Note: Originally published in *Nursing Leadership Forum*, Vol. 3, No. 1, 1998. New York: Springer Publishing Company.

budget (Davis, 1995), with NMs controlling the largest share of resources (Finkler & Kovner, 1993). Much of the discretionary spending occurs at the unit level, where nurses are the largest users of supplies, equipment, and linen (Barnum & Kerfoot, 1995) and thus carry a large role in financial decision making (Huber, 1996).

This is not an inconsiderable expense, since supplies are the second highest expense in the hospital budget (Marquis & Huston, 1996). For instance, the average nursing unit budget is approximately $5 million dollars (Judith A. Farley, July 2, 1996, personal communication), with salaries comprising $2 million or close to half of the budget. Supplies account for approximately $1.5 million dollars. Thus, it can be interpolated that a 10% savings in supplies could result in budget savings of $15,000 on each unit. If a hospital has 10 in-patient units, this could represent a total institutional savings of over $1.5 million. This is not unrealistic since it has been demonstrated that attention to supply use can have significant effects as seen in one study which documented a savings of $1.6 million through a cost awareness program related to the use of supplies and linen (Jeska, 1992).

Nurses thus have unique knowledge to influence the cost of health care (Manss, 1993). Ironically, nurses often have no way of knowing what costs they generate at the time they deliver care and may lack the economic awareness necessary to make cost-conscious decisions (Huber, 1996). Slightly more than half of NMs are found to be in control of their units' budget (Hodges & Poteet, 1991). With the exception of one recently completed study (Caroselli, 1996), no empirical research has looked at the NM's role in unit budgeting in conjunction with such variables as staff nurse economic awareness, and nurse consumption of supplies, equipment, and linen.

Caroselli's (1996) study of staff nurse ($n = 68$) economic awareness and NM budgetary control surveyed four in-patient units with comparable case mix in two urban teaching hospitals. Those surveyed answered correctly only slightly more than half of the questions related to health care economic awareness, which did not vary with age, gender, experience, marital status, or educational level. While two NMs were provided with regular variance reports, a third was given only rudimentary data on a request basis, a fourth was provided with no data at all, and none had any means to monitor costs related to linen use.

Raising cost consciousness may be a budget neutral intervention to decrease costs without a change in direct care activities. Nurse managers are frequently admonished to cut operating costs; while they may succeed, empirical information is lacking as to how nurses can decrease unit expenses by changing their use of supplies, equipment, and linen.

METHODOLOGY

The methodology for this study was a focus group study of NMs. Focus group methodology is particularly appropriate as a confirmatory tool for anecdotally known information, allows the participants to provide readily usable information, and is useful in generating research hypotheses that can be tested in larger scale research (Pedhazur & Schmelkin, 1991).

Recruitment of Participants

Convenience sampling is the most common means of obtaining participants for focus group studies; most groups are composed of six to twelve participants (Stewart & Shamdasani, 1990). Thus, two groups of approximately seven NMs each were recruited from the researcher's personal contacts in New York City urban hospitals.

Developing the Interview Guide

In developing a list of questions to be used in data gathering, the funnel approach was used (more general to specific) and eight main questions (listed below) were formulated so that data of sufficient depth was generated in a short time span (Stewart & Shamdasani, 1990). Participants were also asked to complete a short demographic data inventory.

1. What kind of pressure do you experience to reduce your costs related to the use of supplies, equipment, and linen?
2. How often do you experience it and in what form?
3. What are your "big ticket" items, e.g., high-cost, and/or high-volume supplies?
4. What kind of cost utilization data are you given about these items?

5. How have you encouraged staff to decrease expenditures?
6. Share an anecdote that describes how you were able to decrease operational expenses related to supplies, equipment, and linen.
7. What kind of problems does linen utilization present for you?
8. What resources are available to you as you try to reduce unit operating costs?

Conducting the Focus Group

The session was tape-recorded for later transcription. Confidentiality was assured by requesting that participants not refer to each other by name during the meeting. In keeping with standard procedure for the protection of human subjects, participants were informed of their right to review tapes and to request that all or any portion of the tape be destroyed.

DESCRIPTION OF THE SAMPLE

Table 21.1 describes the sample, which was composed of 13 practicing first-line managers of in-patient acute care units. All practiced in urban teaching hospitals, were female with a mean age of 40 years, averaged over 15 years nursing experience, with nine years management experience, and had been employed on their units for 7 years. The majority were single, had received their basic nursing education in a BSN program, held an MSN as their highest degree, and were certified in a clinical practice area. They generally held the title of head nurse or nurse manager. They estimated that they spent 25% to 50% of their time on cost management, and had acquired knowledge about cost-cutting strategies primarily from coursework or journals and books. They perceived that while their staff were very concerned about cost-cutting strategies, they were only somewhat knowledgeable about this topic.

FINDINGS

Pressures for Cost Containment

The NM has experienced tremendous pressure to "do more with less." Many of the NMs who participated in this study noted that budget admonitions had become standard at leadership meetings,

TABLE 21.1 Description of the Sample ($N = 13$)

	Mean	Range
Age	40.3 years	29–55 years
Professional Experience (years)	15.6	7–33
Management Experience (years)	8.53	1.5–16
Current Position (years)	6.57	1–16.5

Variable	Category	Frequency	Percent
Basic	Diploma	2	15.4
Nursing	AS	1	7.7
Education	BS	6	46.1
	MS	4	30.7
Highest	BS-Nursing	3	23.0
Degree	BS-Other	1	7.7
Held	MS-Nursing	8	61.5
	MS-Other	1	7.7
Certification*	None	4	30.7
	Clinical Practice	7	53.8
	Nursing Administration	4	30.7
Current	Head Nurse	7	53.8
Position	Nurse Manager	4	30.7
Title	Nursing Care Coordinator	2	15.3
Means of	Formal coursework	8	61.5
Acquiring	CE courses	6	46.0
Knowledge Re:	Journals/books	8	61.5
Cost Cutting*	Colleagues	10	77.0
	No response	2	15.4
Percentage of	10–20%	1	7.7
Your Time Spent	20–25%	3	23.0
on Cost	25–50%	7	54.0
Management	> 50%	2	15.4
Staff Nurse	Very concerned	6	46.1
Concern Re:	Somewhat concerned	7	54.0
Cost Cutting			
Strategies			
Staff Knowledge	Very informed	2	15.4
Re: Health Care	Somewhat informed	11	85.0
Economics			

often centering on the use of one particular product such as disposable underpads or butterfly needles, or indicating that budgets must be cut by a specified percentage. As one NM stated, "I've had nightmares about how much money I'm supposed to cut from my budget, and I don't know how I'm going to pull this off. But I have to find a way to make it happen."

Recent layoffs in an organization can act as a powerful motivator for practicing more cost effectively. Some managers seized this opportunity as a "teachable moment" and stepped up their efforts at involving staff in cost-effectiveness strategies.

Organizational Resources/Assistance in Cost Reduction

While many NMs could name various pressures, most could not list actual means of assistance to accomplish budget-related goals. Virtually all participants mentioned the frustration they experienced when a nonclinical department issued cost-cutting directives. For instance, one NM said, "The finance department says I have to cut a certain amount from my budget and they have no clue what it takes to provide care." Another manager said, "With a decreased length of stay and increased acuity, the supply is much more intense and I don't think they ever changed the budgets to reflect that."

Perhaps the most distressing sentiment was expressed by NMs who did not have budgetary control and received little or no budgetary information. As one NM said, "You're told you're accountable, but you don't really have control. It's hard to tell staff to economize if you don't know how much money you're actually spending."

Of those NMs who were able to name resources for cost cutting, NM's mentioned more experienced colleagues who provided information about alternative product choices, and product vendors who exchanged market research data collected by staff for free product trials.

Successful Cost Reduction Strategies

Figure 21.1 lists items used in high volume or of high cost. Figure 21.2 lists strategies employed by NMs to reduce consumption of supplies and equipment. One participant reported a savings of over $7,000 in one year, simply by switching product brands.

FIGURE 21.1 High-volume supplies.

• underpads/ diapers	• urine collection bags
• angio-caths/ butterfly needles	• incentive spirometers
• blood collection tubes	• hemoccult developer
• pens/pencils/ progress note forms	• disposable probe covers

Many NMs cited the importance of scrutinizing monthly expenditure reports to discover inaccuracies; unfortunately, this often necessitated a great expenditure of time with support personnel. Other participants described success in reexamining common practices, such as the manager of an out-patient clinic who discovered that she could maintain infection control standards and yet lower costs by eliminating much of the expensive and unnecessary "red bag" trash handling. Another participant reduced the unit's telephone bill by querying staff about specific phone calls, especially long distance and directory assistance calls and applying sanctions for inappropriate telephone use.

Issues Related to Organizational Redesign

Many hospitals are currently in the throes of restructuring roles and processes, which has cost and consumption implications that in many cases were unforeseen. For instance, the RN is expected to play an increasing role in the fiscal health of the organization as this research clearly demonstrates. This research also demonstrates the great effort that nursing administrators must expend to raise the cost consciousness of the staff nurse who is well educated. This issue becomes much more complex when one attempts cost containment strategies with unlicensed assistive personnel (UAP) who may be less educated.

With the upgrading of the traditional nursing assistant role, many tasks and procedures formerly performed by RNs are now carried out by UAPs, such as sterile dressing changes and suctioning, as well as traditional UAP tasks such as patient hygiene and ambulation. These tasks require disposable supplies and equipment, much of which was among the high-volume supplies mentioned by the NMs participating in this study. As one NM stated, "If I want to cut my use of dressing supplies, I really have to talk to the nursing assistants, who may have no idea about health care budgets." Managers emphasized to UAPs the need to limit the supplies brought into a patient's room, since supplies left in the patient's room on discharge will be discarded even though they are unused.

Those who are closest to a task can bring a unique perspective to cost-saving initiatives. For instance, one NM reported significant gains in her nonchargeable supply budget by following the suggestion of the phlebotomy technicians who felt that ordering sleeves of unsterile 4 x 4s would be appropriate in most cases rather than using individually wrapped sterile pads.

Another issue related to redesign is increased supply consumption when staff learn an unfamiliar procedure. It is known that teaching

FIGURE 21.2 Strategies for reducing supply use.

- eliminate product use, e.g., disposable diapers
- substitute unsterile for sterile/disposable for nondisposable
- limit vendors
- institute product evaluation committees
- comparison shop for lower prices for items of comparable quality
- share supply order
- uncouple items from packaged kits
- establish and reevaluate par levels
- consolidate and hide supplies
- monitor ordering patterns
- limit IV attempts by inexperienced personnel
- produce newsletter on cost data
- limit supplies brought to the bedside
- eliminate stashing of supplies, e.g., linen

hospitals generally have higher costs than nonteaching facilities (Halpern, Bettes, & Greenstein, 1994), perhaps related to the large number of staff in various training capacities. With role redesign, many staff members will become "learners" and thus should anticipate an increase in supplies and equipment. For example, while many hospitals have eliminated IV teams as unnecessarily duplicative of services that could be provided by staff nurses, IV nurses consume fewer supplies and require fewer attempts at needle insertion (Robertson, 1995). Resident physicians are often responsible for IV insertion when IV nurses are not available. A number of NMs participating in this study noted that since residents can increase a unit's consumption of IV supplies, managers often limit residents' attempts at insertion.

All NMs in the study noted that issues related to the personnel budget have a tremendous effect on supply use. As one participant stated, "The hospital made cuts in the dietary department, so now we have nurses passing trays. So the nurses can't get their medications passed or their treatments done on time, so how is length of stay affected? And how cost-effective can they be when they don't have time to think about conserving supplies?"

As hospital mergers and acquisitions become a common phenomenon, some hospitals outsource services rather than performing these services internally. Some experts predict a 15-fold increase in outsourcing (Solovy, 1996). While outsourcing may achieve cost savings, the NMs in this study reported that it also brought problems related to product usage. For instance, in hospitals that provide linen services for other institutions, NMs reported difficulty in receiving their full allotment of linen because the hospital was more responsive to "customer" hospitals.

Many NMs noted that this era of restructuring and cost cutting is also a time of great experimentation and some projects will fail. One participant described a role redesign in which an elevator operator was assigned to other duties, yet subsequently reassigned to his former position when it was discovered that patients were not arriving on time for physical therapy. Similarly, another participant described a failed experiment designed to reduce expenses by substituting a bag of saline for individual IV "flush" bottles which resulted in cross contamination and an increased infection rate.

Effects of Managed Care

With the increased penetration of managed care, the average LOS in acute care hospitals has plummeted, resulting in a rise in acuity in nonhospital settings, such as home care. Patients and families now learn procedures that were formerly carried out by RNs. This has had an effect on the hospital in ways that may not have been previously appreciated. On one unit, patients were discharged with peripherally inserted central catheters. Because these lines require meticulous maintenance, family members needed to learn sterile dressing changes. As the number of patients increased, and as the in-patient LOS for these patients continued to decrease, more supplies were used on the unit because family members need practice to refine line maintenance skills. Thus, savings achieved by a decreased LOS were offset by the use of more dressing supplies and decreased staff time.

Sacred Cow

Hospitals and nursing have long been characterized as "sacred cows," made up of the practices and perspectives which, over time, have become part of the organizational culture, or "the way we do things around here" (Caroselli, 1993). One example is linen hoarding. Staff find it difficult to obtain additional linen if needed between deliveries so that hiding linen is a necessity to prepare for unexpected needs. Managers reported that while it assists staff to address patient needs over a weekend, hoarding had implications for the organization as a whole. For instance, hoarding removed a portion of the institutional linen stock from circulation so that some areas of the hospital were unable to receive par levels. Over time, this resulted in a chronic shortage of linen. Strategies used to modify this behavior included "linen rounds" in which staff were asked to clean out patient areas of unused linen. One manager related an incident in which staff discovered enough extra linen to virtually restock the linen cart. Other managers successfully avoided a daily linen change if possible; prevented patient theft of linen (a significant problem at one institution); and conducted linen counts on a regular basis.

There may be a generational dividing line in the use of disposable supplies. While nurses in their 20s have grown up both personally and professionally with an abundance of disposable products, nurses who are in their 40s and 50s will recall widespread use of reusable equipment. Managers reported that they were able to achieve significant cost savings by converting from disposable supplies to those that could be reused, such as the use of reusable cloth underpads instead of disposable chux. Switching to a reusable product, however, required a tremendous amount of staff re-education, especially among younger nurses. More mature nurses may be a valuable resource in decreasing the use of nondisposable supplies and equipment.

The Rise of Entrepreneurialism in Nurse Managers

Pervasive throughout all of the NMs' comments was a sense of entrepreneurialism about their units, which extended to coalitions within hospitals. For instance, some NMs experienced frustration over inappropriate ordering by a purchasing administrator who consistently ignored the managers' suggestions for ordering standard items. When NM frustration reached a peak, these managers transported unnecessary items in a group to the administrator's office, who quickly modified his ordering patterns.

The majority of the participating NMs indicated that they placed great importance on patient satisfaction, not only as an ideal for patient care, but also as a powerful mechanism for insuring cooperation from departments such as laundry services. For example, NMs who had difficulty obtaining blankets despite multiple requests correlated blanket shortages with subsequent patient complaint letters. As one NM said, "It's great to say . . . that patient complaint letter is related to the time I had to call six people over the space of two hours about this."

Some NMs found themselves performing tasks more appropriate to security staff such as inspecting patient suitcases to prevent theft of linen. One NM estimated that her hospital lost 10,000 blankets yearly, since many patients discharged after delivery returned for the baby's newborn clinic visit with the baby wrapped in a hospital-owned blanket.

Relationships with Physicians

While it has been documented that nurses are the major users of supplies and equipment on typical medical-surgical units, little is known

about the role of physicians in supply consumption. All of the NMs
in the study noted that physicians, especially residents, were responsible for large undocumented supply use, "poaching" from one unit
or hospital for use in another, and supply slippage due to inexpe-
rience in performing procedures such as IV insertion. Nurse managers described residents filling shopping bags with supplies, moving
from bedside to bedside, without charging any patient for supplies.
Several NMs expressed frustration over what they saw as subsidiza-
tion of a neighboring hospital: "That hospital never has any supplies
so the residents stock up on our units and go next door with our
stuff!"

Many managers felt strongly that residents were extremely uninformed about the pressing need for cost containment. Further, NMs
expressed frustration with repeated attempts at changing residents'
behavior and felt that unless residents were compelled to address
cost-effectiveness, perhaps by the chief resident, it was unlikely that
this behavior would change.

A number of managers noted that they attempted to mold residents' supply use behavior by rationing equipment. For example,
one manager indicated that she charged out three angio-caths to
each resident at the beginning of the rotation and told them to return
when they needed more. Many managers indicated that they deliberately hid supplies from residents.

Systems Issues Related to Cost Containment

Several systems issues emerged from this study which had less to do
with specific product use than with the organizations in which the
managers worked. Many managers noted the difficulty in monitoring supply delivery when supply carts are delivered to units during
the night when mangers are not available to verify all orders. Similarly,
most managers noted that the employee who delivers the supply
order to the unit is not one consistent staff member, so that errors
are not picked up as they might be if the same individual serviced
the unit regularly. A number of NMs indicated that they regularly
scrutinized budget reports and reported inaccuracies to the appropriate personnel—which sometimes took 6 months to correct.
Subsequently, budget decisions may be made on inaccurate data.

CONCLUSIONS

This study has revealed a number of significant and successful ventures for cost-effective practice. Given the large amount of time that managers devote to these activities, less time is available for addressing clinical issues. Because cost containment will continue to be an important issue in health care, organizations should consider how these efforts can be facilitated by providing support to first-line managers to manage supply and equipment costs more effectively.

REFERENCES

Ashby, J. L. & Lisk, C. K. (1992). Why do hospital costs continue to increase? *Health Affairs, 11*(2), 132–147.

Barnum, B. S., & Kerfoot, K. M. (1995). *The nurse as executive* (4th ed.). Gaithersburg, MD: Aspen.

Campbell, J. M., & Dowd, T. T. (1993). Capturing scarce resources: Documentation and communication. *Nursing Economics, 11*(2), 103–106.

Caroselli, C. (1993). Assessment of organizational culture: A tool for professional success. *Orthopaedic Nursing, 11*(3), 57–63.

Caroselli, C. (1996). Economics awareness of nurses: Relationship to budgetary control. *Nursing Economics, 14*(5), 292–298.

Davis, B. (1995). Effective utilization of a scarce resource: RN's. *Nursing Management, 25*(2), 78–80.

Deutsch, C. H. (1996, November 6). Taking penny-pinching to the next level. *The New York Times*, pp. D1–D4.

Dison, C. C. (1992). An action plan for nurse executives. In M. E. Cowart & W. J. Serow, (Eds.), *Nurses in the workplace* (pp. 219–234). Newbury Park, CA: Sage Publications.

Enthoven, A. C. (1988). Managed competition: An agenda for action. *Health Affairs, 7*(3), 25–47.

Finkler, S. A., & Kovner, C. T. (1993). *Financial management for nurse managers and executives*. Philadelphia: W.B. Saunders.

Halpern, N., Bettes, L., & Greenstein, R. (1994). Federal and nationwide intensive care units and health care costs. *Critical Care Medicine, 24*(12), 2001–2007.

Hodges, L. C., & Poteet, G. W. (1991). Financial responsibility and budget decision making. *Journal of Nursing Administration, 21*(10), 30–33.

Huber, D. (1996). *Leadership and nursing care management.* Philadelphia: W.B. Saunders.

Jeska, S. (1992). Consultation, education, and quality improvement: Secrets to effective cost management. *Nursing Economics, 10,* 365–368.

Manss, V. C. (1993). Influencing the rising costs of health care. *Nursing Economics, 11*(2), 83–86.

Marquis, B. L. & Huston, C. J. (1996). *Leadership roles and management functions in nursing: Theory and application* (2nd ed.). Philadelphia: Lippincott.

News notes. (1992). *Fortune, 125*(6), 46–50, 54–58.

Pear, R. (1996, May 28). Health costs are growing more slowly, report says. *The New York Times,* pp. A13.

Pedhazur, E. J., & Schmelkin, L. P. (1991). *Measurement, design, and analysis.* Hilldale, NJ: Lawrence Erlbaum Assoc., Pub.

Robertson, K. M. (1995). The role of the I.V. specialist in health care reform. *Journal of Intravenous Nursing, 18*(3), 130–144.

Solovy, A. (1996). No, you do it. *Hospitals & Health Networks, 70*(20), 40–46.

Stewart, D. W., & Shamdasani, P. N. (1990). *Focus group: Theory and practice.* Newbury Park: Sage Publications.

PART IV

Coping With Changing Institutions

Organizational Understanding: Understanding the Practice of Expert Nurse Executives

Constance E. Young, Cynthia Peden-McAlpine, and Rosemarie Kovac

The research literature on the thought processes behind decision-making has generally assumed that reasoning is a linear process devoid of context. In general, the body of literature on executive decision-making states that objective facts are organized in a complex process, rules are applied, and a judgment is made; however, the literature on decision-making of nurse executives is limited. Theories relative to administrative decision-making in the business and nursing literature propose that a logical, deductive, and organized process for decision-making be taught and practiced (Bass, 1960; Gronn, 1983; Henry, 1992; Morris, 1988).

A rift between theory and practice is identified by authors who describe a nonlogical and mystical process of "intuition" used by executives in their practice (Barnard, 1964; Mintzberg, Raisinghani, & Theoret, 1976; Nagelkerk, 1988; Rawnsley & Evans, 1992; Simon, 1987). Simply, some executives do not always follow a deductive process. Indeed these executives cannot reconstruct the format they used in making decisions. These intuitive processes remain largely unconscious and little is known about them.

Note: Originally published in *Nursing Leadership Forum*, Vol. 1, No. 4, 1995. New York: Springer Publishing Company.

This chapter reports the initial findings of a study of the thought processes of expert nurse executives within the actual contexts in which decisions were made.

RELEVANT LITERATURE

The limited number of studies dealing directly with the thought processes behind executive decision-making can be categorized in two research realms: strategic decision-making and intuitive decision-making.

Strategic Decision-Making

Strategic decision-making has been described as a process of linear thinking that can be broken down into general rules. Mintzberg and colleagues (1976), in studying organizational decision-making by persons involved in making strategic decisions, used structured interviews and document review resulting in data that were analyzed into 25 strategic decisions. Flow charts to describe the processes used for making the decisions were then developed.

These findings describe general phases of the decision-making process as: (a) identification, (b) development, and (c) selection. The *identification* phase describes recognition and diagnosis of the problem. The *development* phase identifies two types of solutions: those that are commonplace and those that are more creative and need design. The *selection* phase describes the evaluation of alternative solutions. This study concluded that there is not a simple sequential relationship between the phases of the process.

Nagelkerk (1988) studied the unstructured strategic decisions used by nurse administrators for allocation of resources. Semistructured interviews were conducted with six nurse administrators and transcribed verbatim. Verbal protocol analysis categorized the decision-making process according to Mintzberg's three phases. The findings identify phases as a fluid process of problem recognition over time as a consequence of multiple stimuli. The developmental phase describes a number of types of search activities used by all administrators. The selection phase was consistent with Mintzberg's selection phase. Nagelkerk also identified an additional fourth phase of decision-making termed "implementation," incorporating activities that occur after a choice has been made. She postulates that implementation activities progress in a circular pattern by returning to different phases of decision-making for clarification or modification of the problem decision. Categorizing the phases of decisions, although focused on the outcome of each phase, nonetheless illustrates the creative, nonlinear character of decision-making.

Intuitive Decision-Making

The "intuitive" decision-making characteristics of executives were described by Barnard (1964), who referred to "nonlogical processes" used for decision-making in situations of uncertainty. These "nonlogical processes" involved assessing the total situation that is relevant to the specific organization as a whole. The process of decision-making was said to be an art rather than a science, recognized rather than described, and known by its effects rather than by its analysis. The sense of the whole (in terms of the effectiveness and the efficiency of organizational action and in light of the ultimate purposes of the organization) was the dominating basis for decision. Barnard believed that decisions were interactional and made as a reflection of organizational behavior. These processes, however, were not easily verbalized by the executive. This perspective cogently reflects an important component of current thinking.

Agor (1989) conducted a descriptive study of the intuitive abilities of executives using an intuition scale. He reported that the executives scoring in the top 10% on the intuition scale used information derived from facts and from their years of experience to guide their most important decisions. The executives in this study specified situations and settings in which they found their intuition to be most helpful in making management decisions. These situations are described as those: with a high level of uncertainty, with no previous precedent, and where the variables were not predictable. Additionally, these situations were noted to contain: few facts to provide guidance, limited time for decision-making, and several good alternatives from which to choose. The study also reports that executives at the top of the hierarchy use intuition more frequently than others when making decisions, and that women are more intuitive than men.

Dreyfus (1981) studied the practice of expert managers and found that their intuitive processes fit the Dreyfus Model of Skill Acquisition.

The Dreyfus Model of Skill Acquisition is based on the premise that experience and situational context are key factors in developing expertise. As individuals mature and gain skill in their management roles, they advance through five explicit stages: novice, advanced beginner, competent, proficient, and expert. Each decision-making situation presents the individual with an opportunity to build on earlier knowledge and previously implemented solutions. As the practice becomes more refined, managers advance from the novice stage (where facts and common situational features are recognized and rules are applied for judgment) to the expert stage (where the practitioner responds with rapid, fluid behavior in which past experiences are actively associated with current situations, allowing the managers to anticipate outcomes and act appropriately). With this growth in intuitive response patterns, the decision-maker exhibits an ability to achieve a deep, unconscious involvement with the environment, thereby appearing to respond to problems/dilemmas without having to formally process each situation. In reality, the expert manager has acquired a vast mental portfolio of past experiences, successes, and failures that now inform most of his/her decisions. Deliberation, when employed by expert managers, is characterized as a reflection of one's experiences and raising of issues that these prior experiences deemed important. This activity allows the expert manager to intuitively identify and experiment with options for unusual situations.

Donald Schon (1983) also studied the practice of experienced managers and writes of two competing views of knowledge. He contends that technical rationality is the dominant mode of decision-making used by practicing professionals. This view assumes that professional practitioners solve problems by selecting those technical means best suited to the particular purpose at hand, but the problems that professionals must solve are not presented in stable, determinate forms where the means and ends are known. Schon contends that the manager is more than a technician who follows prescribed formulas to solve problems; he is a craftsman whose practice uses principles and methods derived from management science combined with intuitive judgment and skill. Because practical problems are often unique and unstable, thereby escaping the categories of applied sciences, technical problem-solving is inadequate. Schon's research demonstrated that management decisions involve an artistic process consisting of two activities: "knowing-in-action," a tacit or unconscious process that is carried out in expected or predictable situations, and "reflection-in-action," a process that is stimulated by surprise when a familiar scenario is not resolvable by calling upon past experiences. In such instances, the manager must reflect on personal knowledge, reexamine the features of the phenomenon and how the problem is framed, and review the criteria for making a judgment.

Schon's research demonstrated that, if the performer maintains an open perspective in dealing with the situation while deepening the commitment made to a given frame, the chances of arriving at a deeper and broader coherence of artifact and idea are increased. The performer's ability to do this is dependent on bringing the following constants to the indeterminate situation: (a) an overarching theory, (b) an appreciation system, and (c) an involved stance to inquiry (i.e., reflection-in-action), which for some practitioners becomes an ethic of inquiry.

METHODOLOGY

Hermeneutic methodology developed by Eberhart and Pieper (1994) was used for data analysis in this study. Interpretation of text or text-analogue is a method of inquiry that strives to "understand" or to comprehend meaning of the written word. The interpretive method is derived from the philosophical notion of hermeneutics. Hermeneutics (meaning interpretation) is an ancient Greek word translated as "the process of bringing understanding through language" (Palmer, 1969). Contemporary hermeneutics is an attempt to make clear, or make sense of, a text or text-analogue that, in one way or another is unclear (Taylor, 1971). The hermeneutic methodology is based on the relationships between human experience, goal-directed and intentional human action, and narrative expression. Specifically, this hermeneutic method is focused on the interpretation of the meaning of the actions of the nurse executives fixed in the narrative text.

The methodology designed for the interpretation of action in the text is based on the work of Ricoeur (1977, 1979, 1984, 1985, 1988a, 1988b, 1991), Schon (1983), and Polkinghorne (1983, 1988). These works address a common philosophical perspective on human action which purports that action, informed by meaning, can be captured in text and interpreted to facilitate an understanding of the activity of human experience. The first part of the hermeneutic strategy is designed to reveal the subplots or common elements constituting each plot (the relationship among the elements representing the meaning of the activity) noted in the text. The second part of the interpretive strategy identifies the interrelationship of the subplots and events to portray the sequence of action known as the plot line and thus reflect the activity constitutive of the realm of meaning.

Ten expert female nurse executives participated over time in the study. A purposeful sample was solicited through nomination based on prescribed criteria of expert practice including at least 5 years of practice in a position equivalent to executive vice president of nursing/patient care services. Other criteria for nomination included demonstration of the qualities of transformational leadership (including recognition of the values and needs of others, the ability to communicate effectively and establish reciprocal relationships), and a perception by other nurse executives of success in the leadership role.

Two executives were nominated by a nurse executive/educator/ author with recognized expertise in transformational leadership. Eight other participants were then nominated by asking participants to nominate others with like backgrounds who exemplified the criteria noted above. Multiple interviews were conducted with the participants over time.

The methodology consisted of six phases. In the first phase, each participant was asked to give a narrative account of her executive practice. Participants prepared for the interview by reflecting on situations where there was a clear beginning, middle, and end that exemplified their practice. They were asked to include in the narrative any thoughts and feelings they had regarding the situation and what it meant to them. Each unstructured interview lasted between 2 and 3 hours and was transcribed verbatim into a text for analysis. Identifying information was removed from the transcripts and they were numerically coded for confidentiality.

Phases 2 through 5 comprised the analysis to interpret the actions in the narrative and thus the common plot and subplots. This process revealed the meaning behind the practice of the nurse executives. Phase 2 involved reading the text of all the interviews to get an initial total perspective on the meaning of the text and the overarching plot. Meaning was facilitated through an initial intuition of the plot, focusing on the sequence of actions over time, and a preliminary idea as to the significance of the actions (Eberhart & Pieper, 1994).

Phase 3 involved reading and reflecting on parts of the text to reconstruct, in detail, the sequence of actions over time representing the thoughts of the participants during the experience. This expanded the initial understanding gleaned during Phase 2 to understanding of the experiences from the point of view of each participant.

Phase 4 continued with reading individual narratives to locate parts of the text that provoked thinking and raised questions. These readings led to an understanding of the meaning of the action to the participants. This phase lead to the identification of subplots common to the overall plot (Eberhart & Pieper, 1994).

Phase 5 involved interpretation of the refined meanings of the subplots in relation to each other, and reconstruction of the narrative account of an experience over time. Looking at the interactions of subplots over time revealed the agent's motives and the meaning of the activity of the experience (Eberhart & Pieper, 1994).

Phase 6 concerns the validity of the interpretation. Although there is no precise measure of validity in qualitative research, there was rigor in identifying supportable interpretations through recognition of patterns and coherence of narrative information established through review by a research team. The results of interpretive research remain open and subject to change, using scholarly consensus to test validity (Polkinghorne, 1988).

ORGANIZATIONAL UNDERSTANDING

The overarching activity of nurse executive practice is that of *organizational understanding*. This underlies a significant portion of the practice of nurse executives and informs their thought processes, plans, and actions. Expert nurse executives display an artistry in comprehending the meaning and significance of complex situations, and the concept of organizational understanding is an initial effort to describe the thinking process and actions that comprise that understanding. Organizational understanding refers to the comprehensive understanding the nurse executive has about the people and the institution where she works. This understanding relies on interpretation of information over time, gathered from the organizational situation (its context) in concert with the nurse executive's past experience and education. This process can be likened to a form of practical knowledge, or phronesis, as described by Aristotle. Organizational understanding develops from an ongoing series of thoughts and actions that range from appraisal of the organization to decisions about how to move the organization forward to provide quality patient care services. Organizational understanding is purposeful, continuously informed by thought and action, and constantly under revision. Essential to organizational understanding is the consistent interplay that occurs between thought and action, with actions providing information for reflection or intuitive understanding and thought providing direction for future action. It is noteworthy that when asked to describe their executive practice, these nationally known leaders consistently focused downward on their actions to influence clinical care and practice.

The report of the findings will present three interrelated components of organizational understanding referred to as subplots: (a) ongoing appraisal, through presence and reciprocity, (b) constructing a vision for change, and (c) moving the organization forward.

Ongoing Appraisal Through Presence and Reciprocity

Appraisal of the organization represents the first subplot of organizational understanding. This appraisal process is experientially based and is characterized by the actions of presence and reciprocity. During the appraisal process, expert nurse executives put themselves into situations to see their way through to understand the elements that influence the delivery of patient care services. Ongoing appraisal is participatory because the nurse executive experiences being a part of the situation. The nurse executive uses the qualities of presence and reciprocity to become as close as possible to what really goes on at the juncture of patient care. There is no single way to appraise an organization except for seeing the activities and consequences of work. Work includes those individual tasks, communication styles, interpersonal and intrapersonal connections and cooperation, rationale for a particular approach, and problems and successes that are part of the ordinary life of an organization.

Presence

Presence is repeatedly identified by nurse executives as an essential way to learn about the organization. When learning to understand a new organization, the nurse executive engages in almost a frenzy of activity to get out and become involved in nursing work and to interact with patients and staff. They recall, reflect on, and deeply respect clinical nursing. It is their roots and they consistently return to it to grow in their understanding. This commitment to the heart of the profession is sustained not just by a feeling of responsibility to know but a burning passion and energy that demand their involvement. When their personal involvement lessens, they feel a sense of loss and struggle with finding other ways to appraise nursing's "fit" in the organization, ways that are at least indirectly linked to clinical activities. One nurse executive described it in terms of a journey of discovery that begins with getting in there and getting a sense of what is going on. This means putting themselves directly into situations in the clinical setting and establishing a presence there that allows them to connect with nurses and patients. Presence embodies a quality of immediacy, representing the here and now and therefore reflecting current practices and values. This sense of immediacy also reflects the importance that the expert nurse executive places on being there with clinical providers, of being where the action is.

Presence is not a passive quality but an openness, availability, and willingness to receive information and incorporate feelings from others and from the surroundings. These nurse executives are physically present: They can hear, and see, and touch, and smell. And that is what they do. They watch and listen attentively and if they do not physically touch others, they are nonetheless themselves touched through their active presence in the work of care. While at Harvard University, Barnard (1964) wrote that to understand an organization you must feel it. To feel the organization requires the consistent experience of presence.

A nurse executive described her work since taking a position as corporate vice president in the early 1990s. This position was newly created and intended to link the goals and activities of nursing throughout multiple health care facilities owned by the corporation. Prior to this, the concept of linkage had been virtually nonexistent. In talking about her experience of presence in the early days of this executive position, she commented:

> My sense was that my primary responsibility was to make an assessment on the quality of nursing care that was being delivered and based on that assessment to develop a strategic plan

for the department. And the only way that I could do an assessment and know in my heart that it was a correct assessment was if I went out and started a clinical practice right away—go out, work in all the emergency departments, work in all of their ORs, work in all of their ICUs, really get a sense of what the issues were, how difficult is it to negotiate supplies and equipment, how clear are policies and procedures on what you're supposed to be doing, how good of a relationship is there between nursing administration and nursing staff, how do they relate to the positions, how are they perceived by the hospital administration.

Another nurse executive articulated the notion of presence when beginning in a new executive position in the mid '70s, having moved from a vice presidential-level position in another state:

From the time I came I was interested in patient care and my very first day was spent on making rounds in the nursing unit with one of the clinical directors. . . . I became very involved in nursing and patients from the beginning. . . . I was here to do the best that I could for patients and I had high expectations of staff and their future education and their responsibilities for doing what needed to be done at their level. I realized that I was in a different culture and that I would need to hear from more people [about] where they were coming from as individuals.

Reciprocity

Reciprocity translates the actions that were part of presence into mutuality. The distinction between presence and reciprocity is that in reciprocity there is a sharing of self, which encourages others with whom the nurse executive is interacting to share their concerns, questions, and realities with her. In a recurrent metaphor for reciprocity, the nurse executives continually referred to efforts to get their "arms around the organization." This indicates an intention to embrace the culture of the organization, in order to know it through all of their senses, including the ability to palpably connect with the people and the services provided to the patient. The idea of mutuality, which is the outcome of reciprocity, takes on the following two characteristics: an approachable quality that establishes communications with others, and an openness that communicates respect for the point of view of other. Respect is conveyed through the actions taken by the nurse executive that reflect the point of view or recommendations of others. The positive benefit of this is that mutual respect for individuals, over time, develops into trust on the organizational level.

In reflecting on the importance of sharing information with staff and appreciating their perspective, a nurse executive shares her valuation of the importance of trust.

> There's nothing like firsthand information. There's nothing like sitting down with staff and really getting it from them. Hearing it from them. And I think they feel the same way with me and what happened over the years is the people trust me as I trust them. . . . I always say to staff, "Let's pie in the sky. Let's think about this. How could you change this? What could you do? Or what do you want me to do? What do I need to do for you?. . . ." Trust is very important and you really have to earn it, and you have to be consistent. . . . I speak always of internal integrity. You have to be true to yourself.

Reciprocity involves learning from others. As part of the ongoing appraisal, it is a highly personal and potentially intimate way of communicating with others that ultimately provides a rich resource for understanding the organization on a continuing basis. There is a persistent willingness to see things and people without preconceptions. Respect and openness reinforce that mutuality is genuine. Learning is not circumspect but receptive to everybody and everything. Respect for the nursing staff is powerful in the following description of a nurse executive's actions reflecting presence, mutuality, and learning.

> Yesterday at noon was the first day all week that I did not have a scheduled lunch meeting, and so I walked . . . into the cafeteria for lunch and I looked around to see who can I sit with. And I usually try to see who's there that I need to develop relationships with, you know, enhance relationships. . . . I was fortunate enough to find the nurse manager from the CCU and about four of her staff having lunch and we had a marvelous

time. And what I was able to do was to start talking with the staff
. . . about changing from being appointed to a patient care unit
to a program of care. . . . And so in a half-hour I had this mar-
velous exchange with clinical staff who always understand it . . .
as soon as you start talking. . . . I don't know how to talk about
clinical things any longer . . . and I'm very honest with staff
about that. . . . "You're the experts, clinically, what I need to
know is what do you need from a systems point of view." My practice is really in my head as much as anywhere else. . . . Guess
what they said. "Oh yeah, we've been trying to work that out on
the computer right now." . . . You see, I'm not the one who
comes up with the ideas. They always tell me where to go. They
always lead me in the direction of what's next. . . . They lead
you. You watch your clinical staff, you know what to do next.

The actions that are part of reciprocity and learning from others
are intentional and over time become cyclical, with the nurse executive coming from and returning to the clinical area to openly share
with and to learn from those providing care at the grass-roots level.
In order to successfully move the organization forward, it is critical
that this pattern of cyclical activity be maintained.

Constructing a Vision for Change

Constructing a vision for change is the second subplot associated
with organizational understanding. It describes how information is
integrated and interpreted and it represents the interpretive thought
process used by nurse executives. Organizational understanding is
not possible without integration of information from the appraisal
process and meaningful interpretation. Constructing a vision for
change is composed of two interrelated elements that enable the
nurse executive to envision the possibilities for organizational change.
The first element relates to *how meaning is interpreted within the context of the organization*. The second element is concerned with *how
meaning is interpreted over time*. The interpretation of information
about organizational context over time occurs within a repeating
cycle of appraisal, thought, and action and provides the crucial link
between appraisal of the organization and moving the organization
forward.

Interpreting Meaning Within the Context of the Organization

Interpreting the meaning of organizational context informs the vision for change. This results from the nurse executive's transformation of information from many sources into a meaningful and holistic understanding of the organization. It is facilitated through integration of information drawn from theory and experience. Theory is used in particular ways to inform the direction for change. Knowledge accumulated from within the organization about people and problems, in the past and present, also informs directions for change. The actions of presence and reciprocity are the source of that information.

In trying to describe instituting change in an organization, one nurse executive referenced both a particular theory and past experience relative to constructing a vision for organizational change. In remarking that she loves the process of change and that knowing what to do is intuitive, she says:

> I'm looking at this model and I'm trying to conceptualize it, and I say to myself "this change model won't work here." If I try to implement change, whatever changes I make here, like I had at (another institution), using Lewin's thinking, I will feel like I'm in the middle of a tug-of-war.
> **Q:** How do you know that?
> **A:** I felt it. I can feel the resistance, and I could feel like there was right and wrong . . . and I said, that's not the way to do it. (She then goes on to describe a conceptual framework for change that she remembered reading and described how this seemed to fit with the organization.) I said this is it and the model is very interesting. . . . It's not an organization model, it's a person model.

Nurse executives frequently referenced the use of a general theoretical or philosophic framework that provided guidance to interpret the organization as well as to help inform their direction for change. When asked where she got the idea for development of a new model for practice that was subsequently implemented, a nurse executive replied:

I would have to go back to my diploma education in terms of (its) focus on patients. (The model) came really right out of that. The specifics of the model came from Lydia Hall. She had the professional nurse and the direct care of patients and support of the nurse caring for the patient. She helped not only me but many of us really think very seriously in terms of the proper use of a registered nurse in the workplace and the relationship with the patient. It made so much sense to me because of what I had experienced in my diploma education. I was also influenced by Jean Barrett, and her book *Head Nurse*, to really understand the relationship of providing care and developing systems for that care and the role of the head nurse.

Constructing a vision for change is an open-ended process of interpreting of gathered information. The process is a continual dialogue between theoretical information and information gained from continual appraisal of the organization. This dialogue may be likened to Aristotle's (1980) idea of phronesis, or practical reasoning, involving deliberation between the universal and the particular, resulting in choice and action. In this dialogue the nurse executive deliberates between theoretical information, represented by the acontextual or fixed rules to inform practice, and the information particular to the situation at hand. The dialogue between the "universals" and the "particulars" refines and alters the nurse's boundaries of understanding. The artful integration and interpretation of information is a continuous process of going back and forth between the theoretical and experiential information known through appraising the organizational context. The continuous integration of information into the frame for understanding shapes the direction of future dialogue.

In the process of thinking through the construction of a new approach, the dialogue can create varied constructs about different applications to a particular problem or vision. It is like making different designs from a given set of shapes. Expert nurse executives think about ways to enable people in the organization to do things differently in order to enhance quality patient care. Thinking through an organizational care delivery problem is similar to painting a picture or piecing a puzzle together because the boundaries are less clear and the fit of the pieces of information is neither preset nor is it necessarily limited in the number of choices of fit. Sometimes, like a puzzle, all the information is present and the nurse executive needs to assimilate information in a meaningful fashion, reflecting her understanding about the organization as well as her personal philosophy and expectations. Sometimes, like painting a picture, information is missing and meaning is constructed and then painted over.

Constructing a vision for change is a process filled with ambiguities and uncertainties as the nurse executive tries to construct a nearly complete puzzle or picture from seemingly disparate parts. When asked how she moved from ideas to action, one nurse executive described her thinking as she prepared for a retreat with the nurse managers to revise the organizational structure for unit-level management:

> The way I approached it was, I've certain pieces of data and these pieces of data are trying to paint a picture for me, but part of the picture I try to leave blank. I begin to develop an answer for myself: this is my personal belief, and in terms of someone that's going to build consensus—what can I live with in terms of what the answer is. But I need to do a certain amount of thinking about it on my own. My initial input is based on my past experience and my thought about it. And then it's very important for me to throw these ideas out to other people so that I kind of throw this blank and filled in section. I say, "This is what we know. This is what we can dispute. This is what we have to discover." That usually generates a lot of discussion. I very much need that to happen because when that happens for me, it fills in the top part of what's blank. As I get that interaction the answers come. I'll have an "Ahh, ah!" I'll say, "That's the missing piece. That's what I didn't see." And as they talk, I begin to problem-solve. So I kind of connect all of that stuff and then at the end I generally have what I think is the answer and I'll summarize. But I never can solve it by myself. I need that other interaction.

The nurse executive brings to her role a unique perspective about patient care derived from a baseline of theoretical knowledge and experience that is an integral part of who she is as a nurse and as an executive and the values she holds about her executive practice. It is in this sense that thinking about change is a personal activity that has no precise beginning but moves through an endless and over-lapping cycle of appraisal and thinking and interpretation and action. The expert nurse executive often knows what she needs to know without being conscious of it. Their knowing is a product of internally synthesizing a multitude of data, personal encounters and observations, and past experience contained in a repository of knowledge and understanding about her practice and about organizations.

Interpreting Meaning Over Time

Time provides perspective for interpreting the meaning of events, attitudes, and actions related to organizational understanding. Because there are forces that constantly influence the organization, it is necessary for the nurse executive to continuously appraise and interpret the meaning of organizational context in relation to present, past, and future concerns and implications.

In her new role as a corporate nurse executive, one of the study participants began the description of her practice by saying: "Part of my role is to evolve a story of nursing in terms of what I've learned from the past, what I experience today and what I know needs to kind of happen in the future."

This statement captures the essence and importance of time for the practice of the nurse executive: for understanding, constructing a vision, and moving the organization forward. Time provides the perspective through which organizational understanding is filtered and synthesized to facilitate change, or transform the organization into the future. An organization is not static; it evolves through time. Thus, it is essential for the nurse executive to continuously evaluate the position of the organization along the time continuum. This is done through synthesis of practical and theoretical knowledge. As information is interpreted, there is deliberation about the effectiveness of past and present activities within the organization as they relate to the vision for the future. In this way, future, present, and past interrelate and interface.

A nurse executive references her practice in relation to time, change, and organizational understanding:

The job constantly evolves and changes . . . you have to track the organization's development and its people development and so what you may do at one point in time you would do differently at another point in time and so you're constantly learning. . . . A lot of people will say, "If I took another job I would start doing it differently than I did here." Well you can do it in your own organization also, I mean if you constantly think in terms of a developmental approach—and I believe that's what we've done—is that we constantly try to assess where the organization is as well as where we are as a profession within that organization. And the two things kind of move together, so as a consequence I keep changing and hopefully developing as much as the staff and the organization.

Thinking about change over time is an interpretive activity. The nurse executive interprets the meaning of information through different time frames that are infused by seamless layers of information about people and the organization. It is not only what the nurse executive thinks about, but how she makes sense of the multiple sources of information. Critical to her interpretation is having historical as well as current information about the organization. Future-oriented thinking is partially shaped by information about past activities and their influence on current organizational values, priorities, and actions. Therefore, for the nurse executive there is continuous and simultaneous interpretation of what is happening as shaped by the past and present against what needs to happen in the future. Constructing a vision is ultimately an act of circularity because as change occurs, what was the future becomes the present and then the past.

MOVING THE ORGANIZATION FORWARD

The third subplot in organizational understanding is that of moving the organization forward. Thinking provides the direction for future action, which propels the organization into the future. Contained within the outlines of a broad course of action that is conceptual, such as building a "world class" organization, there are a multitude of problems and approaches to change that are guided by the overarching understanding of the organization. Organizational understanding establishes a framework for realizing how to enable people in the organization to do things differently in order to enhance quality patient care.

The following excerpt illustrates the complex thoughts and actions of the nurse executive in translating her interpretation of the meaning of that organization's context into a future-oriented vision.

> I got feelings of the staff nurses really wanting to help to make things better. . . . Somehow by using my nerve endings, really, I was able to lock onto where the nursing staff and the people there really felt that the hospital should go. . . . So that I went with a lot of those feelings and just really kind of put them into words. . . . My vision for this organization was to make it world class, to have nurses be proud to work here. . . . The idea was to focus our attention and our energies on enhancing the quality of the work life of the bedside nurse who delivered nursing care and direct patient care on a daily basis.

One aspect of a nurse executive's vision is concerned with removing obstacles that interfere with patient care. In talking about the many facets implicated in reducing obstacles to care in a multi hospital structure, and how to direct the change forward, the nurse executive said:

> If every effort of our being in the organization is not totally devoted to removing obstacles from the practicing nurse at the bedside, then we're kidding ourselves about what our value added is, because they're doing the work. They can't remove those obstacles themselves. . . . If they've problems . . . you damn well better be with them and you better be helping them solve that. . . . You have to know what your beliefs are and you have to be able to share that operating premise with everybody that comes in contact with you because if when I say those things to the staff and then I show them the strategic plan and then I show them how every activity we're working on its connected to those three operatives, supporting them, operationalizing the strategic plan and enhancing communication. . . . At least they know what I believe in and I think that's really a key part of getting people motivated and excited about moving forward.

There is both freedom and constraint in the construction of a vision for moving the organization forward. Freedom is associated with the nurse executive's openness to learn and her willingness to think about new ideas, to take risks by fearlessly trying new ideas that may interfere or rock the boat and to make mistakes. She recognizes that she does not know it all, that there is more than one way to achieve a goal, and that indeed situations continually change. Constraint is present through her understanding of and commitment to the vision that is needed to keep the organizational practices current, relevant, and purposeful to the consumer. Constraint is present in her personal belief about the future direction for nursing. Constraint is present in the analysis of just how far and how quickly she can move the clinical practitioners into the future. Freedom and constraint are also influenced by the realities of the organization. Organizational understanding is filled with unknowns and, because of the incomplete nature of that understanding, the thinking and resultant understanding held by the nurse executive about the organization are in a continual state of construction and revision.

Various aspects of freedom and constraint are evident in the next two examples. In this first situation, the nurse executive discusses the freedom and risks associated with the idea of creating a nursing center as a vehicle to move her vision forward and the concerns of staff about quality and money.

I came up with the concept of the Nursing Center. I had no idea how I was going to do it. Most people thought I was going to implement X (the model at a former institution) . . . and I said, "no that's not the way I do it." I go in, I see another piece of paper and I start painting again. . . . Let's play to their strength, because there was no way that I could change that they thought that if you had quality you had to spend a lot of money, that if you didn't spend a lot of money you're sacrificing quality. The Center is going to be to improve patient care and the professional development of nurses. The Nursing Center was formed to do two things: one, to support the mission of the Hospital and the second to implement the values of the Hospital: that patients are the reason that we exist, that people are our strength, that we are going to do things together as a team, that we are going to strive for excellence, and that we will discover new ways of doing things. The Nursing Center then was created to design and make activities happen, to bring the vision forward.

In this second example the nurse executive talks about the importance of her role, risk-taking, and her presence in moving a vision forward in spite of its ambiguities. There is also appreciation of her efforts to balance her presence as a constraint against the freedom of staff to be empowered to implement the vision.

> It is important to know a vision and take care of that, not to always be the person who has all the answers about the shape of that vision, but really engage people who can be committed to the vision, and then want to move it forward and onto creating it, refining it, and taking risks and asking a lot of questions at the time of implementation. To always have a presence whether there is a real physical presence or whether it's a presence of vision, and move in and out in terms of hands-on, not hands-on, as is necessary and appropriate, and really turn the leadership over to the people that are there, but don't ever walk away from it.

In summary, organizational understanding develops as a result of the three components of the interrelationship of thought and action. There is ongoing appraisal of the organization (focused on patient care framed within the past and the present) with the overarching objective of understanding how to move the organization into the future. Appraisal is facilitated through presence and reciprocity. There is integration of theoretical and practical knowledge to construct the meaning and direct change over time. Finally, the consequence of constructing this knowledge is the creation of ideas and plans that move the organization toward improving the quality of patient care.

IMPLICATIONS

This initial report on the practice of nurse executives has identified the importance of organizational understanding within the context of their practice. The thought processes of nurse executives revealed in narratives about their practice illustrate the nonlinear thinking activity integral to understanding the organization. The findings of this study illustrate that the primary philosophic focus of the nurse executive is for the quality of patient care as the fulcrum of understanding. The significance of organizational understanding for nursing education, nursing service, and nursing theory will be discussed.

The actions of *presence* and *reciprocity* are crucial to understanding the organization and implementing a vision at the unit level of patient care. Although presence requires active involvement, it is the act of reciprocity that is a finely honed art (being with others, listening, and questioning) that encourages others to participate in a democratic dialogue about the joys and concerns that surround the everyday experience of providing care. Nurse executives describe the difficulties of finding the time to return to the clinical site. Because this is a rich and requisite source of information essential to maintaining organizational understanding, however, nurse executives need to be cautious about priorities that limit access to this source of information. Creating a rich and honest dialogue with others is both an art and a skill.

Time is an undervalued ingredient that permeates practice. Many of the nurse executives in this study had been in the same institution at the executive level for periods in excess of the more common tenure of several years. Although longevity does not predict success, time is fundamental to organizational understanding and change. It takes time to come to know the history and the people of an institution. Understanding is not grasped instantly but proceeds slowly even as it undergoes change due to the passage of time. Furthermore, changes that are initiated take time to be appreciated, to be effective, and to be evaluated. It takes time to know. It takes time to understand. It takes time to create change. The notion of time as a critical commodity to be acknowledged and used is at odds with the bureaucratic belief that time is an enemy to be controlled and mastered. The current brief tenure of nurse executives (promoted by individual career interests and institutional focus on short-term goals and outcomes) militates against the possibilities of meaningful change and long-term quality care.

It is evident in the findings that the individual personalities and experiences of the nurse executives in great part define how they translate their roles into action and implement their visions. The importance of who they are and what they have experienced relates to the manner and the degree to which they use themselves as recipients and transmitters of information. Their philosophies of quality care and what they value are embedded in their practice as they live it. This suggests that executive practice cannot be guided by absolute rules because understanding occurs within organizational context. Furthermore, information may be incomplete; it continuously changes, and the means and ends are not ready-made or predictable. The thinking processes of expert nurse executives reveal an ability to synthesize salient aspects of theoretical knowledge with practical knowledge derived from their organizational experiences. Their non-linear thinking illustrates the use of more than programmed theoretical information and outcome-oriented goals. The importance of cumulative experience must be underscored as providing the base of their tacit knowledge, or intuitive ability. Experience helps them recognize critical distinctions in particular organizations and aids in constructing creative possibilities for change. To solve problems and develop creative solutions requires a comprehensive understanding of the organization derived from information, time, and reflection.

The practice of each nurse executive was unique, having developed in part from engaging in and interpreting individual experiences. This suggests that there are limits to any teaching rules. Engaging in practice involves what you have become as you live the role. There is a dimension in the continuing development of the nurse executive that cannot be explicated or taught. Nonetheless, the importance of who you are and what you do can be considered through reflection, dialogue, and self-criticism. Nursing administration educational practices need to provide opportunities for students to become aware of their personal styles as well as their leadership styles and how these influence their thinking, interpretation, and action. Models of practice and education that support reflective action create linkages for the practitioner and student among who they are, what they do, and the theoretical frames for understanding quality leadership practices. The development of reflective learning models is necessary to guide educational experiences in schools of nursing and continuing education programs. An important element in learning about the executive role was the opportunity to have had a mentor. The mentors were remembered as making a difference in how the participants thought about their role, their actions, and their responsibility to mentor others. Establishing formal connections with faculty and administrators through strengthening and increasing current practice-education partnerships is a mechanism to facilitate mentoring.

Translating nonlinear thinking to the educational arena requires learning activities and goals quite different from those orchestrated toward finding universal answers to questions ranging from staffing prediction to ethical concerns. Appreciating the importance of experience and context for acquiring practical knowledge suggests that educational programs preparing nurses for leadership positions need to incorporate significant amounts of time for experience-based learning and opportunities to reflect on the interrelationship of theory and practice. For example, a graduate curriculum in nursing administration needs to furnish opportunities to develop the knowledge and skills practiced by expert executives through holistic analysis of an organization, role-playing, and action-oriented projects from the workplace that provide the time to reflect and create possible explanations and solutions.

The findings of this study have implications for the future development of nursing administration theory, offering a beginning basis for the development of theory based on practice. This report is focused on one aspect of nurse executive practice, that of organizational understanding, and its emphasis on clinical nursing management. This study identifies two elements fundamental to interpreting meaning that leads to organizational understanding: the context of the organization and the relevance of time. If meaning is dynamic and changing, the idea of fixed rules to guide practice is questionable. A theory of executive decision-making should be conceptualized to accommodate the finding that time is critical in understanding organizations and an essential to promoting change.

The findings from this study provide a medium for critical dialogue about the differences between the practice of nurse executives in relation to what is known and taught. This study has demonstrated that executive thinking is a way of knowing that is dependent on practice, and that practice can only be known within the context of the organization over time.

REFERENCES

Agor, W. H. (1989). *Intuition in organizations: Learning and managing productively*. Newbury Park, CA: Sage.

Aristotle. (1980). *The Nicomachean ethics*. New York: Oxford University Press.

Barnard, C. J. (1964). *The functions of the executive.* Cambridge, MA: Harvard University Press.

Bass, B. M. (1960). *Leadership, psychology, and organizational behavior.* New York: Harper & Row.

Dreyfus, S. E. (1981). *Formal model as human situational understanding: Inherent limitation on the modeling of business expertise.* Supported by the U.S. Air Force Office of Scientific Research. Under contract F49620-79-C-0063, University of California, Berkeley, CA.

Eberhart, C. P., & Pieper, B. B. (1994). Understanding human action through narrative expression and hermeneutic inquiry. In P. L. Chinn (Ed.), *Advances in methods of inquiry for nursing* (pp. 41–88). Rockville, MD: Aspen.

Gronn, O. C. (1983). Talk as the working accomplishment of school administration. *Administrative Science Quarterly, 28,* 1–21.

Henry, B. M. (1992). *Practice and inquiry for nursing administration: Intradisciplinary and interdisciplinary perspectives.* Washington, DC: American Academy of Nursing.

Mintzberg, H., Raisinghani, D., & Theoret, A. (1976). The structure of "unstructured" decision processes. *Administrative Science Quarterly, 21,* 246–275.

Morris, G. B. (1988). The executive: A pathfinder. *Organizational Dynamic, 16*(4), 62–77.

Nagelkerk, M. (1988). *The processes used in unstructured strategic decisions for allocation of resources by nurse administrators.* Unpublished doctoral dissertation, University of Florida, Gainesville, FL.

Palmer, R. E. (1969). *Hermeneutics.* Evanston, IL: Northwestern University Press.

Polkinghorne, D. (1983). *Methodology for the human sciences: Systems of inquiry.* Albany, NY: State University of New York Press.

Polkinghorne, D. (1988). *Narrative knowing and the human sciences.* Albany, NY: State University of New York Press.

Rawnsley, M. M., & Evans, J. A. (1992). Nursing science and nursing administration: Creating an empowering environment. In B. M. Henry (Ed.), *Practice and inquiry for nursing administration: Intradisciplinary and interdisciplinary perspective* (pp. 55–61). Washington, DC: American Academy of Nursing.

Ricoeur, P. (1977). The model of the text: Meaningful action considered as text. In F. R. Dahlmar & T. A. McCarty (Eds.) *Understanding and social inquiry* (pp. 316–334). Notre Dame, IN: University of Notre Dame Press.

Ricoeur, P. (1979). The human experience of time and narrative. *Research in Phenomenology, 9,* 17–34.

Ricoeur, P. (1984). *Time and narrative* (Vol. I) (K. McLaughlin & D. Pellevar, Trans.) Chicago: University of Chicago Press.

Ricoeur, P. (1985). *Time and narrative* (Vol. II) (K. McLaughlin & D. Pellevar, Trans.) Chicago: University of Chicago Press.

Ricoeur, P. (1988a). The human being as the subject matter of philosophy. *Philosophy and Social Criticism, 14,* 203–215.

Ricoeur, P. (1988b). *Time and narrative* (Vol. III) (K. McLaughlin & D. Pellevar, Trans.) Chicago: University of Chicago Press.

Ricoeur, P. (1991). Narrative identity. *Philosophy Today, 35,* 73–81.

Schon, D. (1983). *The reflective practitioner: How professionals think in action.* New York: Basic Books.

Simon, H. A. (1987). Making management decisions: The role of intuition and emotion. *Academy of Management Executive, 1*(1), 57–64.

Taylor, C. (1971). Interpretation and the science of man. *Review of Metaphysics, 25,* 1–51.

CHAPTER *23*

Be Careful What You Wish for: Caveats and Principles for Responsible Redesign

Mary Crabtree Tonges

Characterized by constant change, today's health care environment can be accurately described as hyperturbulent. This fast, continuous, and pervasive change has important implications for the design of nurses' jobs.

While the positive potential of job redesign is great, there are also important risks and concerns for nurses. As Diane Weaver, president of the American Organization of Nurse Executives (AONE; 1994) noted, "The question is not, 'do we do it,' but rather, 'how can we redesign traditional roles and preserve the important value of providing high quality patient care in a cost-effective manner?'" (p. 2). In seeking answers to this question, the following two points must be kept in mind:

1. Redesigned support services must support redesigned clinical practice.
2. Because education, experience, and preferences vary widely, nurses' individual differences must be accommodated in redesigned nursing roles.

Note: Originally published in *Nursing Leadership Forum*, Vol. 2, No. 2, 1996. New York: Springer Publishing Company.

REDESIGNED SUPPORT SERVICES

It is known that as much as 40% of professional registered nurses' time may be spent performing tasks that do not require their expertise (American Hospital Association, 1988). Increased clinical and nonclinical support to free nurses from these activities has long been recommended by nurse executives (Burn & Tonges, 1983; Spitzer, 1983). Moreover, these recommendations are supported by findings that the dominant controllable factor affecting nursing productivity is the availability of effective support services (Swenson, Wolfe, & Shroeder, 1984). Does this mean that redesigned care delivery systems featuring decentralized teams of multifunctional staff are a wish come true? Maybe, but be careful what you wish for.

The "Strange Partnerships" Phenomenon

As professional registered nurses' time and attention is increasingly being redirected from the performance of tasks to the achievement of outcomes, cross-training unlicensed staff to provide multiple services at the unit level can provide RNs with the support they need to be effective managers of care. Cross-training unlicensed personnel offers numerous advantages in terms of quality and flexibility, as well.

Yet the cross-training of licensed professionals is far less appropriate. If one of the characteristics of a profession is a unique body of knowledge, to what extent can professionals be "trained" to perform competently in other professions' domains? The concept of cross-training, in this case, negates the notion of professional expertise. As illustration, how could one expect a social worker or medical technologist to substitute for a nurse in doing a physical assessment of a patient? And why would a professional be used to do lesser tasks in another field that do not require any professional education? The cost of having more highly paid professional staff members perform tasks that can safely be completed by less expensive technical staff represents a major drawback to this approach.

Many cross-training models include the nurse as a member of a pair or small team of caregivers (Weber, 1991). Some multifunctional "carepair" or team models require that nurses and other licensed staff absorb elements of each others' practice, as well as nonclinical tasks (Watson, Shortridge, Jones, & Stephens, 1991). Schweikhart and Smith-Daniels (1996) describe an example of this approach in which the "intention of fully incorporating multidisciplinary staff into team operations was reinforced by use of the same title, clinical associate, for both RNs and specialized clinicians on the patient care units" (p. 32). They elaborate as follows:

> . . . deployment of multidisciplinary clinicians changes organizational identities, from licensed clinicians to more generic clinical associates in the unit-based care delivery team, as these individuals are cross-trained in many of the skills routinely performed by RNs and other primary care givers. Expanding the task range beyond their specialized skills is particularly important for ensuring full utilization of these clinicians. As explained by one patient care executive, the unique skills of a unit's medical technologist or pharmacist meant that although these individuals would not be sent home if patient census declined, they would be expected to help cover the work of nursing caregivers who were released early. (p. 32)

Apparently nursing's contribution is sometimes viewed as expendable within this context of blurred role.

Using nurses to clean rooms and change light bulbs is advocated by proponents of cross-training on the premise that caregivers should never pass over something they can do themselves (Brider, 1992). If this is the case, can we soon expect to be seeing physicians bathe and ambulate patients as long as they are in the room to do an exam? Given that medicine appears to be exempt from the process, it's not a likely scenario.

Efforts to "break down professional boundaries" in the quest for multifunctional flexibility and efficiency seem particularly focused on nursing and several other health professions. Interestingly, Schneller (1996, p. 129) notes "While the manifest function of redesigning patient care is to improve efficiency and contain costs, a latent function may be to radically change staffing patterns and, consequently, power in health care organizations."

Health service administration authors praise cross-training as a valuable concept imported from manufacturing (Fottler, 1996; Schweikhart & Smith-Daniels, 1996). Yet there are critical differences between manufacturing and service organizations in areas such as the degree of employee-client interaction, the processes used, and the nature of the outputs produced (Mills, Hall, Leidecker, &

Margulies, 1983; Schneider & Bowen, 1985). Mills and Moberg (1982) point out that while the growth in the service sector of our economy is well documented, "the growth of knowledge specifically pertinent to the operations of services has not kept pace with these developments. What is known is that caution should be exercised in applying models derived from and for manufacturing to service operations" (p. 467). While cross training may have been a key element of the successful redesign of manufacturing operations for global competition, I would suggest that there are important differences in the nature of health professionals' work and the knowledge and skills required that may preclude the direct application of a manufacturing strategy.

In discussing patient-focused care service models, Porter O'Grady (1993) offered the following observation:

> All over the country, nursing and other service organizations are in the throes of a frenetic and frantic move to restructure, create strange partnerships, move all the disciplines close to each other, and through some design of osmosis, create a culture of integration, collaboration, and partnership (p. 8).

While collaboration is extremely valuable and should be a high priority, as Porter O' Grady also suggests, nurses' unique contribution to patient outcomes is critical and must be preserved.

Adequate RN Staffing

Inappropriate cross-training is one threat to professional nursing practice; inadequate numbers of RNs is another. The appointment of an Institute of Medicine committee to investigate the need for increased numbers of nurses in hospitals and nursing homes (AONE, 1994) underscored the importance of concerns about the impact of reductions in RN staffing on quality of care and worklife. Regardless of the number of assistants available, it is the professional nurse who must manage patient care and retain accountability for nursing outcomes. There are cognitive limits to the number of patients one nurse can effectively manage, and human information processing capabilities must be taken into consideration when designing new care delivery models and staffing patterns.

As nurses' roles evolve, changes in staffing patterns can be expected. To prevent negative consequences for patients and staff, however, (1) these changes must be carefully analyzed and implemented; (2) appropriate delegation to sufficient numbers of competent assistants is essential; and (3) other factors in the escalation of health care costs must be aggressively addressed, including the price of drugs and equipment, and the volume of resources consumed treating patients in the last few weeks of life.

I am not opposed to redesigning patient care delivery processes, jobs, and systems. There are definitely opportunities to improve the efficiency and effectiveness of health care services; however, these are very complex and important systems, which necessitates careful analysis of potential unintended, negative consequences that may occur in conjunction with the positive, intended effects of changes. Thus, redesign must be thoughtfully conceived, carefully implemented, and rigorously evaluated through systematic assessment of the effects on patients, caregivers, and organizations.

"A NURSE IS A NURSE IS A NURSE" NO LONGER

Although patients' needs must be preeminent, providers should also be satisfied with care delivery. Job satisfaction is based on an individual's evaluation of a job; therefore, it is a function of, or at least positively related to, the degree to which personal needs are met in the work situation (Korman, 1971). Three different types of factors influence job satisfaction: (1) situational variables, (2) individual differences, and (3) individual difference-situational interactions.

A great deal of attention has been devoted to improving situational factors in nursing jobs. Higher salaries, flexible scheduling, clinical ladders, and shared governance have all been attempts to increase satisfaction by changing elements of nurses' work situation. Less attention has been paid, however, to the effects of individual differences among nurses on job satisfaction. Some may assume that nurses are highly similar and operate from a uniform level of satisfaction; however, evidence suggests that this is not the case.

Education, for instance, appears to make a difference. Satisfaction is thought to be related to and based on an individual's expectations. Since education can raise people's expectations, better educated individuals may be less satisfied than others in the same work situation.

Although there is a lack of consensus on this point, more of the available evidence indicates that satisfaction decreases as nurses' education increases (Blegen, 1993; Stamps & Piedmonte, 1986).

This is an important issue. Because of rapidly increasing acuity and technological advances, nurses require a great deal of education to practice effectively today. The resulting change in their expectations is an issue that must be recognized and dealt with in designing nursing roles and practice models for the future.

Yet nurses are, and may continue to be, a particularly heterogenous group. Hofstede (1984) indicates that work values differ based on occupational level and that the number of years of formal education necessary for an occupation is a useful measure of occupational level (e.g., technicians versus professionals and managers). As long as there are three different educational routes to becoming an RN, there are likely to be different types of individuals within nursing who have different values and preferences.

Consider preference for decision-making autonomy as one example. Because baccalaureate prepared nurses have more years of education and are educated in a university setting, their values would tend to be more closely aligned with those of professionals and managers, leading to a higher preference for decision-making autonomy. As this line of reasoning would lead one to expect, McCloskey (1990) found that nurses with more education were most affected by low levels of autonomy and social integration and reported less job satisfaction, as well as less commitment, motivation, and intent to stay on the job.

New nursing practice and care delivery models and decision making structures are being implemented to increase staff nurses' opportunities for autonomy and control. Yet these changes appear to be based on the assumption that all staff nurses are alike in their desire for more decision-making autonomy.

Dwyer, Schwartz, and Fox (1992) studied 151 RNs' preferences for decision-making autonomy in three types of work-related decisions, encompassing both self-direction in clinical practice and personal control over unit management issues. Their findings indicated that the nurses' preferences for decision-making autonomy differed, and these differences affected the relationship between increased autonomy and satisfaction. Nurses with greater preference for autonomy were more satisfied as they climbed the clinical ladder and gained influence over patient care and unit management decisions, whereas those with little or no such preference were less satisfied at higher levels of the clinical ladder. Thus, it would appear to be important to assess nurses' values and preferences before making changes in decision making autonomy intended to increase job satisfaction.

Research concerning the motivational characteristics of staff nurse jobs has consistently indicated that nurses perceive their work to be highly varied and have important consequences for others, but they also report that their jobs are lower in the dimensions of autonomy, feedback, and especially job identity (i.e., a sense of completion or the chance to see a whole piece of work) (Joiner, Johnson, Chapman, & Corkrean, 1982; Roedel & Nystrom, 1988). There is a documented need to make changes in the design of nursing jobs, and the increasing demand for nurse case managers and other types of advanced practice roles represents an opportunity to correct some of these recognized deficiencies. Based on the Dwyer and colleagues (1992) study, however, it is also imperative that structures and systems be designed to provide opportunities to achieve different types of person-job fit for different types of nurses within the same organization.

There is a need to accommodate those who have more education and/or higher needs for autonomy by creating appropriate practice roles and opportunities for control over unit management. This should not be accomplished, however, at the expense of reduced job satisfaction for other types of nurses. Although 27% of the total supply of RNs have baccalaureate degrees, 64% of the nurses graduating in 1990 were from associate degree programs (National League of Nursing, 1991). These numbers provide a persuasive argument for using a more "cafeteria-style" contingency approach, which should result in increased levels of average overall satisfaction with this aspect of nurses' jobs.

WHAT WORKS AND WHAT DOESN'T

One Nurse's Perspective on Redesign

Like most things in life, this is not a black and white issue. Because hospitals and other health care organizations are unique entities, there are few absolute rules regarding the best way to design and implement new models of care delivery. Generally speaking, how-

TABLE 23.1 Generally Speaking, What Works and What Doesn't: Principles for Responsible Redesign

WORKS	DOESN'T
1. Champion who can inspire others with vision and enlist commitment	1. Coercive manager
2. Giving staff available facts about problem and enlisting their help in developing solutions	2. Dictating plan from on high —OR— Abdicating administrative responsibility
3. Picking brightest and busiest for team	3. Assigning important work based on who has the most time
4. Theory-driven, research-based model development	4. Copying others without regard for organizational differences
5. Changes that support quality patient care and quality of work life (i.e., good for patients and good for staff)	5. Strange combinations of responsibilities (i.e., housekeepers cross-trained as phlebotomists); adding to work loads without streamlining processes in other ways
6. Demonstration units with strong first-line managers and a need for change	6. Rapid, house-wide implementation
7. Preparing all the key players (e.g., developing RNs' delegation skills)	7. Training only for the new roles (e.g., technicians or multifunctional workers
8. Model with consistent core features individualized to meet specific needs of different units/services	8. Everybody do their own thing
9. Evaluation research to measure outcomes and continuing redesign based on results	9. Anecdotal evaluation (i.e., "everybody likes it")

ever, certain approaches tend to be more consistently successful than others. Selected responses to the question, "What works and what doesn't?" based on my experiences are summarized in Table 23.1.

Several of these recommendations require further comment. From a process, as well as a content perspective, facilitating staff involvement in designing the model is critically important. As Margaret Wheatley notes, "I don't work with any processes now that start with the assumption that a few people can design something that will be of benefit for the rest of the organization" (Flowers, 1993, p. 55). Yet she also indicates that "the real challenge is creating these processes that engage greater and greater numbers of the organization" (Flowers, 1993, p. 55). Although engaging large numbers of organizational members in the development of new designs can be a cumbersome and expensive endeavor, neither dictation from above nor abdication of leadership responsibility are viable alternatives. We must, therefore, continue to search for cost-effective approaches to fostering participation.

Explaining the rationale for incorporating theory and research in the model development process may also be helpful. Theories are basically explanations for events of interest in a particular area. As such, they speak to the relationships thought to exist between different factors and how they are expected to affect each other. Even though they are not always articulated, implicit theories underlie efforts to create new programs. Decisions are made to restructure systems and jobs in particular ways because it is expected that desired outcomes will be produced (e.g., decreased length of stay, reduced cost, increased satisfaction, etc.). These decisions indicate that certain relationships are thought to exist (e.g., If I change A and B, C will increase).

Because theories guide our decisions, it is useful to be more explicit about our beliefs and expectations. This can be accomplished by identifying our assumptions and hypotheses, which in turn provides a basis for examining whether available evidence supports them. The results of this process can be quite informative and sometimes surprising. For example, it is widely assumed that there is a positive relationship between job satisfaction and productivity, that is, happy employees do a better job. Yet a meta-analysis of data from hundreds of studies of the job satisfaction-performance relationship suggested that in most situations these two variables are only slightly related (Iaffaldano & Muchinsky, 1985).

As previously noted, numerous interventions have been directed toward changing situational factors in nurses' jobs. If efforts to increase job satisfaction are based on the assumption that this will improve performance, those initiating the program are likely to be disappointed. On the other hand, there is evidence to suggest that job dissatisfaction is strongly linked to turnover among nurses (Diamond & Fox, 1958; Price & Mueller, 1981, 1986). Therefore, decreased turnover and a reduction in related recruitment and orientation costs are reasonable outcomes to expect from actions that effectively increase satisfaction. In summary, it is important to identify the theoretical assumptions influencing the development of a new care delivery model, and determine whether research supports them.

Having discussed the case against developing a new model on the basis of "gut feelings" and intuitive appeal, it is important to note that launching new programs because they work someplace else can be a major problem. Prior to attempting to replicate a program thought to be successful in another organization, it is advisable to find out as much as possible about that facility's circumstances and objectives for the project, as well as the depth and sophistication of the evaluation undertaken to assess achievement of those objectives. To accomplish a successful replication rather than copy a fad, it is essential to ensure that the desired results were, in fact, produced, and to assess similarities and differences between the two organizations likely to affect the outcomes of the program (e.g., strategic plan, payer mix, resources, medical staff organization, etc.).

Demonstration units are recommended for several reasons. Although it is not unusual to encounter organizations in which key players are clamoring for housewide changes yesterday, there is much to be gained from experimenting with new ideas on a smaller scale, in one area, and making needed improvements prior to a full-scale rollout. To take maximum advantage of this approach, the experimental unit should be selected with great care. It should be a place that needs changes to solve problems related to the objectives of the model (e.g., improved staffing or support services), but also provides a trial that has a high chance for success. In other words, choose a basically well-run unit with a competent first-line manager that happens to be having some temporary difficulties, as opposed to the most troubled unit in the hospital where nothing is likely to work, or the unit that is so excellent it would be difficult to improve.

The notion of trying new approaches and making them better also relates to the recommendation about evaluation. This should be an iterative process in which feasible ideas are tried and evaluated, and the information provided by the evaluation is used as a basis for continuing redesign. This process requires systematic collection and analysis of qualitative and quantitative data related to the objectives of the program. Anecdotal information is less reliable and may create distortions that obscure potential problems and opportunities.

As a last example, the caveat against picking people in the organization who seem to have more time available to manage a key project is based on the observation that there may be reasons why they are not as busy (e.g., they present a performance obstacle or problem). Thus, it is advisable to pick the best and brightest, who are also frequently among the busiest people in the organization. To make this work, one also has to be willing and able to free up those selected for the project and provide them with sufficient resources, in addition to time, to successfully complete their charge.

Other mistakes commonly made in organizational change projects include:

- Delegating a redesign project to an individual or group without an explicit set of goals. The design team should be able to come up with alternative approaches, but it needs some top-level direction about the objectives of the project and the parameters within which it is to work.
- Failing to recognize that the changes in care delivery and roles must be supported with changes in other administrative systems. If staff are expected to behave in new ways, this behavior must be reinforced through changes in training, orientation, job descriptions, performance appraisal, compensations systems and other management tools.

CONCLUSION

Times of great change are times of great opportunity because organizational resistance to change temporarily decreases. However, this fluidity also creates the risk that a less desirable change may happen very quickly. The moral of the story is to be careful what you wish for—be sure that changes in care delivery are in the best interest of patients and acceptable to caregivers—because your wish just may come true.

With the formation of integrated service networks, health care organizations are becoming increasingly complex, and redesign will become even more challenging. Although there is no guaranteed formula for success, the caveats and principles presented here summarize what works for me and are offered as guideposts for the journey to responsible redesign.

REFERENCES

American Hospital Association. (1988, October). *Proceedings of the invitational conference on the nursing shortage: Issues and strategies.* Chicago, IL.

American Organization of Nurse Executives (AONE). (1994). Committee on the adequacy of nurse staffing begins work. *AONE News, 3*(6), 1.

Blegen, M. (1993). Nurses' job satisfaction: A meta-analysis of related variables. *Nursing Research, 42*(1), 36–41.

Brider, P. (1992). The move to patient-focused care. *American Journal of Nursing, 9*, 27–33.

Burn, E. D., & Tonges, M. C. (1983). Professional nursing practice in acute care settings. *Nursing Administrative Quarterly, 8*(1), 65–75.

Diamond, L. K., & Fox, D. J. (1958). Turnover among hospital staff nurses. *Nursing Outlook, 6*, 388–391.

Dwyer, D. J., Schwartz, R. H., & Fox, M. L. (1992). Decision-making autonomy in nursing. *Journal of Nursing Administration, 22*(2), 177–183.

Flowers, J. (1993). The power of chaos, a conversation with Margaret J. Wheatley. *Healthcare Forum, 36*(5), 48–55.

Fottler, M. D. (1996). The role and impact of multiskilled health practitioners in the health services industry. *Hospital & Health Services Administration, 41*(1), 55–75.

Hofstede, B. (1984). The cultural relativity of the quality of life concept. *Academy of Management Review, 9*(3), 389–398.

Iaffaldano, M. T., & Muchinsky, P. M. (1985). Job satisfaction and job performance: A meta-analysis. *Psychological Bulletin, 97*, 251–273.

Joiner, C., Johnson, V., Chapman, J. B., & Corkrean, M. (1982). The motivating potential of nursing specialties. *Journal of Nursing Administration, 12*(2), 26–30.

Korman, A. (1971). *Industrial and organizational psychology.* Englewood Cliffs, NJ: Prentice-Hall.

McCloskey, J. C. (1990). Two requirements for job contentment: Autonomy and social integration. *Image, 22*(3), 140–143.

Mills, P. K., & Moberg, D. J. (1982). Perspectives on the technology of service operations. *Academy of Management Review, 7*, 467–478.

Mills, P. K., Hall, J. L., Leidecker, J. K., & Margulies, N. (1983). Flexiform: A model for professional service organizations. *Academy of Management Review, 8*, 118–131.

National League of Nursing. (1991). *Nursing datasource 1991, Volume I, Trends in contemporary nursing education.* Division of Research, New York.

Porter O'Grady, T. (1993). Patient-focused care service models: Perils and possibilities. *Journal of Nursing Administration, 23*(3), 7–8, 15.

Price, J. L., & Mueller, C. W. (1981). *Professional turnover: The case of nurses.* New York: SP Medical and Scientific Books.

Price, J. L., & Mueller, C. W. (1986). *Absenteeism and turnover of hospital employees.* Greenwich, CT: JAI Press.

Roedel, R. R., & Nystrom, P. C. (1988). Nursing jobs and satisfaction. *Nursing Management, 19*(2), 34–38.

Schweikhart, S. B., & Smith-Daniels, V. (1996). Reengineering the work of caregivers: Role definition, team structures, and organizational redesign. *Hospital & Health Services Administration, 41*(1), 19–36.

Schneller, E. S. (1996). Contemporary models of change in the health professions. *Hospital & Health Services Administration, 41*(1), 121–136.

Schneider, B., & Bowen, D. E. (1985). Employee and customer perceptions of service in banks: Replication and extension. *Journal of Applied Psychology, 70*, 432–439.

Spitzer, R. (1983). Legislation and new regulations. *Nursing Management, 14*(2), 13–21.

Stamps, P., & Piedmonte, E. B. (1986). *Nurses and work satisfaction.* Ann Arbor, MI: Health Administration Press Perspectives.

Swenson, B., Wolfe, H., & Shroeder, R. (1984). Effectively employing support services: The key for increasing nursing personnel productivity. *Modern Health Care, 14*(16), 101–102.

Watson, P. M., Shortridge, D. E., Jones, D. T., & Stephens, J. T. (1991). Operational restructuring: A patient focused approach. *Nursing Administration Quarterly, 16*(Fall), 45–53.

Weaver, D. (1994). Toward effective work redesigning a collaborative effort. *AONE News, 3*(5), 2.

Weber, D. O. (1991). Six models of patient-focused care. *Healthcare Forum, 34*(4), 23–31.

CHAPTER *24*

The "Three Rs" Revisited: Reengineer, Redesign, and Restructure

Mary Crabtree Tonges

The nineties were a decade of great change and complexity, characterized by the new "three Rs": reengineer, redesign, and restructure. Although these techniques remain popular, there is some ambiguity as to their distinguishing features, interrelationships, and implementation. This article presents definitions of these terms and an analysis of their similarities, differences, and potential integration.

SYSTEMS-BASED STRATEGIES FOR HEALTH CARE MANAGEMENT

Senge (1990) has suggested that the complexity we are experiencing is created by our own increasing capacity to generate more information than anyone can absorb, foster more interdependencies than anyone can manage, and accelerate change faster than anyone's ability to keep up. This dynamically complex environment requires a new approach to management, known as systems thinking, which Senge defined as a conceptual framework to make the full patterns of complex interrelated actions clearer and help people see how to change them (Senge, 1990).

A growing awareness of systems thinking is apparent in both business (Goodstein & Burke, 1991) and health care literature (Flowers,

Note: Originally published in *Nursing Leadership Forum*, Vol. 2, No. 3, 1996. New York: Springer Publishing Company.

1990; Tonges & Madden, 1993). Given our increasing appreciation of systems thinking as an appropriate approach to managing in a turbulent environment, it is not surprising that some of today's most popular and successful strategies are systems based. For example, reengineering and care and case management reflect a systems-oriented approach. Each of these strategies recognizes and addresses the multiple interdependencies that transcend departmental boundaries in contemporary health care organizations.

DIFFERENTIATING THE THREE Rs AND OTHER MANAGEMENT TOOLS

Although there is some conceptual overlap among these three techniques, key distinctions can also be made. These distinctions provide a basis for differentiating the three Rs and other popular management tools.

Reengineering

Hammer and Champy (1993), two prominent experts, have defined reengineering as "the fundamental rethinking and radical redesign of business processes to achieve dramatic improvements in critical contemporary measures of performance, such as cost, quality, service, and speed" (p. 32). According to these authors, the distinguishing characteristics of reengineering include:

1. *Process orientation*—Reengineering focuses on an entire series of steps involved in getting something done and cuts across departmental boundaries.
2. *Ambition*—This is a technique to employ when major improvement is sought, as there are much easier ways to achieve small gains than organization-wide change.

    For example, to achieve a 5–10% cost reduction, managers usually take steps that would not be considered extreme, such as limiting overtime or finding less expensive supplies, as opposed to reinventing the way the firm does business. Reengineering is not the technique of choice when you are just trying to do the same things in the same way for a little less money.

3. *Rule breaking*—Reengineering involves surfacing inherent assumptions about the way work has to be done and destroying old rules, leading to genuine innovation rather than surface changes (i.e., it's not the proverbial "rearranging the deck chairs on the Titanic").
4. *Creative use of information technology*—Information technology (IT) is the enabler that makes it possible to work in totally new and different ways (Hammer & Champy, 1993).

Word processing provides a good example of this characteristic. Because of the ease with which documents can be composed at the screen of a word processor, which may also be portable, many administrators now type or at least draft their own documents and send a file or disk to a secretary. This represents one of the biggest changes in the way that business material has been produced since the invention of the typewriter.

Redesigning

The second technique, job or work redesign, is defined as "changing the actual structure of the jobs that people perform" (Hackman & Oldham, 1976, p. 44). The objective of job design is to incorporate intrinsically motivating factors, such as autonomy and variety, in the structure of a job. Job design theory suggests that performing well in a job with these characteristics is a rewarding experience for individuals with strong needs for growth and achievement (Hackman & Lawler, 1971). As a result, employees' intrinsic motivation, job satisfaction, and performance are expected to and have been shown to improve (Hackman & Oldham, 1976).

Job redesign and reengineering have distinct differences: reengineering focuses on business processes at an organizational level and employs IT as the lever that makes new ways of working possible, whereas job redesign focuses at the level of individual jobs.

Dienemann and Gessner (1992) have suggested that there are two basic theoretical perspectives that can guide a redesign effort: job redesign and system redesign. Job redesign, as defined above, is the primary focus of this discussion; however, a brief comment on system redesign may also be helpful.

Sociotechnical System (STS) redesign is an example of a systems approach to redesign. STS is a framework or perspective that looks at work as a system and considers both the technical aspects (the work and how it is accomplished) and the social aspects (the relationships among the people doing the work) (Davis & Trist, 1974).

As an example, the work of a nursing staff is to provide nursing care for their patients. The delivery of this care can be organized in several different ways, such as in a functional, team, or dyad nursing care delivery system. Each of these approaches represents a different combination of technical and social factors. While organizing nurses and assistants as a functional delivery system may optimize the efficiency of some of the technical aspects of the work, a team or dyad approach would probably strengthen social elements of the system, fostering better coworker relationships and team work.

The goal of STS redesign is to develop alternatives that foster both high productivity (technical system) and high job satisfaction (social system). Hallmark characteristics of STS interventions include: (1) group-oriented reorganization of social systems, (2) increased workgroup autonomy and reduced external supervision, and (3) concern with fit among subsystems (Beekun, 1989).

The STS approach to redesign was originally developed in the 1950s (Davis & Trist, 1974) and clearly preceded today's reengineering movement. The two techniques share a broader systems perspective, and both emphasize an iterative process in which knowledge gained from trying new things is used as a basis for continuing innovation (Tonges, 1995). The major differences appear to be, again, the key role of modern IT in reengineering and the attention to social dynamics in STS redesign, which the reengineering approach seems to lack.

Restructuring

Although restructuring is related to, and often seen in conjunction with reengineering, it is not the same thing. Restructuring changes things like the number and types of departments and managers and the way organizational decisions are made.

Shared governance is an example of a popular organizational restructuring initiative in health care. This form of restructuring flattens the administrative hierarchy by eliminating levels of middle managers and increasing staff decision-making (Blouin, 1994).

After business processes have been reengineered, it is frequently necessary to change the organizational structure, and other administrative systems, to support the new processes. It is important to note, however, that the changes created through reengineering are what drives the changes in structure. Thus, departmental restructuring in the absence of process changes is not reengineering.

Other Management Tools

In addition to distinguishing reengineering from restructuring, Hammer and Champy (1993) have identified differences between reengineering and several other popular management tools, including automation, downsizing, and Total Quality Management/Continuous Quality Improvement (TQM/CQI):

- Automation entails doing the same things, often the wrong things, faster. Hence, Hammer's (1990) advice is to wipe the slate clean of existing procedures, i.e., "don't automate, obliterate" (p. 104).
- Downsizing involves doing less with less in response to a decline in demand, such as a lower inpatient census, whereas reengineering strives to do more with less.
- Although TQM/CQI and reengineering are techniques that focus on changing processes in an effort to improve customer service, TQM/CQI assumes that the system is basically sound and seeks incremental improvement. Reengineering, on the other hand, is a "start from scratch" approach to radical change. Thus, it would make sense to integrate these approaches by first reengineering your business processes and then employing TQM/CQI to maintain and gradually improve the new systems.

INTEGRATING THE THREE Rs

Reengineering, redesign, and restructuring are different, but complementary. As Figure 24.1 illustrates, the most logical approach to integrating these techniques may be to:

1. Begin with reengineering as a means of creating new processes for accomplishing work
2. Design jobs to carry them out; and
3. Restructure the organization (and other administrative systems) to support their implementation.

Prior to the introduction of reengineering in the early nineties, many organizational change initiatives began with an STS approach. Now it seems that STS concepts and techniques may be successfully applied between individual job redesign and organizational restructuring, as a bridge back to the macro level that focuses on connecting individual jobs to the social system of the organization.

Unfortunately, universally accepted definitions of the three Rs do not appear to exist. Given the proliferation of new management tools designed to cope with the hyperturbulent business environment, it is not surprising that confusion concerning these concepts persists. For example, some may say that redesign is related to rearranging existing functions, while reengineering has to do with creating something completely new; however, systems theorists and STS work redesign practitioners have long recognized the need to make a fresh

FIGURE 24.1 Interrelationships among the "Three Rs."

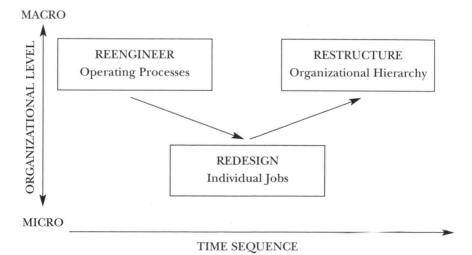

start and focus on the objectives to be achieved, rather than attempting to correct problems within an existing system (Mohr, Thomas, Ranney, & Lamb, 1989; Nadler, 1981).

Systems tend to seek stability and resist efforts to change them; therefore, efforts to improve a dysfunctional system through incremental adjustments may prove fruitless. Worse yet, the current system may be based on faulty assumptions and fundamentally flawed. Focusing on making changes within an existing system places artificial boundaries on one's thinking. Trapped within the limitations of the current system, one is easily blinded to the possibility of more creative alternatives.

What *is* new about reengineering is its emphasis on IT as an essential enabler. Perhaps the radical departure from conventional approaches, made possible by emerging IT capabilities, creates the false impression that reengineering generates the new, while redesign modifies what already exists.

Reengineering, redesign, and restructuring are currently being used to create a new infrastructure for the delivery of health care. Core processes that are common to the care of all patients are being reengineered (e.g., entry into the system, diagnostic and therapeutic procedures). Changes in these core processes are being accompanied by changes in the design of health care jobs and work teams and the structure of health care organizations.

These organizational changes will provide a new foundation for further streamlining of the processes of care for specific case types. This second wave of clinical process improvement will be accomplished through strategic implementation and enhancement of care and case management systems (Bower, 1993; Zander, 1992).

Dienemann and Gessner (1992) classified nursing case management as a health care system redesign initiative. Care and case management initiatives definitely fit these authors' description of system redesign as involving multiple departments, roles, and relationships, and creating changes that result in new organizational systems. These innovations also create new jobs, such as case manager, and changes in the motivational characteristics of existing jobs (e.g., staff nurse, nurse manager, and clinical specialist), and may thus represent a blending of system and job redesign.

THE HEALTH CARE CONTEXT

With or without reform legislation, the drive to control costs is creating radical changes in the health care industry. As Toner (1994) pointed out, "The choice never was between change and the status quo, but over who will make the changes, and how, and with what kind of regulation, if any" (p. 1).

Change has accelerated to a pace where cycles have been replaced by rapid, extreme fluctuations. In the midst of this maelstrom, nurses are being affected in numerous ways. Although it is amazing to anyone who worked through the severe nursing shortage of the late eighties, the hospital market is so tight that many new graduates have difficulty finding jobs (Sherer, 1994). One is reminded of the old saying about the weather in Chicago, "If you don't like it, just wait, it'll change."

Despite the turmoil, at least two things are clear. In this time of change, the three Rs will continue, and nursing will encounter both risks and opportunities. If we can maintain a clear vision of our identity and contribution, avoiding the risks and seizing the opportunities, the potential for advancement for our patients and our profession is tremendous.

SUMMARY

In summary, the three Rs are neither interchangeable nor incompatible. Reengineering identifies core business processes, such as order fulfillment, and employs information technology to create new and better ways to accomplish this work. Job redesign changes the structure and motivational characteristics of individual jobs, and STS redesign seeks a balance between productivity and quality of work life. Finally, restructuring changes the framework of communication channels and decision-making mechanisms that support organizational operations. Putting the three Rs together thus involves reengineering the work, redesigning the jobs and interconnections among them, and restructuring the organization.

REFERENCES

Beekun, R. I. (1989). Assessing the effectiveness of sociotechnical interventions: Antidote or fad? *Human Relations*, 877–897.

Blouin, A. S. (1994). *Organizational culture in hospitals with shared governance.* Unpublished doctoral dissertation, University of Illinois, Chicago.

Bower, K. (1993). Case management: Work redesign with patient outcomes in mind. In K. J. McDonagh (Ed.), *Patient-centered hospital care: Reform from within.* Ann Arbor, MI: Health Administration Press.

Davis, L. E., & Trist, E. L. (1974). Improving the quality of work life: Sociotechnical case studies. In J. O'Toole (Ed.) *Work and the quality of life* (pp. 246–280). Cambridge, MA: MIT Press.

Dienemann, J., & Gessner, T. (1992). Restructuring nursing care delivery systems. *Nursing Economics, 10*, 253–258, 30.

Flowers, J. (1990). Understanding how our actions shape our world. *Healthcare Forum, 33*(2), 12–17.

Goodstein, L. D., & Burke, W. W. (1991). Creating successful organizational change. *Organizational Dynamics, 19*(4), 5–17.

Hackman, J. R., & Lawler, E. E. (1971). Employee reactions to job characteristics. *Journal of Applied Psychology, 55*, 259–286.

Hackman, J. R., & Oldham, G. R. (1976). Motivation through the design of work: Test of a theory. *Organizational Behavior and Human Performance, 16*, 250–279.

Hammer, M. (1990). Reengineering work: Don't automate, obliterate. *Harvard Business Review, 68*(4), 104–114.

Hammer, M., & Champy, J. (1993). *Reengineering the corporation: A manifesto for business resolution.* New York: Harper Business.

Mohr, B., Thomas, G., Ranney, J., & Lamb, S. R. (1989, July 17–26). *A sociotechnical approach to designing high performance organizations.* Bethel, MA.

Nadler, G. (1981). *The planning and device approach.* New York: Wiley.

Senge, P. M. (1990). *The fifth discipline: The art and practice of the learning organization.* New York: Doubleday.

Sherer, J. L. (1994). Job shifts. *Hospitals and Health Networks, 68*(19), 64–68.

Toner, R. (Oct. 2, 1994). Ills of health system outlive debate on care. *The New York Times*, Section 4, pp. 1, 4.

Tonges, M. C., & Madden, M. J. (1993). Running the vicious cycle backwards and other system solutions to nursing problems. *Journal of Nursing Administration, 23*(1), 39–44.

Tonges, M. C. (1995). The evolution of reengineering. In D. Flarey & S. S. Blancett (Eds.), *Reengineering nursing and health care.* Rockville, MD: Aspen.

Zander, K. (1992). Critical pathways. In M. Melum & M. Sinoris (Eds.), *Total quality management.* Chicago: AHA Publishing.

CHAPTER **25**

Nurse Administrator Vulnerability

Ruth Davidhizar

Nursing administration positions, whether in service or education, are becoming increasingly vulnerable. Vulnerability may be related to a new administration, change in philosophy of the present administration, the nurse executive's performance, competition with a subordinate or peer, or a combination of these factors. Regardless of performance, being fired or terminated, or being asked to resign and realizing that resignation is the only option, are all situations that easily may confront the nursing administrator working in the 1990s.

Vulnerability, however, is not new to the 1990s. In 1981, Schorr wrote an editorial for the *American Journal of Nursing* entitled "Nursing Leaders: An Endangered Species?" Schorr (1981) wrote about the vulnerability of nursing leaders in general and deans in particular. As a result of her concern, a resolution expressing concern about the "Encroachment on Nursing Prerogatives" by physicians and hospital administrators was passed at a national deans' meeting, and a task force was established to study the matter. Five years later, Barritt (1986) identified that this action did not solve the problem and it should have been addressed more generally to cover both external and internal factors. Although little is written on this subject, the issue of vulnerability of nursing executives continues to be a problem.

Anticipatory planning is important before a nurse enters an executive position. Nurse administrators should think about the dismissal process while the job is going well in order to make thoughtful and

Note: Originally published in *Nursing Leadership Forum*, Vol. 1, No. 4, 1995. New York: Springer Publishing Company.

rational decisions (Weaver, 1988). The process of leaving a job is the true test of leadership skills. Schwartz (1979) noted, "Anybody can hire a man, but the test of true leadership is how one handles the dismissal." This is true for the people on both ends of the dismissal, particularly true if the dismissal is your own. Thus, planning for termination is an important task of the nurse administrator either before taking the job or while it is going well. Planning wisely in the midst of the turmoil that may surround leaving is very difficult.

VULNERABILITY IN EXECUTIVE POSITIONS IN SERVICE

Discussion here will be limited to the nurse executive who holds the highest nursing position in the organization. Titles of nurse administrators vary significantly, whether in service or education. Some terms, such as nurse administrator or nurse executive, are used to describe the top nursing administrator in both service and education, yet other terms are used in service primarily (see Figure 25.1). Titles may change with corporate restructuring or changes of administration in an attempt to better describe the altered role of nurse administrator (Mackenzie, 1987).

For simplicity, the title Director of Nursing (DON) will be used to incorporate all the service titles in the rest of this article. Vestal (1990) notes that top health care executives stay in jobs an average of 3 years, resulting in an annual turnover rate of about 30%. It even appears that the rate is increasing (Sabatino, 1987; Vestal, 1990). Chief exec-

FIGURE 25.1 Terms to describe nurse administrators.

Service	Education
Director of Nursing	Dean of Nursing Department/
Vice President of Nursing	School
Patient Care Services	Chairperson of Nursing
Vice President	Department
Patient Care Coordinator	Head of the Nursing Department
Assistant Vice President of	Chairperson of the Nursing
Nursing	Division
Assistant Administrator	
Associate Administrator	

utive officers (CEOs) today frequently have new role expectations for those around them. Thus, a new CEO may be predisposed to question whether an "in-place" nurse executive can effectively change to meet the new requirements. The nursing executive, then, is highly vulnerable to being fired, or requested to hand in a resignation, when the top administration changes. Some administrative health care executives think that it will be easier to get staff to think differently if all the top management people are changed simultaneously. Even if there were no complaints about the nurse executive, the nurse executive may be asked to leave.

In a study by Freund (1985), it was noted that over a 10-year period, hospitals averaged 2.5 DONs. The majority of hospitals (57%) had one or two DONs whereas 19% had four or more in the 10-year period. Termination or requested resignation was cited as the most frequent reason past DONs left their positions (40%). A study in 1990 by Witt Associates estimated nurse executive tenure to be 4.7 years, a decrease from the study done 2 years prior.

Vestal (1990) notes that the phenomenon of executive firings has become so commonplace in the business world that the stigma of losing a job is not as problematic or demoralizing as it was in the past. It is suggested that if the firing or termination process is managed well, the consequences for the nurse executive can in fact be quite positive (Vestal, 1990).

With the changes in corporate health care structures, and with the focus on bottom-line management, even if the nurse executive stays when a new corporate administration takes over, the role description is likely to be significantly altered.

For example, many nurse executives are finding that they are responsible not only for delivery of patient care but also for the management of complex additional corporate structures and relationships.

VULNERABILITY IN EXECUTIVE POSITIONS IN COLLEGES AND UNIVERSITIES

Schorr (1981) noted that nursing deans are even more vulnerable to job loss than nurse administrators in service. Today, it would be difficult to estimate which group is more vulnerable, but both are seriously at risk. Deans also may encounter a change in administrative structure and a philosophy that it is easier to start with all new administrators if a change in philosophy and approach is being implemented. In addition, job vulnerability is increased by a number of other factors. Since the 1970s there have been increasing budgetary restraints for administrators of nursing programs in universities and colleges. The dean is often the bearer of the bad news to the nursing faculty. Consequently, the dean is often blamed by nursing faculty for the decrease in allocation of resources. Institutional conflicts can become personalized as deans and other administrators are made scapegoats for the frustration and anger of faculty (Barritt, 1986).

The blend of teaching, research, and practice (the "three-legged stool") required by the university has often been difficult for the nursing faculty to attain (Association of Academic Health Centers, 1980). As funds for personnel, research, and capital improvements have continued to shrink, many nursing schools have had to close programs that were begun without permanent university budget lines. The nursing dean often ends up being blamed for these retrenchments.

Copp (1995) notes that the decision for a dean to step down, whether it be the dean's choice or a decision made by others, is a very significant one not only for the dean but for the institution. In most settings the dean remains in the school as faculty, peer, and colleague. This requires an adjustment on the dean's part, on her predecessor's part, and on the part of the faculty. Copp (1995) notes, however, that this change can be a positive one for both students and colleagues if it is well managed.

NURSE EXECUTIVE'S PERFORMANCE

Confronting the changes and demands of the present tumultuous health care industry or the dramatic changes in institutions of higher learning requires ongoing adaptability, the ability to negotiate conflict, skill in helping others reconcile differences, and political savvy. It requires a nurse executive who is responsive yet who can set limits. The nurse executive must be able to handle outside forces that impact on the organization and department, as well as provide strong leadership to the staff supervised. Not everyone succeeds; some nurse executives misjudge how to keep up with the times and misread how the "winds" within the organization are blowing (Barritt, 1986).

Others may deteriorate in their ability to handle ongoing administrative challenges. This may be the result of illness, accident, or the increasing complexity of the job. Both subordinates and superiors may recognize the downward spiral and may need to adjust to the nurse executive's inability to competently lead. Whereas some staff will be overprotective and cover up the administrator's faults, other staff are all to eager to identify the administrator as incompetent. Administrative action may be fast or slow in coming, depending on the strength of the documentation of incompetency and the appeal process within the institution.

COMPETITION WITH A SUBORDINATE OR PEER

Another area of vulnerability for the nursing administrator rests in the desire of a subordinate for the top position. A nurse executive may or may not recognize that a subordinate employee has an eye on replacing, is working toward replacing, and may actually be planning to replace the nurse executive. When the nurse executive has no plans or wishes to leave the position, this can be not only surprising but unnerving. How can administrative respect be maintained if employees think the nursing administrator will not remain in the job? The directions the nurse executive gives may not be taken seriously if staff feel the nurse executive will not be there when the plan is actually put into effect. How can administrative authority be maintained if the administrator's directions are undermined by the would-be successor? Employees may feel they don't want to make the possible successor angry and consequently may be hesitant to respond to the nurse executive and go against the would-be successor's direction.

The nurse administrator may suspect an employee has an eye on the top job, even if they are personal friends. This suspicion can be intensified if the employee talks to others about spending time with the CEO outside the work environment talking about work issues. This can be further magnified when the employee acts negatively and is nonsupportive of the nurse administrator. The nurse administrator may suspect that the subordinate is using their personal friendship to collect information on the nurse executive's faults in order to cast a negative light.

If a new administration has been brought in, the subordinate may quickly try to identify with the new administrative team. The subordinate may try to become visible as a positive change agent and, ignoring any chain of command, seeks out the new administrators to discuss ideas for positive change.

In another scenario orchestrated by a subordinate who wishes to have the nurse administrator's job (either in service or education), complaints from subordinates may be taken straight to top administration. In the college setting, senior faculty may short-circuit the system and go to central administration with their complaints about the nursing dean. Under the pretext of being "unable to communicate with the dean" (Barritt, 1986), faculty may become increasingly adamant to administration that the problems in the nursing department are related to and caused by the dean.

RECOGNIZING WARNING SIGNALS

Astute nursing administrators are aware when there is a shift in loyalty or a lack of support from higher administration and/or subordinates. They recognize the risk of being fired or terminated. In fact, there are usually multiple signals that warn of the future action. Nursing administrators are typically sensitive to the signs and symptoms that indicate their job is in jeopardy (Biordi & Gardiner, 1992; Vestal, 1990). Not only are signs recognized but action must be taken quickly to resolve the issues, improve performance, or at least facilitate the nursing administrator's managing of the termination process on his or her own terms (Blouin & Brent, 1992a, 1992b, 1992c; Kerfoot, Serafin-Dickson, & Green, 1988; Zimmerman, 1994).

For a few, it is only when the job is lost that recent events fit together and the nurse administrator realizes that significant clues were missed or not believed and acted upon. In this case, the former nurse administrator may tell colleagues, "I never saw it coming." "I had no warning." "I had no idea that this would happen to me." Or, "I saw many of the warning signals, but I didn't believe it could be happening to me after all I've done for that organization."

Of course, some nurse administrators who tend to personalize the actions of others may perceive warning signals where none exist. Such administrators may assume their jobs are in jeopardy when in fact they are not. Ironically, acting in a suspicious manner can quickly turn others against the nurse administrator and actually put the job in jeopardy.

The following items are risk factors that may indicate that the nurse executive's position is in jeopardy, whether it be by firing or a negotiated decision. In an excellent article, "Fired! Managing the Process," Vestal (1990) lists some 12 warning signs. Some of Vestal's warning signs have stimulated the following discussion of nine categories believed by the author to be particularly significant.

1. Changes in Administration

When a new administration takes over, the nurse executive should carefully explore with the new CEO or president if compatibility exists as to goals and mission for the organization. Factors such as congruency of leadership styles and philosophy or management must also have a good fit. There should be a match on strategic priorities. Sometimes it is immediately evident that the new administration is not supportive of the nurse executive and/or the nursing department. For example, the organization of the nursing department may be restructured without consulting the nurse executive. The nurse executive may feel forced to leave rather than compromise leadership principles and positional authority within the department.

2. Major and Unresolved Disagreements With Superiors, Peers, and Subordinates

When the incidence of clashes with both superiors and peers increases and reconciliations become less and less satisfactory, the astute nurse executive should carefully evaluate the dynamics of what is going on. These clashes may be an indication of a deeper problem and of a general lack of support for the nurse executive. Frequent clashes will result in an increasing disharmony.

Another type of lack of support occurs when the superior withdraws resources, for example, decreases the budget, which puts the nurse executive in a position of compromised effectiveness. Lack of support may also occur when the nurse executive is moved to a smaller office or to one far away from corporate headquarters or distant from the persons supervised. Taking away space is yet another way to show nonsupport, for example, requiring the nurse executive's supervisors to move into tighter quarters, reducing availability of conference rooms or classrooms, or cutting back on break room space. Yet another way to show nonsupport is for educational funds for staff or travel money to be slashed from the budget request.

3. A Decrease in Collaboration From Others

Lack of support may not only be demonstrated by clashes with others and their failure to agree on satisfactory resolutions but also by negativism, lack of cooperation, and a general lack of willingness to collaborate from others. For example, when the nurse executive presents an idea, it may be received with lack of acceptance or disapproval even if the idea seems sound.

4. A Widening Gap Between Philosophical Beliefs With Higher Administration

An increase in philosophical differences may show up at department head or administrative meetings. Directions given by top administration may not fit with the leadership style with which the nurse executive feels comfortable. Although the nurse executive may make efforts to gain support, the basis for disagreements continues unresolved.

5. Unresolved Role Conflict

Role conflict between the nurse executive and top administration may be experienced when new responsibilities and role expectations are given to the nurse executive. If the responsibilities are not congruent with the nurse executive's beliefs about role, such role conflict may continue unresolved and lead the nurse executive to unrest and unhappiness. For example, the nurse executive's position may be changed into clinical program director with decreased focus on nursing and more emphasis on the interdisciplinary team.

6. Use of Subordinates on Administrative Projects

The nurse executive may find out that top level administrators have assigned nursing staff to administrative projects without going through the proper channels. This can indicate a serious lack of respect and willingness to abuse the organizational chain of command. If leaving the nurse executive out was deliberate, it may result in staff receiving orders or instructions without going through their supervisor, undermining the nurse executive's authority. If the response of the top administrator to the nurse executive's objection is to take the nursing staff member out of the nursing department, the handwriting is on the wall.

7. Lack of Response From Superiors to Requests for Appointments

When higher administration is repeatedly not available or is "tied up" with other matters, the nurse executive should recognize that this action shows lack of support. When the nurse executive's requests continue to be denied, the lack of cooperation and an indication of disrespect are serious.

Failure to respond to the nurse executive's proposals and/or white papers may be another indication that he or she is being put out of the loop. Even if the nurse executive has excellent ideas, they cannot be accomplished without administrative support and resources.

8. An Increase in Evaluations

When the nurse executive is told that a special evaluation of performance is going to be done (a review that is not consistent with the agency routine), this is always a signal of trouble. The nurse manager may question this process and even refuse to submit to it. Even if the nurse administrator wins the argument, the issue is unlikely to pass. An alternative method of scrutiny is usually implemented.

9. An Increase in Work Responsibilities

Another common pattern is one that often fools nursing executives and makes them feel flattered. In this pattern, they are given more assignments, for example, major responsibility for preparation for an accreditation visit or the assignment to prepare major grant applications. Whatever the specifics, the new assignments are heavy, critical, and numerous. Such tactics may be a setup for failure. This is especially true if the added responsibilities involve jobs that require new resources that are not forthcoming or if the assignments include "no-win" projects. Another version of this pattern is taking away the nurse executive's assistants but still requiring the same amount of work. A dean of nursing, for example, may be given the major responsibility for preparing for the university or college self-study report for reaccreditation only to find that follow-up has not been made to recommendations on the last self-study and there is inadequate time to put the changes in place and to show a positive track record.

A related pattern occurs when the nurse executive is given responsibility for additional departments beyond nursing that already have major problems. Again, if adequate resources to solve the problem do not accompany the added responsibility, it may be a setup for failure or to "prove" the nurse executive inadequate for the job.

TACTICS TO REDUCE VULNERABILITY

There are a variety of tactics that can be employed by a nurse executive to reduce vulnerability to job loss. In fact, even when a nurse executive feels that there may be some concern about vulnerability, taking such tactics can increase job security.

1. Focus on Enhanced Communication

Keeping superiors and subordinates informed on what the nurse executive is doing and why is a significant way to improve and maximize interpersonal relationships. Input from subordinates and superiors should be solicited before new projects are undertaken. In addition to communicating in writing, it is important to communicate verbally and to work at developing strong relationships. The nurse executive should be affirming, should communicate respect, and should focus on upholding others rather than taking them for granted. If retrenchment is needed, the nurse executive should solicit feedback from faculty or staff on how this should be done.

2. Keep Department Goals Congruent and Complementary to Goals of the Organization

It is important that goals be congruent and complementary so that the nurse executive does not feel at odds with the CEO. Astute observations should be made on which direction the organization is heading, and then the direction of the nurse executive's department should be brought in line with complementary goals.

3. Assess the Costs of the Department Versus the "Payoffs"

When one is "under the gun," it is not the time to undertake expensive programs with questionable payoffs. When tactics to reduce vulnerability of the nurse executive seem timely, an effort should be made to keep extra or unnecessary costs at a minimum. It is also helpful if the nurse executive points this out, "We decided that this is not the time to try to implement a project that we are not sure will take off; we'll put that on the back burner for a while."

On the positive side, it is exactly the time to implement projects that will deliver a fast and welcome payoff. Even a series of small "wins" can change others' perceptions of one's performance.

4. Solicit Publicity That Makes the Department Look Good

This is a wise time to put extra effort forth in getting good press on innovative nursing programs. Placing supervisors in prestigious community positions or even drawing attention to a recent appointment to the American Academy of Nursing can enhance the pride the CEO feels in the nursing division.

5. Bring in External Monies for the Organization

This is the time to write a grant that has been on the back burner and that has a good chance of being funded. Grants, contracts, or having programs/projects that earn money for the institution can enhance the image of the nursing department and ensure its place of priority on the CEO's list of important departments.

6. Keep Contemporary

The nurse executive should not take this time to step back and be minimally involved in organizational and community events. Efforts should be made to network with peer nurse executives and to maintain good networks in the larger organizations outside of nursing.

7. *Networking*

Networking with non-nursing peers in the organization and community can help build support for the nurse executive. This should include influential persons in the community, board members, and others whose positive view of your achievements will become known and a deterrent to the CEO "removing" the nurse executive.

SUMMARY

Recognizing warning signs of job vulnerability is key if the nurse executive is to remain viable and effective in an organization. It is important to recognize not only signs but actions that may indicate that the administration may not be satisfied with performance or may think a change is in order. Risk factors include changes in administration; major and unresolved disagreements with superiors, peers, and subordinates; a decrease in collaboration with others; a widening gap between one's philosophical beliefs with those of higher administration; unresolved role conflicts; unauthorized use of subordinates on administrative projects; lack of response from superiors to requests for appointments; an increase in one's performance evaluations; and even an increase in work responsibilities.

On the other hand, tactics that can be taken to reduce vulnerability can be: focusing on enhanced communication, correlating goals of the department with goals of the organization, increasing "payoffs" of the department, bringing in external monies, keeping contemporary with peers as well as those in the organization and community and, finally, building a network of support. By maximizing tactics to reduce vulnerability, it may be possible to minimize and even alleviate an impending job threat.

REFERENCES

Association of Academic Health Centers. (1980, October 6). *Meeting minutes.*

Barritt, E. (1986). The vulnerability of deans. *Nursing Outlook, 34*(1), 40.

Biordi, E., & Gardiner, D. (1992). The handwriting on the wall: Warning signs of impending job loss. *Journal of Nursing Administration, 22*(11), 15–20.

Blouin, A., & Brent, N. (1992a). Nurse administrators in job transition: Contractual considerations. *Journal of Nursing Administration, 22*(5), 8–10.

Blouin, A., & Brent, N. (1992b). Nurse administrators in job transition: Negotiated resignations and severance assignments. *Journal of Nursing Administration, 22*(7/8), 16–17.

Blouin, A., & Brent, N. (1992c). Nursing administrators in job transition: Managing the exit. *Journal of Nursing Administration, 22*(10), 12–13, 24.

Copp, L. (1995). When the dean steps down. *Journal of Professional Nursing, 11*, 197–198.

Freund, C. (1985). The tenure of directors of nursing. *Journal of Nursing Administration, 15*(2), 11–15.

Kerfoot, K., Serafin-Dickson, R., & Green, S. (1988). Managing transition: Resigning with style from the nurse manager position. *Nursing Economics, 6*, 200–220.

Mackenzie, N. (1987). Nurse executive survey results. *Apsen's Advisor for Nurse Executives, 2*(5), 2–3.

Sabatino, F. (1987). The revolving door: CEO turnover. *Hospitals, 61*(19), 80–84.

Schorr, T. (1981). Nursing's leaders—an endangered species? *American Journal of Nursing, 81*, 318.

Schwartz, D. (1979). *The magic of thinking big* (p. 210). North Hollywood, CA: Wilshire Book Company.

Vestal, K. (1990). Fired! Managing the process. *Journal of Nursing Administration, 20*(6), 14–15.

Weaver, C. (1988). Nurse executive turnover. *Nursing Economics, 6*, 283–285.

Witt Associates, Inc. (1990). *Today's nurse executive: Report of a survey* (p. 9). Oak Brook, IL: Author.

Zimmerman, P. (1994). Advice for dealing with a job loss. *Journal of Emergency Nursing, 20*(2), 83–84.

CHAPTER 26

Where Will I Go?
Displaced Nurses Relate
Their Experiences

Martha Greenberg

INTRODUCTION

Registered nurses have been experiencing displacement, the non-voluntary transfer or reassignment of the registered nurse to another unit or position, or layoff, termination, and severing of nursing personnel as a result of the closure of hospitals and other agencies and the physical relocation of departments or units. The purpose of this qualitative study is to describe the human experience of change from the perspective of displaced nurses. Thirteen registered nurses employed at eight metropolitan New York agencies described their experiences of displacement. Their interviews were analyzed using grounded theory methodology. Five themes emerged in the displacement experience: finding out, weighing options, coping with negative emotions and loss, support, and giving advice. Implications for education, practice, and research are discussed.

Retrenchment, reengineering, reorganization, restructuring, mergers, downsizing, and job redesign in health care have created change in the delivery and organization of nursing services. From the mid 1980s to the present, a declining U.S. patient census, shortened lengths of stay and changes in reimbursement structure affected decisions in the private and public sectors to close or merge hospital units

Note: Originally published in *Nursing Leadership Forum*, Vol. 5, No. 1, 2000. New York: Springer Publishing Company.

and restructure positions and organizations (Barnes, Harmon, & Kish, 1986; Begany, 1994; Geddes, Salyer, & Mark, 1999; Ingersoll, Cook, Fogel, Applegate, & Frank, 1999; Krugman & Preheim, 1999; Urden, 1999). In the early 1990s there was a shift away from a job market where nursing positions were plentiful and where, for the most part, there was job security. The agencies where these nurses worked began job freezes, bought nurses out of their positions, or urged them to retire in an attempt to reduce costs. In some agencies, staff nurse positions were frozen and people were not replaced when attrition occurred. Displacement occurred because buildings and units were closed or moved, agencies were merged or bought out, and departments and positions were eliminated or combined.

This resulted in the nonvoluntary transfer or reassignment to another unit or position, or in layoff, termination, or severing of nursing personnel (Barnes, Harmon, & Kish, 1986; Begany, 1994; Ireson & Powers, 1987). In 1994, 71 percent of nurses responding to a national survey no longer felt secure in their positions (Meissner & Carey, 1994). Presently, local and state workforce surveys (Bowen, Lyons, & Young, 2000; The Center for Health Workforce Studies, 2000) indicate that health care reform continues to affect job security and job availability. Displacement persists as a significant problem facing nurses.

Although there is some empirical indication that nurses' job satisfaction (Armstrong-Stassen, Cameron, & Horsburgh, 1996; Krugman & Preheim, 1999; Urden, 1999), job security (Meissner & Carey, 1994), morale (Shindul-Rothschild, 1994), trust, and commitment to an employer (Anderson, Baker, & Beglinger, 1998; Armstrong-Stassen, Cameron, & Horsburgh, 1996) are negatively affected by restructuring, reengineering, and job redesign, the literature conveys little of the human aspects of displacement that nurses experience. Qualitative methods were used by Tillman and colleagues (1997) to explore how uncertainty of staff nurses in the turbulent change environment affected their ability to provide patient care. Qualitative methods were also used by Geddes and colleagues (1999) to examine the impact of hospital and nursing unit characteristics on the delivery of care and on patient and nursing administrative outcomes. Factors contributing to an uncertain environment revolve around issues of workload, workplace identity, and the impact of reengineering on care delivery.

The present study addresses the experience of displaced nurses. What is the nurse's participation in the change process? How are displacement decisions handled within organizations? How do nurses feel about being displaced? What support is offered? Qualitative methodology is used to explore the perceptions of nurses about their displacement. Leaders who are able to demonstrate a genuine understanding of the human side of displacement can design effective strategies to lead nurses through this time of turbulent change.

METHODS

The School of Nursing Institutional Review Board approved the study, and procedures to protect human subjects were followed throughout.

Sample

Participants were registered nurses from the metropolitan New York area who had experienced displacement. The sample consisted of four staff nurses, two nurse educators, one nurse researcher, one advanced practice nurse, and five nurse managers. Twelve nurses were female and included American Blacks ($n = 3$) and Caucasians ($n = 9$). There was one Caucasian male.

Participants ranged in age from 26 to 55 years. Highest education completed was AAS ($n = 2$), BSN ($n = 4$), MS ($n = 6$), and PhD ($n = 1$). Nursing experience ranged from 5 to 27 years. Participants were employed in eight different agencies; two were urban and three suburban medical centers, two were suburban community hospitals, and one was a university.

Data Collection and Analysis

Participants were recruited via word of mouth and flyers during a 7-month period in the late '90s. Unstructured face-to-face and telephone interviews were conducted. Nurses were asked to tell their experience. One nurse submitted an audiotape of her experience without a formal interview. Interviews averaged about 90 minutes in length and were audiotaped. Follow-up interviews were conducted as needed for clarification or to check themes. The interviews were transcribed by a typist and verified for accuracy by the researcher.

The constant comparative method (Strauss & Corbin, 1990) was used for data analysis. Data were reviewed line by line through open coding to identify categories, their properties, and dimensions. Codes were ascribed. As data collection and analysis progressed, codes were grouped together to refine categories and categories continued to be refined throughout analysis. A graduate student who participated in data collection and analysis also reviewed codes, categories, and concepts. Credibility of data was established by the following techniques: multiple sources, formal audiotaped interviews, and member checking.

RESULTS

Five themes in the displacement experience emerged from participants: finding out, weighing options, coping with negative emotions and loss, support, and giving advice.

Finding Out

Finding out incorporated the circumstances around the displacement and the realization by the nurse of the transforming culture of health care and nursing and the risk of displacement. In the Northeast during the early 1990s, the climate within health care organizations changed from one of economic concern to one of crisis and a focus on cost containment. Processes for delivering nursing and other services were examined, portending the reengineering, restructuring, and downsizing that later followed.

The discovery and subsequent realization by the nurse that s/he would be displaced was typically preceded by lack of information. With the exception of one educator, nurses were not included in planning or decision-making to change existing functional-organizational structures. Lack of a larger perspective about the reasons for change in their agencies formed the nurse's professional employment reality. A nurse educator accurately reflected the thoughts of the majority of the participants when she said:

As someone being displaced, I didn't understand what was the whole picture. Why can't they sit down and say, "This is what we have to do. This is what the whole picture is and this is why we have to do it." That was never done.

Basically employees were left in the dark and typically, as one nurse put it, "they really didn't update the nurses about what was going on and what the plan was; everything was up in the air." For change to be embraced, nurses had to understand management decisions and have some information about the change. Receiving little information about restructuring was interpreted as disorganized and unpremeditated change.

In some cases organizations rejected input from staff and viewed their opinion as factious. One middle manager characterized this rejection in exclusionary terms, saying, "We stopped getting invited to meetings before we were actually told we weren't going to have positions." Managers' concerns about the effects of reorganization on staffing and patient care were often seen as antagonistic to the change. One manager with a job share position was told in no uncertain terms to look elsewhere for employment, if she resisted the change. She explained:

It was massive changes; people had concerns and the repeated response was just variations on the theme 'If you're not with us on these changes, you need to find someplace else to work.' And that was essentially the tone throughout the change until I left. I really objected to that. I thought we had concerns, we needed to discuss them. Not, 'If you're not with us on this, you need to find someplace else to work.'

Lack of information and subsequent power had negative ramifications for those managers relegated to informing their staff of the displacements. Managers were unable to adequately answer nursing staff since the managers were uninformed. A former manager recounted angrily:

There were different levels of staff—weekend people who worked strictly weekends. They called them into a meeting and told them they were no longer going to have that position, that they had to apply for a part-time position, no more strictly weekends.

And we were never told they were going to do that. Not even ask us our opinion, but at least warn us they were going to do that. And then the staff who were weekend people came to us upset or in tears, whatever, "Why'd they do this," and we had a blank look on our face because we had no idea they were going to do it, so we looked incredibly stupid.

Nurses began to suspect displacement when rumors about layoffs, closure of units and entire facilities, or phasing out of positions circulated within the institution. This unofficial communication alerted the nurse of impending displacement, but in so doing created anxiety and insecurity. The collective bargaining unit in one institution attempted to quell rumors by posting flyers. One nurse said:

There's a lot of stress. You can feel the anxiety in people because of the not knowing, the rumors. Even [name deleted] posted around "Do not listen to rumors."

Denial was a common response to rumor and innuendo and occurred when the nurse believed that s/he was immune to transfer or termination. A staff nurse said, "When I got hired, I heard that it [the place] would probably close but you always hear stuff and you never quite believe it." One manager whose position was phased out received several warnings of potential termination that he denied. He related:

She would say off the cuff, 'You know, this is coming, you'd better be careful because if you don't fix this, the next one that's going to go is you.' I always thought, 'They're not going to get rid of me,' but they did.

Secrecy was common and extended from directives to keep quiet to written oaths of nondisclosure regarding information classified as sensitive, e.g., budget cuts. A manager said, "We had to sign an oath that it would be kept under the strictest confidence and not be shared with anybody, in order to squelch any rumors that would happen and cause discontent among the staff." An educator was directed to keep quiet, saying, "I was told, I was asked not to talk about it, not to discuss it at the time with my peers, with my friends, or whatever."

Nurses found out about their displacement in a variety of ways, ranging from letters, telephone, face-to-face communication from a supervisor, or group meetings. Formal communication of transfer or termination occurred at various times throughout the calendar year. Several nurses heard by letter just before a significant holiday, which was especially difficult. One staff RN recalled:

> December 23rd they told me (1995) that I was losing my job. Like two days before Christmas they told me 'You're going to be losing your job.'

Some received the news of their displacement suddenly during their work shift, with little warning beyond rumors, leaving them feeling dazed with few choices. One young staff nurse said, "I don't know if . . . the hospitals think that it's more beneficial to make it more abrupt so that people just feel like, "Well, what else are we supposed to do?" Nurses tried to orient and reorient themselves to the sudden shift in their employment status and sought information from their superiors about their future, but they were often frustrated in their attempts. One nurse characterized this confusion in rather incredulous terms, relating excitedly:

> In early March I was working and I got this phone call at one o'clock in the afternoon. I was going to go to lunch and all of a sudden it was like "Don't return back to the floor." And I was like, "Where do I go?" And she said she'll get back to me or they'll let me know and I went home at the end of day, I unpacked my locker, I cleaned everything out. I really took 9 years of stuff home.

One nurse was notified of her layoff on an FYI (for your information) sticky note! Months following the layoff notification she voiced her bewilderment, and shaking her head, said, "I came in on a Friday morning and it was sitting there on my desk, with a little "FYI." And I come in at 7:30, so it wasn't as if I could take it and go."

Formal meetings, individually and in a group, were another way of finding out about the displacement. Participants reported that finding out individually or in a group did not soften the blow; the news was always upsetting, a shock, and final. A staff nurse recalled: "It was mid-morning. I had only been there for an hour. I was called off the unit for a meeting and then I had to go back to work. I was upset—I remember I was crying a little bit with the nurse manager."

An assistant nurse manager, a position that she shared with another nurse, was not formally told about the phase-out of her position. She and her job-share partner were forced to solicit information from the new positional head. She found out at the end of a staff meeting:

> The new director took over the cardiac care center. I figured she must be going from each unit to each unit to get to know the people who were there and running the units. Maybe I was being naive, and I thought eventually she would come to CCU and want to meet the charge nurse, the assistant nurse managers who were running that unit, and at least introduce herself, which never happened. Then the notice went up that she was going to have a meeting to speak to all the CCU staff, so we all went, as many as could get off the floor at the time. And she still did not speak directly to the charge people and then the meeting was over with, and we stayed and said, 'We'd like to discuss our positions. We keep hearing about how there aren't going to be any charge people and we're wondering does that include the assistant nurse managers. And if we're not going to have a job, what are we going to do?' And I felt as though if we hadn't directly asked, I think we would have waited a long time before somebody said something to us. So I was a little miffed by that. Her response was, 'Oh, you're the job-share people.' I said, 'Yes, we are.' And she said, 'Well, in the new world (and that's what they kept calling it) there really won't be assistant nurse managers, there'll just be self-directed work teams.'

Managers were often in the dark about specific details of institutional change and thus unable to inform nursing staff accordingly. This was particularly true with initial change as opposed to the second or third rounds of reengineering. Since the process concerning retention decisions was new and often chaotic, and decisions concerning the process for retention took so long, managers lacked information to give to their staff. One manager fretted about the trying position that she was in where she was unable to give her staff accurate information:

> It made my job that much harder working for staff, telling them what to expect because I didn't know even though I had been going to meetings.

As reengineering progressed, some administrators realized that lack of participation in the change process and little information heightened employee anxiety. In subsequent changes, staff nurses were given a voice and participated in the change process. One manager said:

> For the second displacement, we knew exactly what was going to happen. The staff was prepared for it. A lot of forethought went into it, a lot of thinking how to make it work best and a lot of education, so everyone was more or less prepared and knew what was going to happen. The second time there was a staff member who was much more involved and we could help in sharing information in dispelling myths.

This staff education, communication, and participation, however, did not characterize the displacement experience for most of the nurses in this study. One young staff nurse accurately depicted most of the study sample when she said there was a "total lack of communication."

Weighing Options

After hearing of their displacement, participants weighed their options and chose among new work assignments when positions were available. In agencies where positions were available, there was an air of urgency surrounding the decision-making process and participants were required to make their decisions immediately. One nurse remembered:

> They talked to me and they kind of gave me a choice at that time. They didn't say that I could think about it for a day really. I guess maybe they were making decisions quickly. I don't know. I don't know of any other reason they wouldn't inform us in advance so you could have a day to think about it.

Sometimes the information given to the displaced nurses was incorrect or misleading, yet they were expected to make an immediate decision. One nurse was called on her day off to attend a meeting at her agency to make her choice. Her agency had collective bargaining. This is part of her report:

I had my child with me, sitting around for hours on my day off, in a room, with the Director of Nursing. . . . And they had given handouts and the handouts were incorrect and every time we went to a meeting they gave me a list of available positions on different floors, which was never correct. And they made us wait 3 hours in that room with my child on my day off, with a lot of other people. But one thing that they did was they would not go on to the next person until they got in touch with the person before them to choose where they wanted to go.

Recognizing that decisions have an impact on their personal and professional life in the short and long term, participants did not always make their decisions alone. They consulted with their spouses, boyfriends, colleagues, parents, and/or children. For example, a nurse said:

I called my husband. You know he's part of my life. He knows my whole life is going to change. Before I made the decision, I made sure it was okay with him. It wasn't like I had nobody to depend on, or have depending on me. I have children and a husband and my life was changing. My hours were changing.

Some nurses saw opportunity in change and made their choice based on the chance to learn new skills and advance professionally. One said, "One of the other reasons I joined the floor is because they were having a ventilator support unit and I thought that'd be a good opportunity for me to learn that." Others decided based on personal factors, for example, "I went to work in same day medical ambulatory care, because I was going to school and that was no weekends and no evenings and I thought that would help with the stress of going to school."

The options for a nurse with an advanced degree or specialization were found to be severely distasteful and limited. Several nurses with advanced degrees viewed displacement bitterly, often requiring them to return to a former status or role. An inservice educator with a master's degree was offered a staff position. She refused the position, saying:

She told me I would be offered a comparable, challenging position. That position was going back to the Intensive Care Unit, which was where I came from and the same position I had been in.

For those nurses whose positions were phased out, one option was to find work in a different position in the institution, or in a different agency. Location and commutation were factors that these nurses pondered as they weighed their options. One manager said, "When I got laid off, the issues were still there, 'Where do I go? Do I go back to the city? Do I try the other 20 hospitals in Westchester? There's nothing in Rockland.'"

Decisions made by displaced persons are often ambivalent and some nurses chose to settle for a position simply because a job was offered. Several nurses related this idea, saying, "It may not be the position that I want or the shift that I want, but it's a job. You know what I mean? I'm given a job. It's up to me whether I decide not to take it. But they're giving me a job."

As participants weighed their options, they realized that seniority often determined employment or unemployment. Seniority represented some degree of job security and it was the major way nursing service made decisions about displacement. A staff nurse said:

> They keep coming around "What's your date of hire?" And two people were hired on the same day, same hour. They do it to the minute, could you imagine, to the minute. But that is actually the only way they should do it. They have to know who came first because you can't let somebody go if there was somebody who was hired after them, or before them. So it really comes down to the wire. Who was hired at 12:00 instead of 12:01.

Once seniority was ascertained within the organization, "bumping" occurred. Bumping was taking another nurse's position of the same title and, at larger medical centers, within the same department. Bumping was perceived as a mixed blessing: The nurse had a job but did not necessarily continue to use the same education or skill set learned and mastered. Seniority determined retention and pecking order for choice of positions. Qualifications and merit were meaningless. Several participants echoed the seeming disregard for expertise as a consideration in displacement. One nurse commented, "The one thing I don't understand is they move you out of a position which you were trained for, and have not just basic nursing skills, because somebody else has more seniority than me, to now retrain somebody else." A manager concurred, saying:

I lost people who were used to the unit, used to the patients, well qualified to administer chemotherapy, and knowledgeable about oncology, only to have to turn around and hire new people. And put them through the orientation process. They have to learn how to administer chemotherapy.

Nurse manager participants were as much in the dark as to institutional plans as their staff, especially when it was the first time for massive change. During the first reorganization in her institution one manager reported attending administrative meetings with collective bargaining representatives that elucidated a retention process that was disorganized and unclear. She said:

There was so much undecided and so much right up to the last minute. It was just like an upheaval to me as far as I was concerned, of how it was going to be done. There was a lot up in the air, there seemed to be a lot of confusion. How was it going to be done; was it going to be done by seniority? Were people going to be put in, I guess sort of like apply. I didn't know what the process was going to be the first time because there was negotiation between administration and the union, and it was a long time (almost to the end) before it was decided just how it was going to be done.

Coping With Negative Emotions and Loss

Reports of severe anxiety and insecurity during displacement were common. This was particularly true with nurses who had been working in the agency many years, had been out of the job market for a long time, and were unsure of retaining a position in the agency. One nurse reported: "It brings a lot of anxiety and a lot of feelings of 'God, what happens if you lose your job?' People have families and livelihoods and it's a very scary time now." Another nurse said, "I've never been without a job and the thought of having to enter the job market, not knowing what was going to happen in three weeks—whether I would be working or not working. . . . It was a difficult time for my husband and myself." Part of the anxiety seemed to be related to starting over, "I worked at [name deleted] since 1985. I had a job and was content where I was, so it's been a while. I had to approach the director of the ICU to see if there was a position available. She intimated to me that she was doing me a favor taking me back into the ICU." A nurse educator related, "It's difficult because you're like starting all over again in a place you've already been."

Although the worry often surrounded potential or actual loss of a job, nurses were also concerned schedule changes. One nurse, recently accepted into a graduate program, said:

I was more concerned as to whether I was keeping my flextime, which is working 12 hours basically, three days a week, because I didn't really want to see myself doing 8 to 4. To me a 9 to 5 business kind of job—that's not what I went into nursing for. What I saw was that 'Oh my God, this is going to happen. It's going to suddenly affect me. I may not be able to do everything I want to do; I love this schedule, why is this happening to me?' You didn't know what to expect.

Many nurses experienced change as loss and began a grieving process that ebbed and flowed even as job security was somewhat assured. Multiple losses, i.e., status, esteem, self-confidence, sense of self, security and control, relationships, and place, occurred repeatedly. Lost status and esteem occurred more often for nurses who felt uncomfortable moving from one specialty to another, particularly if they had not encountered these units or patients since their initial nursing education. One nurse described the loss following her third displacement, from psychiatric nursing to medical-surgical units, with resentment because of her loss of status, role, expertise, and esteem. She said, 'Every day I went to work I was like 'I don't want to be here, I hate this.' They weren't giving me credit for what I knew, and instead of utilizing my skills, it was like I was a nothing. I went from a place where I was in charge of like a staff of four people, to a place where I was a piece of [expletive deleted], you know, like I was a nothing."

Nurses used family analogies to discuss the relationship costs of displacement, for example, "my family from my old floor" and "I don't feel like a member of the family, I feel like a stepchild. And you know, quite frankly, I wish there was a divorce." After two displacements, one manager described the breakup of "family" and her grief:

I felt a sense of loss; I was losing nurses that I had come to know and respect, who I knew were clinically competent, and they really had become like a family on the unit. So, losing these nurses I did feel a deep sense of loss, personally, and also for the staff. I watched the other staff members who had not been displaced—they grieved for their colleagues who were going on to other units.

After moving to a new unit nurses often returned to their former units and the secure friendships with former coworkers to eat lunch and socialize. "The first few months I was there, I would run down to the seventh floor to say hi to everybody. I keep in contact with them. I initially spent my lunchtimes with nurses on the seventh floor because they were my friends." A staff nurse said:

It was very hard initially because I was comfortable with all the nurses on the eleventh floor; we had developed a relationship, they knew me personally. The year before . . . I had gone through a lot, and to now have to somehow lose this relationship and go to another floor. You're happy, you're comfortable, you form relationships, and now the relationships are broken.

Another common source of anxiety was assimilation. They changed agencies, floated to new units, had no locker space, or offices were moved or taken away. An educator remarked, "I switched out of an office, so I moved my office to a different floor where I'm not as readily available. I feel a little bit more displaced that way." With the transition and loss of security and group belonging, they encountered feelings of alienation. One nurse said, "I had nowhere to put my stuff; I just felt animosity." Another said, "Going from one institution to another was a lot different; there was a lot of prejudice against us. You know, 'You're the people from [name deleted], you're the ones that are invading our territory.'" They viewed themselves as homeless people, experiencing relationships as superficial and professional competency as suspect. "I don't know who I'm going to work with. I don't know each unit. It feels like I never have a home, and people don't get a chance to know me, and when they see me floating here and floating there, they don't know me, and don't know what I'm capable of."

A number of nurses said that when they were notified about the displacement they felt angered by the loss of control imposed by the unknown. This response was more frequent among nurses in leadership positions who reported phase-outs of their positions, a possible return to staff positions, or leaving the institution. They blamed other administrators in the organization:

> I was angry. I tried to anticipate and plan ahead; I don't usually fly by the seat of my pants. That was my reason for researching the position in the beginning, thinking that it would be a position I could grow in and have longevity and whatnot. So I was very angry that after having spoken with those individuals, to find out 5 months later that the position would be gone.

Anger brought about by the loss of security and control that surrounds displacement put the nurse in the position of embittered employee. Strong feelings of betrayal and victimization were reported:

> You know, I thought, well look at this, man, they're really screwing me, and I really felt victimized, and I felt like basically I was a piece of nothing, a piece of [expletive deleted]. . . . Now and then I talk to other people and see that this has devastated not only me but a lot of other nurses. I guess we all have different stories, but we have all the same feelings, you know, being victimized.

Participants reported financial loss, including pay cuts and loss of fringe benefits. The fact that this occurred just before a major holiday made the loss even more traumatic. A nurse practitioner remarked, "It was like a $250 a week cut, so that was a big deal . . . but to take that cut with the holidays coming and everything else, that was like another incredible stress." A manager said:

> I wasn't being released until July 2nd. I mean it was right before the holiday, my birthday was in July; I didn't even bother going on vacation. I was so careful with my money, like I didn't want to sponge. I had saved enough, but I own a house, I have a mortgage to pay, so I was working per diem . . . and I was working corporate nursing and things just to get through the summer. And I had school bills to pay. I lost all my insurance and all my benefits because I couldn't afford to pay them.

Overwhelming ambiguity and fear of the unknown were physically and emotionally challenging and were manifested in physical and emotional symptoms or problems. Relationships suffered. One staff nurse reported asking her husband to move out. Prior substance abuse problems or chronic physical problems were exacerbated or new medical conditions occurred. A number of nurses also indicated experiencing psychosomatic symptoms such as headaches, weepiness, exhaustion, and insomnia. One nurse reported "stress headaches, tension headaches, like the muscles up here and tightness around the head, all of that with this displacement thing—it's really incredible." Another said, "It's very stressful. I couldn't settle in. I have been just unhappy; I haven't been sleeping well." These responses were more frequent with nurses who were terribly discontented with their new positions; however, those who faced the change as an opportunity to learn new skills also complained of constitutional upset:

> I'm not getting any sicknesses that occur when I come into the building, like nausea or persistent headaches, but it's just, 'God!' I'm more exhausted—I tend to sleep a lot when I'm on my way to work. . . . I sleep during the day on my lunch breaks, I don't really eat on my lunch breaks—I tend to sleep. When I get home I'm exhausted from working. It's just very tiring and I don't really remember this occurring when I was on my old floor.

Rebelling and acting out were reported. Calling in sick or increasing the use of sick days were indicators of dissent. For one nurse, simply avoiding the work environment and her coworkers and decreasing her productivity and eagerness for her work was her way of rebelling. She said, "I was a person who was always in the hospital by 7:30 to hang out with the staff that was coming on for the day shift, and I mean now I come in at quarter to eight, eight o'clock on the nose. I don't see any point of coming in early. I don't want to come early. What's the sense?"

Support

Participants were offered or sought support to cope with negative emotions and losses. Informal support consisted of talking with coworkers, colleagues, friends, and family who offered a sympathetic ear. Colleagues commiserated with the nurses as they vented their anger, fears, and loss. Participants said repeatedly that peer support was very meaningful to them and although talk did not change their situation, they felt better knowing that their colleagues were sympathetic. An educator said:

> Actually I had a lot of support from my peers. I have to say they were very angry, very upset. They felt that I had paid my dues and was entitled to more than what happened. You know that I had worked there while I was in school, they knew all of that, and that I had kind of earned that position. There are people who are still angry and will still mention it to me that they feel that I got a raw deal over what happened.

Participants sought out peers from their former units and others who had been displaced since some administrators were cold and indifferent and didn't even acknowledge their job loss. As one staff nurse said "I think there's support in the ranks, but not in supervision or authoritative ranks." One nurse was still furious about supervisory indifference one year after her experience. She broke out in hives when she said, "The response was absolutely nothing, from the director of nursing, from the CEO. There was no 'I'm sorry this had to happen. Is there anything we can do?' Nothing. I heard nothing from the director of nursing or anyone else."

Not all administrators were unresponsive. Some nurses spoke about seeking and receiving support from an immediate supervisor and were pleased with the leader's empathic reaction. For example, a staff nurse said, "I don't want to come across and say all these people are unsympathetic, because that's not true. The head nurse . . . she seems to be supportive of the staff because everybody's going through turmoil." Participants did not necessarily expect managers to be entirely supportive, however, since they perceived the supportive role of the manager as being dichotomous with the evaluative role. One said, "The head nurse was somewhat supportive too, as much as she could be because she was kind of in the management role, too."

At times when family, colleagues, and others did not acknowledge the nurses' losses and grief, support was perceived as unsympathetic and unhelpful. The most common and least helpful response encountered was the idea that each should be grateful that they were employed as a nurse and still "had a job." This response demonstrated a total lack of empathy, especially when delivered by fellow nurses. Participants reacted with extreme hurt to the idea that their position and status, specialized knowledge and experience, or education was interchangeable. They felt belittled by the idea that after many years of hard work and advancement in the profession they should be thankful for any employment in nursing and simply "get over" their loss and grieving. This staff nurse typified the comments of others:

> During the period of displacement I heard from certain management individuals I "should be happy that I've got a job. There are nurses who don't have jobs." Let me tell you, if nothing else, that just made me more sickened to the whole process of being displaced, because I know and I think 99% of the nurses know that the hospital needed us. It's just that I think that I would have sat down with somebody who is sympathetic, who understood that this isn't where I wanted to be and sat there and talked to me about it. 'Well, maybe you could find other solutions,' or whatever, you know 'Did you ever think about this?' Instead of talking about like "Get over it; this has been a year now."

Formal support services were for the most part severely lacking. Services that existed were perceived as overburdened, redundant, or self-serving for the institution, so they were either not used or used perfunctorily. Services included: counseling and psychiatric liaison, unit facilitators, and résumé and job application assistance. One nurse felt that she was supporting the psychiatric liaison service provider, saying:

> I met with this woman. She wanted me to meet with her; she felt it would be a good idea, I said fine. So I met with her. She was very nice—she, too, needed support. I mean what we were doing was supporting each other in different roles. I thought it was a riot because I was actually supporting her. It was a hilarious situation, but the stress level was so high that people were just needy of one another for the emotional support.

In several institutions facilitators assisted with staff problems and morale, or trainers educated staff to new philosophies and processes.

These people and practices did not necessarily support the problems unique to the displacement; rather their role was mediation or training.

When assistance was available several participants chose not to use the service, thinking that they were not at a point of dysfunction or great need. Typically these nurses looked inward for self-help and felt as expert as the counselors they might seek.

> I knew what was going to help me was to get myself motivated and find the right job. So to go there and just talk to someone to me didn't seem to make sense. If I was like really depressed and nonfunctional, then that might have been an option because then you would need some help. But I knew what my problem was and I knew how to make it better, and I could talk to my friends—nurses who were friends of mine, so I didn't feel like I needed to talk to somebody else.

Two participants used self-help groups. One nurse attended for continued substance abuse problems and the second attended one meeting of a group for displaced nurses sponsored by a state nurses association. She only attended the meeting once and never returned since she experienced survivor's guilt. She explained, "The [name deleted] Association had put a flyer out about a support group for displaced nurses. When I went, there were only about 10 or 12 of us in the room, and I was one of the few with a job, so I felt like perhaps I shouldn't be there."

Collective bargaining and advocacy units provided limited assistance to the nurses who worked in agencies represented by state nurses associations or health care workers "unions". Nurses perceived "union" or collective bargaining representatives as overseeing the process and ensuring that everything was "legal." Nurses working in represented institutions felt a somewhat greater degree of power and assurance that the displacements would be reasonably fair. Nurses who were not represented said they had no recourse and felt even less power during displacements than did nurses in comparable positions working in agencies where there was representation.

Giving Advice

Giving advice involved imparting their knowledge about displacement to colleagues who might undergo displacement. As they processed the change in their professional and personal lives, participants offered advice to their present and future colleagues who might also face the prospect of displacement. As one nurse so aptly said, "I learned 'don't put your head in the sand, don't ignore that this is going on, don't ignore that this has an impact on people.' It affects job performance, it affects sick calls, affects people's mental status. This downsizing thing transcends everything. It even transcends into your home life, too." Specific recommendations from their learning experience were offered, for example, communica-

FIGURE 26.1 Displaced nurses' advice to colleagues.

Communication

     Open communication
     Inform all employees of the "whole picture"
     Be honest about finances, the longevity of positions,
        expectations regarding budget cuts
     Hold information sessions and meetings
     Prewarn to avoid shock
     Encourage input
     Do not discourage communication with colleagues

Support

     Refer to human resources; provide outplacement
     Encourage and provide formalized support and networking
     Be sensitive—do not inform during the work shift; do not
        inform in a group

Be Proactive

     Keep résumé up to date
     Diversify and learn new skills
     Avoid a "pity party"
     Be assertive, aggressive, and creative in pursuit of your goals
     Learn business skills

Informed decision-making

     Allow time to weigh options
     Make informed decisions—talk to managers, staff ,
        familiarize self with new setting
     Depersonalize the process—accept that change happens

tion, support, being proactive, making informed decisions, and depersonalizing the process. These are amplified in Figure 26.1.

DISCUSSION AND DIRECTIONS

This study described the career-altering change experienced by nurses who were displaced. Displacement was perceived as an erratic and arbitrary process that often undermines the self-worth and expertise of professional nurses. Knowing about the experience of displaced persons and the themes of displacement, nursing leaders can anticipate the experience and help employees to cope and adjust. The following recommendations are suggested for coping with displacement.

Displacement Support Programs

Health care organizations can incorporate clear, organized, and carefully developed displacement support programs into the change process. Staff development programs before, during, and after relocation are critical in helping nurses maintain a sense of self-esteem and job security (Ireson & Powers, 1987). A displacement orientation program can minimize nurses' level of anger, self-confidence, and productivity (Barnes, Harmon, and Kish, 1986). This could include weekly discussions about adjustment, socialization, working relationships, and gaining the larger perspective of change in health care. Support can include psychological counseling, outplacement services, and workshops for morale building.

Stress Management, Empathy Training

Findings indicate that survivor syndrome leaves survivors with little empathy for coworkers. Hospitals, educational institutions, and nursing organizations can provide stress management or empathy training for survivors. The high degree of indifference encountered by displaced nurses and the relative lack of empathy from their colleagues left these nurses feeling grief-stricken and isolated. Coworkers believed that these nurses were lucky to remain employed which left the nurse feeling angry or guilty and further increased the need for support. Internalizing this belief about their "luck" as survivors further hinders the ability to grieve the loss. Survivor syndrome (Curtin, 1996) accounts for feelings of anger, depression, fear, distrust, and guilt as survivors are under pressure to do more with less.

Open, Humane Communication

Most participants felt their supervisors were unable or unwilling to communicate with them and reported low supervisor support. Nursing managers are also a vulnerable group in that they experience high levels of displacement, sometimes precluding the ability to be supportive of others. Nursing administrators should learn how to provide information and emotional support to their staff (Ingersoll et al., 1999), which can lead to higher levels of organizational commitment and job performance in those nurses who remain in the organization (Armstrong-Stassen, 1994).

One of the crucial strategies in downsizing is communication. Administrators must provide nurses with information about what is happening and what will take place in the future to ensure a context of caring (Armstrong-Stassen, Cameron, & Horsburgh, 1996) and a satisfying work environment (Urden, 1999). Although contradictory to sound managerial practices, during organizational change interpersonal communication may be poor, and policies and plans may be developed after the fact. In the present study there was a perceived lack of planning in terms of displacement and communication that failed to lessen feelings of helplessness that arose due to restructuring. The high degree of secrecy and the relative lack of leadership from administrators both concerned and confused these nurses. An emphasis on open communication, respect, honesty, and trust would have had a positive impact on their communication needs. Curtin (1996) implored managers to increase employees' sense of control by providing every bit of available information to staff even if it means posting information in restrooms. Although some of the lack of communication experienced during displacement might be unintentional, the secrecy appeared to be intentional and perhaps even related to organizational philosophy.

Besides an apparent deficiency in planning institutional change, there was an astounding neglect in managing the human side of change (Kanter, 1985). Nursing administrators need to provide ample opportunity for nurses to participate in all aspects of change, to help them adjust to displacement. In the final analysis, it is more humane to empower nurses with information, even if the news is negative.

Employment Policies/Practices

The results of this study point to the need to examine the influence, resources, and effectiveness of collective bargaining groups and nursing organizations, especially their impact on employment policy and practices. Agencies employing nurses need to consider uniform policies for transfer, hiring, or firing decisions during displacement. Nurses who are displaced must rely on the discretion of their employer or on seniority, if they are represented by collective bargaining. They can and should play a more active role in their career management (Donner, 1995; Donner & Wheeler, 1993) by shifting their perspective from employment security to employability security or increased value in the job market (Kanter, 1989). The ability to learn new skills or apply them in different arenas of nursing, as several of these participants reported doing, can help secure one's future. As well, educators need to prepare students to work in an ever-changing world, teaching flexibility, teamwork, collegiality, and career management.

SUMMARY

Displaced nurses recognize that today's world of health care is marked by ubiquitous change, insecurity, and business efficiency. Nonetheless, they embrace a caring ideal of loyalty and devotion to patients and the profession, and to the work environment. A major finding of this study is that nurses were ill-prepared to deal with the magnitude of professional and personal change brought about by displacement. Experienced nurses found leadership support inadequate. Nurse executives can use strategies aimed at clear information and communication, definitive planning, trust, and support. Leaders who demonstrate respect and humanity amid the chaos of organizational change can ensure that displacement does not serve as a harsh contradiction to the caring imperative that symbolizes nursing.

REFERENCES

Anderson, A., Baker, C., & Beglinger, J. (1998). Managing organizational challenge and change: Closing an inpatient unit. *Nursing Administration Quarterly, 23*(1), 15–20.

Armstrong-Stassen, M., Cameron, S. J, & Horsburgh, M. E. (1996). The impact of organizational downsizing on the job satisfaction of nurses. *Canadian Journal of Nursing Administration, 9*(4), 8–32.

Barnes, D. J., Harmon, P., & Kish, J. P. (1986). A displacement orientation program: Effect on transferred nurses. *Journal of Nursing Administration, 16*(7–8), 45–50.

Begany, T. (1994). Layoffs: Targeting R. N.'s. *RN.* July, 37–38.

Bowen, M., Lyons, K. J., & Young, B. E. (2000). Nursing and health care reform: Implications for curriculum development. *Journal of Nursing Education, 39*(1), 27–33.

Curtin, L. (1996). Surviving survivor syndrome. *Nursing Management, 27*(10), 7–8.

Donlevy, J., & Pietruch, B. (1996). The connection delivery model: Reengineering nursing to provide care across the continuum. *Nursing Administration Quarterly, 20,* 73–76.

Donner, G. (1995). Supporting staff in times of change: Career development strategies. *Canadian Journal of Nursing Administration, 8,* 46–57.

Donner, G., & Wheeler, M. (1993). Career planning. *Canadian Nurse, 89,* 26–27.

Geddes, N., Salyer, J., & Mark, B. (1999). Nursing in the nineties: Managing the uncertainty. *Journal of Nursing Administration, 29*(5), 40–48.

Ingersoll, G. L., Cook, J., Fogel, S., Applegate, M., & Frank, B. (1999). The effect of patient-focused redesign on midlevel nurse mangers' role responsibilities and work environment. *Journal of Nursing Administration, 29*(5), 21–27.

Ireson, C. L., & Powers, P. H. (1987). Relocation: The impact on staff nurses. *Journal of Nursing Administration, 17*(5), 15–20.

Kanter, R. M. (1985). Managing the human side of change. *Management Review,* April, 52–56.

Krugman, M., & Preheim, G. (1999). Longitudinal evaluation of professional nursing practice redesign. *Journal of Nursing Administration, 29*(5), 10–20.

Meissner, J. & Carey, K. (1994). How's your job security? *Nursing 94,* July, 33–38.

Shindul-Rothschild, J. (1994). Restructuring, redesign, rationing, and nurses morale: A qualitative study on the impact of competitive financing. *Journal of Emergency Nursing, 20,* 497–504.

Strauss, A., & Corbin, J. (1990). *Basics of qualitative research.* Newbury Park, CA: Sage.

The Center for Health Workforce Studies. (2000). *Meeting future needs of New Yorkers: The role of the State University of New York.* University at Albany: Rensselaer, NY: Author.

Tillman, H. C., Salyer, J., Corley, M. C., & Bates, B. A. (1997). Environmental turbulence: Staff nurse perspectives. *Journal of Nursing Administration, 27*(11), 15–22.

Urden, L. D. (1999). The impact of organizational climate on nurse satisfaction: Management implications. *Nursing Leadership Forum, 4*(2), Winter, 44–48.

This research was supported by funds from Pace University, Lienhard School of Nursing Dean's Summer Research Fund. The assistance of Daniah G. Jean-Francois, MSN, who helped in data collection and analysis is gratefully noted. A special thank you to Dr. Harriet Feldman for her comments and editorial assistance.

CHAPTER 27

Serving on a Board Overseeing a Closing Institution

Kathleen M. Dirschel

Most nurse leaders sooner or later find themselves serving as board members on one or more, usually health-related, institutions or organizations. But what are one's tasks and vulnerabilities if that organization becomes insolvent and is closed during one's board tenure? In today's health care environment, nurse board members may find themselves faced with just that reality. It happened to me; it may happen to you.

One seldom agrees to serve on a board of an institution that may fold, but no one truly knows the status of an organization until accepting a board appointment, when one becomes privy to otherwise confidential information. Nor in today's market can even the best board prevent some organizations from becoming insolvent when faced with shrinking resources, increasing competition, and a changing clientele. This chapter speaks to the issues involved when the closing organization is a hospital, although the same principles would apply to other health-related organizations.

What are a board member's responsibilities in such a circumstance? One's main role is what it has been all along: to assure that management does what it says it is going to do. Additionally, the board member must be equipped to assess and evaluate the fiscal and operational status of the organization, and be prepared to do this on a moment's

---

Note: Originally published in *Nursing Leadership Forum*, Vol. 3, No. 1, 1998. New York: Springer Publishing Company.

notice if the organization's financial picture is changing rapidly. There is little time for the luxury of incremental learning and little security in relying on financial interpretations by others, whether they be the institution's administrators or other board members. One cannot afford to get swallowed up in someone's overoptimistic interpretation of figures that actually signal an opposite message.

Fiscal and managerial oversight does not imply a passive, review-oriented role these days. Especially in cases of fiscal vulnerability, oversight must be proactive, often involving guiding the managerial actions of senior staff. It may be necessary to identify and clarify the respective roles of the senior executive officers and board members, so that there is no overlap, and, more important, no gap in information input to the board or in administrative actions taken on strategic plans dictated by the board.

When an institution is threatened, senior staff may not want to provide the board with the bad news, especially if they fear that they may be blamed or vulnerable to firing. Hence it is very important that the board work at maintaining open, honest, sharing communication with the administrative staff, particularly with the chief executive officer. The board should look for and identify hidden agendas on the part of senior staff. In examining the lines of communication, the board must learn how decisions are really made because channels may or may not follow the lines of authority represented on the organization chart.

When an organization is at risk, the board should ensure that it has input into all critical decisions. That means that board members must take the time to read and interpret the minutes of all organizational meetings, including ferreting out any obvious gaps in information. None of this is entirely separate from the obligations of a board member in an institution that is doing well operationally and fiscally. In all cases the board member must have a keen nose for the degree of fiscal solvency and cushioning available as well as knowledge of the number of similar organizations in the area and their competitive programs.

One must also have a clear sense of the institution's care indicators and their trends, including how such information is tracked. Having a board member serve on each committee that deals with quality control is one useful tactic. In addition to the care indicators revealed in quality control tools for patient care outcomes, the board member will want to know the numbers of (and areas of) board-certified physicians and the numbers of (and level of preparation of) nursing staff. The hospital's admissions and discharges, particularly in its strongest and weakest arenas, are also important data. Knowledge of the community and its perceptions of the institution are critical. Do community individuals and groups see the institution as offering easy access and receptivity to patients? Is its consumer orientation evident? Or is the institution working against itself?

One also wants to know what programs are doing well, which ones are not, and why. An eye must also be kept on who is leaving the institution and why. Often those who perceive a coming storm prefer to leave before being associated with the loss. Often this is not simply a loss of numbers but of critical players—those who can easily acquire other positions because of their known value

WHEN THE ORGANIZATION STARTS HAVING PROBLEMS

As soon as problems are recognized, it is key that the board check the real income against projected income for the immediate period and against projected expenditures for one or more upcoming quarters. There must be a careful monitoring of the earnings/expenditure ratios each month. The board cannot be satisfied with excuses for a negative ratio. There needs to be an active, immediate and concrete plan, implemented immediately with board approval. Often senior staff will want to give the situation more time because a correction may be painful for all involved. Hence it is easy for these officials to encourage the board to "play for time" instead of taking the hard but timely measures necessary.

The board must demonstrate fiscal accountability, a tough "show me the money" attitude. If necessary, the board should get an outside auditing firm, especially if there is any suspicion that figures may have been cooked to present a rosy picture. Sometimes this lack of candor about the financial condition is more than merely putting things in the best light. There may even be false information given to the board. The ledger sheets must be accurate for the board's satisfaction, accounting for all income and expenditures, including any loan repayments.

When serious financial problems are recognized, retrenchment is the obvious first step. Agreement on how to retrench is a more difficult matter; employees and departments will suffer. Senior staff may be hesitant to make hard decisions that will affect those closest to them in the organization. Hence, the board will have to judge the merits of any proposed retrenchment plan carefully. Because it is difficult to implement retrenchment plans, there must be active, aggressive board oversight for the process.

WHEN FILING FOR CHAPTER 11

The board's role is unique and difficult when filing for Chapter 11 because it must preside over the liquidation process, including determining pension benefits, managing lawsuits from employee unions, paying creditors, and paying legal and crisis management consultants.

When closure and bankruptcy petitions are filed, there must be adequate notice of closure and corresponding notices of termination of employment to all involved employees. These notices need to be sent consistent with the provision of the WARN Act which requires certain employers to give at least 60 day advance notice of plant closings. Employees could thus be entitled to 60 days of pay beyond the immediate closure, assuming that there are no liens on the funds that would override that principle.

Sales of assets is an important issue in bankruptcy proceedings, and the board has a serious responsibility to assure that assets are identified and income is directed to meet debts. Assets include instruments and equipment as well as buildings and properties. In some cases, income-producing programs can be sold. Pharmaceutical and other supply inventories are included among assets.

The receipt of charity care monies from the state is an issue requiring negotiation. In general, charity care reimbursement is issued by the sponsoring state the year after the services have been rendered. If the hospital is in bankruptcy proceedings, however, some states have proven unwilling to pay for outstanding services rendered in the previous year, taking the position that the charity care monies are proactive rather than retroactive. This issue could result in a multimillion dollar issue seriously affecting what is available to pay creditors.

MANAGING EMPLOYEES

Once hospital bankruptcy is filed, patients are discharged from the facility, usually within 48 hours. Obviously, this requires a great deal of planning for both finding appropriate transfer sites and for the process of transfer. Subsequent to this time, employees will continue to work on a daily basis, cleaning, taking inventory, preparing assets for liquidation. Even if the number of employees has been significantly reduced by earlier retrenchments, payment for the 60 days post-bankruptcy filing is required for all employees actively on the payroll at the time of the filing.

It is important to remember that health benefits, as well as the pension benefits, of employees must be paid. Appropriate monies must be set aside for this purpose.

Resolution of the pension plan is another major hurdle. With the loss of senior executives as occurs in bankruptcy proceedings, the ongoing administration of the pension plan can be worrisome. Distribution of pension funds to those who retired prior to bankruptcy should continue according to schedule. Those who retire immediately postbankruptcy or anytime thereafter may have a difficult time activating pension payouts without an astute pension fund manager. A member of the board with such experience could be that pension manager; however, that may not be the wisest move legally. Issues of equity, rights, and obligations are difficult, and the board cannot afford the slightest taint of self-interest in the resultant decision making.

The board also has a moral obligation to help physicians and other salaried employees of the institution to locate other positions, if possible. What kinds of, or percentage of, employees might be taken on by neighboring institutions? What can the home institution do to negotiate such positions? What about physicians and their various research programs? What are the logistics of program transfers, especially when grant funds are involved?

As soon as the decision for closure is made, the organization should begin to consider the future of its employees. This may include helping people prepare résumés, arranging employment interviews, and other types of outplacement services.

BOARD LIABILITY

A final issue for consideration is the role and responsibility of the board and the potential personal liability after bankruptcy is filed. Most boards have directors and officers (D&O) insurance to protect their members' personal assets in the event of a suit; however, no insurance protects a board if taxes aren't paid. Then the board members may be personally liable. Also, D&O insurance (depending on the contract) may pay for legal fees once a minimum outlay is met.

Board members must consider this reality in their planning. The original setting of the minimum is the responsibility of board and is often in the $10,000–$20,000 range.

Sometimes before a bankruptcy decision has been made by a board, senior staff may have been shifting money internally—possibly with full intention of replenishing the borrowed funds; however, such machinations may get caught up in circumstances where those best laid plans simply don't work. The board may discover serious financial shortfalls in any number of areas.

There may not be malice, but there may well be free fall, and all possible areas where funds could have been divested to pay for daily survival needs require board scrutiny.

SUMMARY

Serving on a board when an institution closes provides one with a wealth of frustrations and anxieties, both concerns for the institution, its employees, its clients, and oneself as possibly financially vulnerable. In today's economy more and more board members may find themselves faced with this uncomfortable task. Hopefully this chapter will make such a board member aware of some of the pitfalls and some of the necessary actions, minimizing the damage and chaos that inevitably results. Even when a closing is well orchestrated, the process is painful, but a well-designed board oversight plan can minimize problems and frustrations.

CHAPTER 28

Mergers: Your Role as a Nurse Executive and Leader of the System

Carolyn Hope Smeltzer and Penny M. Vigneau

Mergers and acquisitions continue to be a necessary strategy for the survival of many health care systems throughout the country today. The process is time consuming and intense. The nurse executive has a vital role throughout the process to provide leadership to physicians and staff. The nurse executive must work with a consultant through the efficiency study, verification of efficiency, clinical consolidation, and implementation phases of the process. All the while, the nurse executive must maintain a balance of focusing on her own organization while developing a strategy for the new, merged organization to follow. By taking a leadership role in this process and developing a systems perspective, the nurse executive will assist the merged organization in achieving its cost, quality, and service goals.

In today's fast-paced health care environment, organizations are utilizing the services of consultants to keep up with the pace of change. Nurse executives are increasingly being asked to participate, provide data, and carry the message of change to staff and physicians. The nurse executive must take a leadership role in determining the needs of the organization, and thus assisting with the scoping of the project as well as with the selection of a consultant. The purposes of this article are to describe the process and results of mergers in particular, and discuss the role of the nurse executive in general and in

Note: Originally published in *Nursing Leadership Forum*, Vol. 3, No. 3, 1998. New York: Springer Publishing Company.

developing a relationship with a consultant. This chapter is based on the experiences of both authors in consulting engagements across the country.

BACKGROUND

Mergers and acquisitions are occurring at an increasing rate. This has been spurred by numerous factors, primarily cost cutting. Employers and payers of health care are stabilizing or reducing their health care budgets and support any merger that will reduce health care costs in a community.

Costs can be reduced via the elimination or reduction of duplicative administrative and clinical functions. Duplicative capital outlays can be reduced or eliminated as well. Finally, applying best practices from one area across all areas of the new system can also reduce costs. Some examples include cost per case, hours per patient day, and supplies.

Applying best practices across the system will enhance quality, thus enabling the new organization to compete more effectively in the market and gain some negotiating power with payers and employers. This is why the nurse executive must be intricately involved in the merger process. As the leader for patient care and quality, the nurse executive must ensure that the quality results of the merger or acquisition are not overshadowed by the cost factors.

Consultants are engaged early in the merger process to determine the actual cost savings that can be generated from the merger. As an objective third party, a consultant can obtain data from the two organizations and analyze potential cost savings from the merger. A consultant can later facilitate the process of clinical consolidation, making decisions as to how and where services can be consolidated.

SELECTING A CONSULTANT

The nurse executive should be involved in the selection of the consultant. Although the skill and knowledge that a consulting team brings to the merger process is crucial, there are other characteristics that should be considered when selecting a consultant. Table 28.1 highlights criteria by which consultants can be selected and during which stage of the selection process these criteria can be evaluated.

During the proposal phase of the selection process, the nurse executive can begin to analyze the expertise and past experience of the consulting groups. In addition, the process should make sense for the organization and not be a "boiler plate" from other engagements. The nurse executive can get a sense of the time frame expected to complete the process and the proposed involvement of staff and physicians.

The consulting teams that are invited to make presentations to the executive committee should provide adequate details about past experience and results. The nurse executive and other key executives should assess how well the consultant listens to the issues and concerns these executives have, how they modify their approach to fit with the organization's culture and processes, and how well the consulting team works together. The nurse executive should also concentrate on clinical consolidation activities with the consulting team. Although not all of the consultants need to have clinical expertise, they must be able to gain credibility with physicians and staff who are clinicians. Expertise in market analysis, facilities, and clinical operations is necessary.

TABLE 28.1 Characteristics in Selecting a Consultant

	Proposal	*Presentation*	*References*
Expertise of Consulting Team	X	X	X
Credibility		X	X
Past Experience	X		X
Prior Results	X	X	X
Ability to Communicate	X	X	
Ability to Listen		X	X
Time Commitment	X		X
Not "Boiler Plate"		X	X
Open to "New Ways"		X	X
Homework Done in Advance		X	X
Culture Fit	X	X	
Synergy/Team Effectiveness	X	X	X

Finally, when checking references, executives can verify their perceptions with other organizations that have used the consulting team in the past. Again, the consultants' ability to listen and communicate, their appreciation of the organization's culture, and their ability to facilitate processes and achieve results should be analyzed.

MERGER PROCESS

As highlighted in Figure 28.1, there are numerous phases involved in a merger. Beginning with the assessment of efficiency and following through to implementation, the process can take approximately 2 years. The timeline reflects an interactive process, involving staff and physicians from all levels of the organization. At every phase, the leaders of the organization should facilitate the process while the consultants set the stage for objectivity and define a process for the institution to achieve its objectives.

The first phase, a feasibility study, typically involves high-level analysis of duplicative administrative functions. The consultant analyzes where overlaps in administrative functions occur and determines the costs that can be saved by reducing one of the positions. This is where the initial cost savings are determined to justify the merger to the Department of Justice.

The nurse executive should ensure that following this high-level study, verification of the efficiency study occurs. In this second phase, the nurse executive interfaces with the outside consultants on a regular basis to verify the cost savings predicted in Phase 1. The efficiencies are verified department by department, with the nurse executive and the nursing management team helping the consultant understand roles and staffing. In most cases, this phase of the process will identify additional savings that can be achieved through

FIGURE 28.1 Phases of the merger process.

Phase I	Phase II	Phase III	Phase IV
Assessment of Efficiency	Verification of Efficiency	Clinical Consolidation	Implementation
3 Months	4–5 Months	5–6 Months	8–9 Months

the elimination of duplicative positions as well as through the consolidation of clinical programs.

By getting involved up front in the process, the nurse executive takes control of the process and begins to emerge as a leader—one who is "in the loop"—of the clinical services staff. The nurse executive has the opportunity to establish and carry out a vision for the merged organization. Rather than feeling threatened by the consultant, the nurse executive should utilize the expertise of the consultant to assist in creating understandable messages, based on data, to physicians and staff.

Following the verification of efficiency, nurse executives and staff from both organizations will need to come together to determine how duplicative clinical services can be consolidated. In this phase, clinical consolidation, data are compiled from the consultants and used by clinical service teams to make decisions as to how and where services will be consolidated. The staff ultimately believe that if the service goes to a site where they are not currently practicing they will be laid off. Therefore it is crucial that the nurse executive assure staff that the best people, policies, and procedures will be moved to wherever the best facility happens to be for that service. It is important that physicians, as well, see the nurse executive take a stand for the "best practice" as well as for the long-range welfare of the system.

The clinical consolidation phase involves the development of a database made up of four key elements for decision making. This database includes physician interviews, as well as market, operational, and facilities analyses. The nurse executive must work closely with the consultant to make sure accurate data and information are obtained.

Physician interviews should be conducted prior to Phase 3. Interviews are conducted to obtain information as to where clinical services could possibly be consolidated, to provide physicians with an avenue for input, and to identify where barriers to the process may occur. Physicians should be asked a series of questions to include:

1. What services do you think could be consolidated after the merger?
2. What criteria should be used to determine which services should be consolidated?
3. Where should the above identified services be consolidated?
4. What criteria should be used to determine where services should be consolidated?

5. What barriers to clinical consolidation do you foresee?
6. What community and operational issues should be addressed in the process?

The results are quantified into the database and sorted by physician specialty, practice location, criteria, consolidation opportunities, and barriers.

Market analyses should be conducted for key service lines as well as for the hospitals as a whole. These analyses will assess the need for inpatient capacity in general as well as for specific service lines. Analyses should be conducted to determine postmerger utilization forecasts for radiology, medical oncology, cardiology services, and other outpatient services. The nurse executive can assist the consultants in understanding day-of-week and seasonality issues, as well as target occupancy levels. Quantifying this data and sorting by primary service area and product line will allow for a thorough analysis. These data will assist clinical service teams in making decisions regarding service needs down the road.

A high-level *operational review* is required of clinical services, so that the consultants understand how service is delivered at each of the current sites. Key aspects of care delivery must be considered when making decisions as to the scope and size of consolidated programs. Patient load, staffing quality, and satisfaction should be compared by unit and service line to highlight consolidation opportunities and challenges. In addition, interrelationships between clinical services must be understood and incorporated into the consolidated model. The nurse executive can assist the consultant in understanding these issues. These are more data that clinical service teams will use in determining how and where services should be consolidated.

A *facilities review* must be undertaken to highlight strengths and weaknesses of current program facilities, building and renovation code restrictions, and opportunities for expansion. Facilities renovations are the driving costs of consolidation and the least easy to change. Therefore, it is essential that the consulting team include a facilities expert to make appropriate assessments. It should be reiterated that people, policies, and procedures are portable to whichever site presents the best facility option.

Through an integrated planning approach to clinical consolidation, and implementable plan emerges. During this phase, the four components of the database are presented to teams of physicians and staff from each of the merging institutions. It takes approximately six meetings for the clinical service teams to review the four components of data and make ultimate recommendations regarding how and where services will be consolidated. Table 28.2 represents the meeting structures. In the first meeting, the clinical service teams develop a vision for the merged program based on where they feel their service is going in the future. Having the group invest time in developing a vision for the merged organization fuels an excitement about the range of possibilities. After understanding the market, operational, and facilities analyses, the group can make informed decisions. Finally, by understanding and incorporating patient and physician requirements, the new organization can ensure success. The nurse executive is instrumental in facilitating these discussions.

In the final phase, implementation, the nurse executive should again lead the charge to engage a group of staff and physicians to determine the best way to admit and discharge patients, to assure postdischarge follow-up, and to prevent illness and hospitalization whenever possible. The goal of this phase is making consolidation happen, since the decision as to where the consolidated service will be located has been made, as have the scope and size of the service. Now, with direction from a clinical steering committee, the clinical service teams must decide upon staffing, schedules, policies, proto-

TABLE 28.2 Meeting Structure

Meeting	Topic	Strategies
1	Vision/Charge/Scope of Integration	• Conceptual/High Level • Regulatory Issues
2	Market Forecast	• Future Expectations • Growth/Change Factors
3	Operational Requirements	• Interdepartmental Relationships • Other Resource Requirements
4	Conceptual Facilities Options	• Review Criteria • Conceptual Models
5	Site Recommendations	• Implications Discussion • Recommendations
6	Implementation Plans	• Efficiency Savings Targets • Timelines, Roles, Responsibilities

cols, and clinical pathways for the consolidated program. Service, quality, and outcome targets must also be determined.

A clinical steering committee that makes decisions for the system as a whole should obtain input from the particular service lines before making decisions that the clinical service lines must implement. These decisions affect how care will be delivered across the organization. The nurse executive is in a perfect position to obtain input and provide feedback. Again, the focus must remain on cost, quality, and service as guiding principles.

ROLE OF THE NURSE EXECUTIVE THROUGHOUT THE PROCESS

Figure 28.2 depicts groups and areas of focus where the nurse executive takes a leadership role during the merger process. Between the merger, the nurse executive from each organization is focused on staff and physicians in the prior organization, that organization's strategy for meeting customer and community needs, and clinical practice issues. In the initial stages of the merger, however, the needs of the community become a focus of both nurse executives. Common practice issues are highlighted and there is a desire to engage all physicians in the process. Nurse executives, however, must not lose their focus on their individual staff and strategies for meeting patient needs.

During clinical consolidation and integration, nurse executives begin to think more as a merged system. They begin to see staff, physicians, and strategy as a means for the new organization to create value and competitive advantage in the marketplace; however, there may remains some alignment with a particular facility. It is at this stage that key leadership positions are being discussed and decided and political jockeying is bound to occur. The successful nurse executive, however, will keep an eye on the goal of the merger and the vision established by the clinical service teams. Ultimately, by championing this process, the nurse executive will develop a valuable, marketable advantage, whether with the current system or elsewhere.

Once the merger is complete and a new nurse executive is chosen, the focus on staff, physicians, strategy, and practices established

FIGURE 28.2 Emphasis of the nurse executive throughout the merger process.

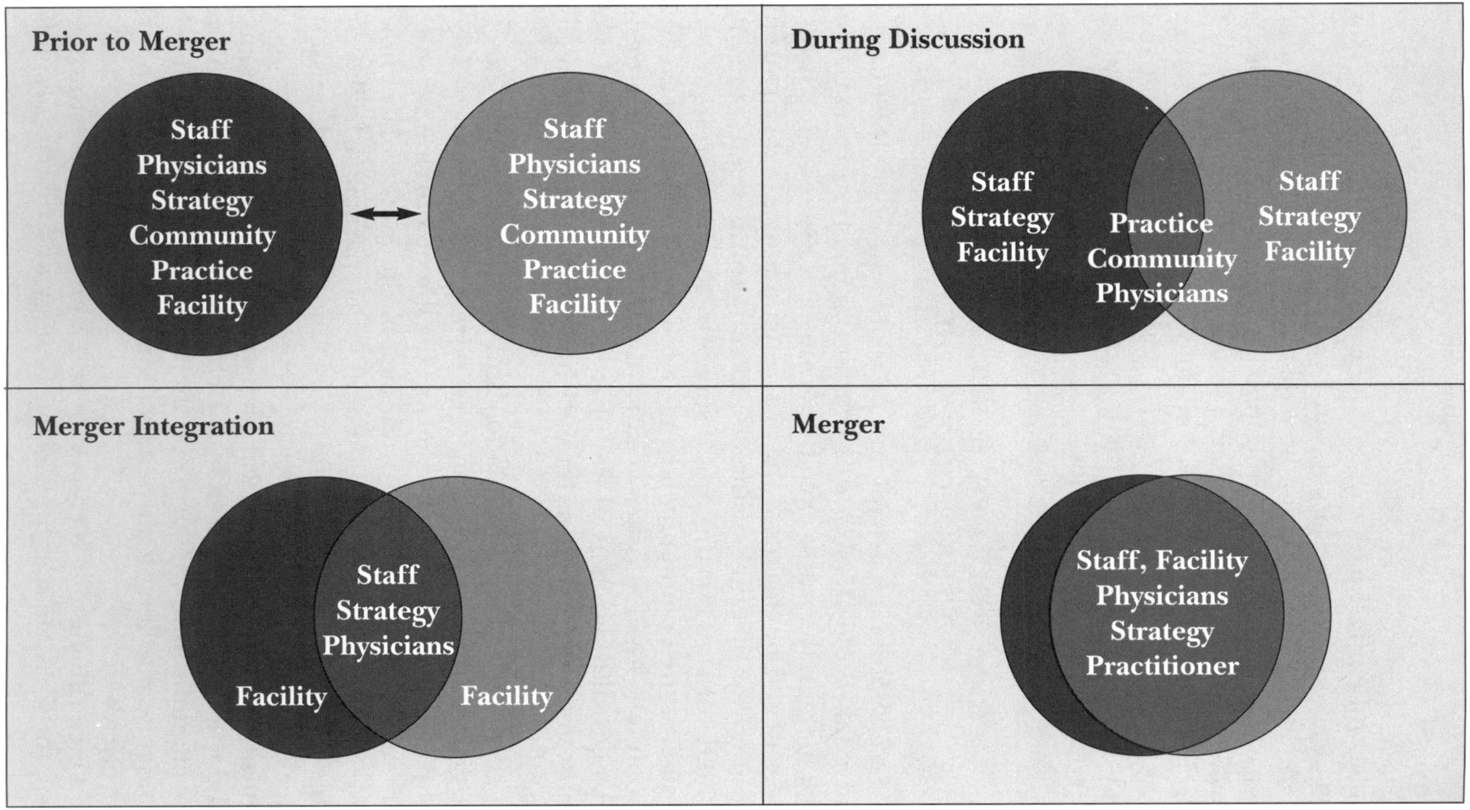

throughout the merger process and developed for the new organization becomes even more critical. A system's perspective must be portrayed and the value of all system components communicated. By ensuring that the chosen model meets everyone's need—cost via efficiency study, quality via best practices, and service via physician and customer requirements—and that the program is sized appropriately at the best facility, the nurse executive can move forward with the task of making integration happen.

CONCLUSIONS

The nurse executive's role during a merger is central, multifaceted, and a significant challenge. Throughout the merger process, the nurse executive must provide leadership and support. The expertise of consultants can greatly impact on and facilitate data analysis and the process of the merger itself. The nurse executive plays a key role in supporting physicians and staff by involving them in the process and addressing their feedback. A "systems hat" must be worn and must include a commitment to the best practices and people rather than to a particular site, placing community, patient, and physician requirements at the center of all discussions.

By leading the way through the phases of the merger process, the nurse executive ensures that the outcome of planning meets the preestablished goals of cost savings, quality, and service. The marketability of the nurse executive is ensured as well, either within the newly merged organization or by other organizations going through the merger process.

SUGGESTED READINGS

Anderson, S. T. (1998). How healthcare organizations can achieve true integration. *Healthcare Financial Management, 52*(2), 31–34.

Alexandria, V. (1998). Beth Israel and Deaconess merger: An all-at-once effort. *Executive Solutions for Healthcare Management, 1*(1), 7–11.

Callaway, M. M. (1997). Integration in the real world. *Healthcare Forum Journal, 40*(2), 20–27.

Carlson, G. L. (1998). Mission possible: You can create a strong post-merger culture. *Healthcare Executive, 13*(2), 52–53.

Connor, R. A., Feldman, R. D., Dowd, B. E., & Radcliff, T. A. (1997). Which types of hospital mergers save consumers money? *Health Affairs, 16*(6), 62–74.

Clinical integration: The whys and hows of restructuring to create value. *Hospitals and Health Networks, 69*(1), 52.

Herzlinger, R. (1997). Retooling healthcare: 'Focused factory' model can help build a patient-friendly, service-driven system. *Modern Healthcare, 27*(7), 96.

Pritchett, P. (1997). *After the merger: The authoritative guide for integration success.* New York: McGraw-Hill.

CHAPTER 29

Consensus and Community: Achievable in American Health Care?*

Claire M. Fagin

This year is the 50th anniversary of my graduation from Wagner College with a Bachelor of Science in Nursing. Who could have forecast that it would be marked by this splendid honor from New York University?** Fifty years ago I had one of the best jobs of my career in nursing, one I loved so much that I would leap out of bed in the Bronx before 6 a.m. so that I could get to Bellevue early. I worked on PQ5 with emotionally disturbed adolescents. That experience helped determine what I would do in nursing for more than 20 years and stimulated my work at NYU as a student and faculty member. So Bellevue receives a share of my gratitude for this honor.

My choice to be a nurse, baffling to my parents and friends, has given me immense opportunities to develop and redevelop my career in ways that would have been unimaginable to me when, at the end of World War II, I was as impressed with the posters of the blonde Cadet Nurse as I was by the actual work that would be involved. But what a lucky decision! Nursing has given me the most wonderful opportunities in patient care and academia.

---

* Edited Presidential Lecture of November 12, 1998, New York University, The Humanities Council and The School of Education, Division of Nursing.
** Presidential Medal.

Note: Originally published in *Nursing Leadership Forum*, Vol. 4, No. 2, 1999. New York: Springer Publishing Company.

It has been my source of superb and lasting friendships and col-leagueship. And, nationally and internationally, I have been fortu-nate to have a place at the table in the public and corporate sectors. In short, I would not be standing here before you today to receive this honor if I had not made this seemingly quirky career choice so many years ago.

TWO AMERICAN TABOOS: CRITICIZING THE MARKET, SUPPORTING UNIVERSAL HEALTH CARE

So given the opportunity of receiving this wonderful award and speak-ing to a stellar audience, I have thought long and hard about how I would take advantage of my time with you. I decided to take on two interrelated American taboos. One taboo is: We are not allowed to criticize the market shortcomings in providing answers to all our problems, including those in health care. The other taboo is: We can't have a serious, in-depth discussion about some form of tax-sup-ported universal health care system as the solution to our health care problems. The unwillingness of policy makers, movers and shakers, joined episodically by the public, to address the notion of universal health care is an example of what Walter Burnham calls "excluded options" in American political discourse.

Let me state my views on these two taboos at the outset. First, I believe that in health care, the for-profit market approach is inappropriate and immoral. Second, I believe that we must consider, plan for, and implement a system of universal health care for the 21st century.

The market paradigm is inappropriate in health care. Remember, the *sine qua non* of market discipline is that people can vote with their feet when they don't like the product. Forty-two percent of the insured report no choice in health plans and "employers forcing employees to change plans brings the percentage of insured without effective control of plan choice to 63%" (Gawnade et al., 1998). Further, choices on qualtiy are virtually impossible since "the available tools to accurately measure performance of providers are quite limited" (Eddy, 1998).

Markets are amoral in general, that is, sentimentally neutral, but in health care this general amorality has the potential to become immoral. The buyers, industry, and government want to reduce costs. The sellers, the managed care organizations, must reduce costs to remain competitive and provide profits to shareholders. Caregivers become implicit and explicit rationers of care who often benefit directly from rationing, a factor that is unique in the American system and exists nowhere else in the industrialized world. Thrown into the brew is ERISA (Employee Retirement Income Security Act), making managed care organizations legally unaccountable for shortcomings in the care they deliver. Put all this together and you have an ideal formula for immorality. I find it hard to come to grips with a system that profits by denying services, removes services from needy clients, blackmails or greenmails the subscriber and the federal government to pay more for these services, then returns profits to shareholders rather than devoting them to increasing access, innovation, and quality of care within the system.

The government and we, the public, have become hostage to employers and insurers in health care. To liberate ourselves, we need to reinforce our views of citizenship and particularly health care citizenship. The concept of citizenship, like its sister term, community, is one of those notions that stands for something we know, even if we have trouble explicitly defining it. Most of us view ourselves as good citizens and want to be part of finding creative solutions to what we see as our common problems. These solutions will come with a price. I believe Americans are willing to pay the price—as individuals and communities—if the vision of what they are paying for is compelling and fairly presented to them.

In 1998 we spent 14.2% of our GNP on health services, as contrasted to Canada's 9.2%. Yet more than 44 million of our citizens are uninsured, among them some 10 million children under 18 years. Add to this problem the unknown number of underinsured, and the issue becomes one of self-interest rather than only of helping the underserved.

A sense of community, as an inherent part of every citizen's understanding of our health and social fabric, is in direct opposition to the popular view of the American's rugged individualism and autonomy. But that popular idea has little utility as we try to solve major social problems. In health care our common denominator is that we will all get sick some day and that we will all need care. If not sooner, then later, and if later, that care will be longer and cost more. More important, denying care to the sick diminishes us as human beings and as a society. We have to convince people that universal health care is not about us against them, about the well-to-do against the poor and uninsured. It is about all of us. Private enterprise cannot deal with the financial burdens of expanding populations of care and will never agree to pay for what it will cost to appropriately care for all of us. Further, and perhaps most dangerous, a for-profit dominated system, grounded in price competition, forces the not-for-profits and the public sector to join in the same behaviors. We risk losing the safety net which the teaching hospitals and public sector institutions have traditionally offered the poor.

No, we may not have universal health care this year or next, but it must be on our policy agenda. Our plans should be flexible and balanced. We will succeed in the longer term; therefore, strategies for incremental changes must be ready for ongoing implementation. Universal health care is inevitable. It is only a question of when.

SIGNS OF TROUBLE IN THE MARKET APPROACH

Universal health care will eventually succeed because the market approach is doomed to fail. Let me highlight five signs of trouble that lead me to this conclusion.

First, the job market is changing rapidly and dramatically. In the next century we will find that employment and health benefits cannot be linked as they were in the past. We are seeing evidence of this development as more and more people are involved in shorter-term jobs, contract employment, and the like. (Some companies are considering eliminating completely segmented benefits and giving lump sums from which employees can choose what benefits they want.) We are seeing rising numbers of uninsured Americans, many working, who cannot afford the health insurance options offered by their employers. The issue of the uninsured is coupled with the failure or shortcomings of the Kennedy-Kassebaum legislation to provide a solution. The General Accounting Office of Congress has told us that people who exercise their rights under the law are often charged premiums far higher than standard rates. One insurer said it reserved the right to charge high-risk individuals five times the rate charged healthy people.

Second, managed care, once considered the solution to our escalating cost problems, is on a slippery slope and showing signs of deep strain and overreaching, particularly in relation to Medicare and Medicaid. Managed care companies (or should I say managed cost companies since this is what we have) are opting out of Medicare and Medicaid contracts and, in other cases, reducing the benefits offered to attract Medicare clients.

Third, the American Association of Retired Persons (AARP) reports that Medicare beneficiaries of average income spend almost 20% of their income on out-of-pocket health care expenses, and poor beneficiaries spend, on average, more than one third of their yearly income on out-of-pocket costs. The Balanced Budget Act has added to the problems of Medicare clients and is forecast to increase costs and reduce benefits.

Fourth, the Labor Department reported that the health benefits index surged 0.8% in the third quarter of 1998 (Miller, 1998). Premiums for employer based health insurance increased 5% in 1999. The overall rate of increase in health spending for 1998 was higher than the growth in gross domestic product (GDP), a sign that the past few years when expenditures grew more slowly than GDP may be ending (Ginsburg, 1999). Out-of-pocket spending for premiums, coinsurance, and copayments grew 5.3% to $187.6 billion last year, the first time since the late 1980s that out-of-pocket growth outstripped costs for private health insurance. Analysts posit that the cost-saving gains from managed care have already been realized. A sharp rise is predicted in health care costs over the next decade (doubling to $2.1 trillion by the year 2007), caused by increases in demand for new and more expensive prescription drugs and stockholder pressure to raise premiums to boost earnings (Department of Health and Human Services, 1998). Meanwhile, in a related area, we are already seeing physician management businesses deserting the market because of poor earnings and losses. Pressure for more return to shareholders will certainly lead to increasing public dissatisfaction with increases in premiums, out-of-pocket costs, and the demand that the government kick in more money to pay for Medicare.

Fifth, a majority of HMOs lost money in 1998. HMO losses have hurt industry stock according to Bloomberg Business (1998). The current situation was forecast several years ago by some of the early entrants to the business who knew when to get into the business and when to get out. Return to shareholders is not where it was in the glory days, and with much of the fat taken out of the system through cookie-cutter reductions in labor force and cuts in hospital and home care, there is nowhere left to go except to even more extreme rationing of services and higher prices. Further, insurance companies predict higher costs will result from patient protection legislation.

Aetna's classic comment in response to these problems tells the story: "We shouldn't be in the business of losing money, and we are not going to be" (Burton, Lagnado, & McGinley, 1998). Or, as Malik M. Hasan, chief executive officer of Foundation Health Systems, put it, "A war is coming which will make what has happened until now look practically like a picnic" (Inglehart, 1997).

It would appear that managed care, or as currently conceived, managed cost, has neither expanded the populations who receive care nor saved money for individuals and families. In fact, as I have stated, the market has shifted costs to these consumers through greater out-of-pocket costs, higher deductibles, higher co-payments, and dehospitalization, leading often to great personal burdens and costs for families losing work days to care for their sick at home. If anyone has benefited by the market incursion into health care, it would appear to be large corporate buyers, the pharmaceutical companies, some shareholders, and some hospitals.

So, all told, the forecast does not appear to be rosy for the for-profit companies and possibly for the entire managed cost system. The market approach is imploding and will fail completely in health care within the next decade. The worst thing that could happen, however, would be that the failure of the for-profits would lead to the demise of the total concept of carefully evaluating, coordinating, and managing care. This outcome is possible since the public is unable to differentiate between managing care and managing cost, between not-for-profit and for-profit organizations. And, after all, why should they be able to, when the market approach is dominant and struggling for survival has changed the behaviors of many of the not-for-profits.

PUBLIC WORRIES AND THE BURDEN OF CARE

In the last five years the public has told us in survey after survey that they are worried about the health care system. A survey done by the Kaiser/Harvard/Princeton coalition (Blendon, 1998) found that the majority of Americans believe that the government should protect users of managed care. This poll also revealed that the majority of Americans believe that managed care will damage quality of care for people like themselves and that they will not receive the services they need when they get sick. These perceptions do not come from media stories but from word of mouth and from people's own experiences and that of friends and families.

Two studies done by the American Hospital Association (AHA) report that the public is particularly frightened about the reduction of professional nursing care (AHA and Picker Institute, 1996). They believe that business personnel, who do not understand the complex dynamics of health care delivery, have cut professional nursing services and that patients do not get sufficient professional nursing care to make them feel safe, comforted, and properly cared for.

Some of us are calling this phenomenon the "burden of care." Caregiving by professionals and by families contains within it the possibility of immense richness and human connection but also the potential for crushing burdens. Several situations turn caregiving into punishment rather than a satisfying link in the human community. If the caregiver is not morally, emotionally, and educationally prepared, then caregiving becomes an experience of frustration and, perhaps, an act of control. The public worries about this problem. They tell pollsters in poll after poll that they trust nurses more than any other health care provider, and they distrust the forces that are threatening the decline of an essential social service.

I do not want the management of care to fail. While decrying the for-profit motive of our current players, my intention was not to throw out the baby with the bath water. In fact, the advent of truly managing *care* gives us a shot at developing a revised system, which can be the basis for expanding care. Neither the fee-for-service system of the past nor private enterprise at large can be used as models on which to build a system of expanded access.

MANAGING COST VERSUS MANAGING CARE

The issue is not "managed care" per se. Most of us believe that genuinely managing care is an appropriate concept to address the problems of a fragmented, disease-oriented, fee-for-service system with disincentives for cost constraint. In reaction to those problems, however, we have gotten an inappropriate, for-profit, managed cost system where nurses and physicians have lost control—and sometimes ceded control—over care decisions to managers who understand so little about patient care that they think they can manage it from afar. It is another brand of the assembly line model developed by Taylor and suggests that health care delivery is equivalent to factories. Where this happened first, in California, we are seeing turmoil in care and the "aha!" recognition on the part of administrators that they have gone too far.

No, we don't want to get rid of managing care, but we need clear thinking on organizing and delivering care in the future. In fact, there are opportunities at present to develop and articulate strong patient care systems that are cost effective and do no harm—our obligation to society. There is all too often a linking of managed care with what is wrong rather than what is right and could be improved upon to make for a more equitable, qualitative, comprehensive and cost-effective system. We have seen examples of such systems two decades ago in California, Washington, and Minnesota, at the least, in this country. These states had strong not-for-profit systems that were models for all recommendations for health care system change. The hardball competition of for-profit companies in their marketplaces, however, changed all the rules under which Kaiser, Puget Sound, and others operated. Having no access to the market for funding to expand and innovate on services, and forced to compete with the for-profits, they could not survive unless they cut corners and costs, and, in some cases, privatized for access to financial markets.

We have to start admitting that the market approach to managing cost is a failed model. But because of our love of the market, and the taboo of discussing market failure, my guess is that attribution for its failure will be placed on design flaws in coordinating mechanisms such as gatekeepers, use of emergency rooms, lack of access to specialists, and the like. People will not put the blame on the profit making for shareholders that resulted from early cost cutting, but on the whole notion of managing care. In other words, managed cost will give the very notion of managing care a bad name.

More cries will be heard that these failures show that America cannot offer universal health care because we can't afford it. You don't think that for a minute, and neither do I. It's pure baloney to think that an equitable system of care, which provides a basic safety net for all of our citizens, is impossible in this innovative, rich country. But we need to be able to take a hard look at our sacred cows.

In our country the sacred cows are pharmaceuticals, organized medicine, health care consulting companies, health insurance companies, and the politicians who support and are supported by them. They have won out each time major change has been contemplated. Experts in economics, medicine, and the social sciences have not been able to come up with solutions that have captured the public's attention and most have not even tried. Criticism has seemed easier. In fact, criticism is one of the most wonderful intellectual exercises all of us revel in.

So now that I have shared my views on the for-profit mode and why it will fail sooner rather than later, do I dare suggest any solutions to our continuing crisis in health care? This lecture forces the issue for me, so I will end with five proposals for the future.

SOLUTIONS FOR THE FUTURE

Insist on Universality of Care

First, universality. I certainly don't have the temerity to say that I can invent a universal system where exalted others have failed; however, I do have the temerity to ask you to speak plainly and loudly, in your personal and professional lives, about what we should expect in this country. We must insist that solutions to our pressing health problems be found. We must maintain a focus on our common purpose of improving health care for all, incrementally, but with the strategies in place for a cohesive and coherent system. Such a system would include: primary, secondary, and tertiary care over the lifespan; programs for prevention of disease; building people's capacity for self-care (but not confusing that with asking people to nurse and doctor themselves when they are really sick) by giving individuals information about health and health care they can understand and use; and guaranteeing accountability from all providers of care.

The subject of universal care has never been compellingly and fairly presented. It must be on our agenda despite the naysayers. After all, that's what political struggles are all about. We should pressure every legislator to respond to the question of how we are to take care of the health care needs of our citizens.

Preserve Management of Care

Second, management of care must survive. The concepts behind it are appropriate. But to have a healthy citizenry we must be able to expand access to care for the entire community. To do this, our health care system must manage care, indeed, must ration care in order to provide basic benefits to all. The question is how are decisions made about appropriate care and whom do they benefit. A system grounded on the principles and philosophy of care, not profit, can provide the framework where providers are able to look at the whole patient and the trajectory of needs across the lifespan—prevention and wellness, care during acute illness, rehabilitation and convalescence, chronicity, and death.

I believe, with many others, that smaller, regionally based, not-for-profit managed care organizations can ultimately offer a sound basis for organizing a new system. It is important to develop a funding stream for the not-for-profit mode for money and survival.

Strengthen the Power of Patients and Families

Third, we must strengthen the power of patients and families, the users of health care. Today, the real buyers of health care are the government and the corporate purchaser. To have clout, the individual and family must learn to influence the buyers through the ballot and at the negotiating table. The public has not yet become engaged in strong, broad-based coalitions for universal health care. There is not yet a strong, national voice. Without such coalitions, people are caught up in their individual disappointments and satisfactions, and professionals are open to attack as vested interest groups.

Although medical consumerism is a growing force, it is most effective in organized groups with a natural constituency focused on specific conditions. According to Inlander (1998), there are some 600,000 such groups in the United States. We have all seen the effectiveness of many of these groups in gaining funding for breast cancer research, winning policies to give access and better care to the disabled, and changing the priorities of research funding by the National Institute of Mental Health. Activism, if even minimally reflected in the behavior of the average citizen, could have a strong impact on the quality of health care offered by managed care systems.

The employed insured group is extremely powerful. Despite the seeming intractability of the managed cost scenario, managed care organizations are vulnerable to patient complaints and eager to meet the standards of their large private contracts. But HMOs *must* be held to the same rules of accountability as the rest of the health care system, that is, nurses, physicians, and all other providers who are liable for their mistakes. The loophole in ERISA that allows HMOs to operate differently must be repealed.

Support Providers Who Are Allies

Fourth, we must challenge the overwhelming power of groups like the American Medical Association and some pharmaceutical and health insurance companies, which have skewed congressional thinking for half a century at least away from a universal, government sponsored health care system. Conversely, we must support and strengthen the efforts of nurses, doctors, and other clinicians who have joined with one another and with patients to fight to regulate the current system. Campaign reform is one part of the answer to this dilemma.

Make Nursing Models the Core of Health Care Practice

Fifth, I said earlier that I would not be getting this wonderful award if I were not a nurse, if nursing had not given me untold opportunities throughout my life. But how many times during my 50 years as a nurse have I and others said, "This is nursing's moment," or "Nursing is at the cusp of its maturity," or "The window of opportunity is open for nursing now," or "Nursing is the right answer to the public's needs." All of these statements and others were correct but the moment passed or important conditions such as unrestricted practice and independent reimbursement were not in place. But now, for the most part, these conditions are in place and the problems that persist in health care cry out for nursing solutions.

We have emphasized preventing disease. We have emphasized providing access to affordable basic health care in the home, in our schools, and in the workplace. And we have emphasized providing long-term quality care to the chronically ill and the elderly. Understanding prevention in its primary, secondary, and tertiary modes permits nurses to help people attain and maximize their health. Knowledge about human behavior and the responses of people to their illnesses are essential in assisting individuals with cancer, heart disease, and arthritis to live optimally in their day-to-day lives.

In short, the models of practice required to deal with major health problems we face today are nursing models of practice. In my mind, there is no question that nursing models of practice will be the central core of the health care delivery system of the future. There is no question that demand for nursing care will grow as America ages, as home care expands, and chronic illnesses increase. I do have a question about who will perform the major roles in nursing care and control the economic management and quality of nursing models of care.

From the standpoint of any patient or family member, the answer should be the nursing profession. From the standpoint of nurses ourselves, the answer must be the nursing profession. We must continue to perform the major roles in nursing models of care. That is a given. We must also accept the challenge of controlling the economic management and quality of these models wherever they occur. In nursing homes, in community nursing centers, in hospitals and in the home, we have the right and the responsibility to the public to assume such control if we are to be accountable for the safety and quality of nursing practice. But first and foremost, we must maintain the central core of our profession. That is our direct connection to patients as their caregivers of first and last resort.

In closing, I ask all of us to acknowledge and respond to the realities that have led to the growing revolt of patients and clinicians against the mismanagement of care. The facts I have shared with you about the current implosion of market medicine have been gathered over the past several years from a variety of sources. I see the two taboos, the market in health care and universal health care, as opposite sides of the same coin. With a worsening picture for large segments of the population, I believe that as an informed citizenry, we must plan for a more enlightened health care future. It is no longer naive and overly optimistic to talk about universal health care. What is naive is not to recognize how much all our futures depend on the quality of the health care system. If we and our fellow citizens are to get needed care and if those of us who are clinicians are to be allowed to give it, we have to have the courage to shatter these American taboos about the market and universal coverage.

Our health care scene is fluid and changing. It is set in sand, not stone. This is a perfect time to influence change that builds on our sense of community and strengthens our capacity for citizenship. Together, as we move into the 21st century, I know we can and we must move toward a system of health care for all.

REFERENCES

American Hospital Association and Picker Institute. (1996). *Eye on patients*. Boston, MA: Author.

Blendon, R. J. (1998). Understanding the managed care backlash. *Health Affairs, 17*(4).

Bloomberg Business. (1998). *American Health Line* [On-line]. Available: www.americanjournal.com

Burton, R. M., Lagnado, L., & McGinley, L. (1998, August 11). HMOs Medicare cuts jolt patients. *The Wall Street Journal*, p. B1.

Department of Health and Human Services. (1998, November 10). Health Care Financing Administration release. Washington, DC: Author.

Eddy, D. (1998). Performance measurement: Problem and solution. *Health Affairs, 17*(4), 7.

Gawnade, A. A., Blendon, R. J., Brodie, M., Benson, J. M., Levitt, L., & Hugick, L. (1998). Does dissatisfaction with health plans stem from having no choices? *Health Affairs, 17*(5), 184–194.

Ginsburg, P. B. (1999, November). Tracking helath care costs. Long-predicted upturn appears. *Brief, Center for Studying Health System Change*. Washington, DC: Author.

Inlander, C. (1998). *This won't hurt*. Allentown, PA: People's Medical Society.

Inglehart, J. (1997, June 19). Listening in on the Duke University Private Sector Conference. *New England Journal of Medicine, 336*(25), 1827–1831.

Kilborn, P. T. (1998, July 6). Large HMOs dropping poor and elderly. *The New York Times*, p. A1.

Miller, R. (1998, October 30). 1% jump in wages lifts inflation fears. *USA Today*, B1.

Index